The **Skillful Leader**

Confronting Mediocre Teaching

ALEXANDER D. PLATT Ed.D.

CAROLINE E. TRIPP Ed.D.

WAYNE R. OGDEN, CAGS

ROBERT G. FRASER Ed.D. , J.D.

Ready About Press
Distributed by Research for Better Teaching
Acton, Massachusetts

The Skillful Leader
Confronting Mediocre Teaching
Copyright © 2000 Ready About Press

Distributed by Research for Better Teaching, Inc.
One Acton Place
Acton, MA 01720
978-263-9449 *voice*
978-263-9959 *fax*
pubs@rbteach.com

Library of Congress Catalog Card Number: 99-075800

ISBN 1-886822-07-7
ISBN 978-1-886822-07-8
18 19 20

Cover and text design: Catherine Hawkes
Composition: Vanessa Gerhard
Production Management: Post Publishing Services
Developmental and copy editing: Merry B. Post

Contents

Preface   v
Acknowledgments   ix
About the Authors   xi

Chapter 1.   Introduction   1
Chapter 2.   Confronting Institutional Mediocrity   15
Chapter 3.   Profiles of Mediocrity   35
Chapter 4.   Selecting Data Sources   69
Chapter 5.   Describing Strengths and Problems   91
Chapter 6.   Designing an Improvement Plan   119
Chapter 7.   Model Contract Language   141
Chapter 8.   A Principal Confronts Mediocre Teaching   153
Chapter 9.   Detecting and Preventing Mediocrity in New Teachers   165
Chapter 10.   Evaluation in the Early 2000s   181

Epilogue   Voices of the Students   193

Appendix A   *The 3C's Supervisor's Survey on Competence, Conviction, and Control*   199
Appendix B   *Unpromising Institutional Practices Survey*   203
Appendix C   *Grading Your Evaluation Procedures*   205
Appendix D   *Grading Your Evaluation Procedures (Annotated Version)*   207
Appendix E   *Improvement Plan Worksheet*   211
Appendix F   *Model Final Summary Evaluation Report Form*   213
Appendix G   *Performance Roles of Teacher and Related Competencies*   215

Bibliography   222

This book is dedicated to the many excellent teachers who set high standards for teaching and learning.

Education—free, public, equal, accessible and good quality—is part of the American promise. We want the best for our children. Our public rhetoric calls out for excellent teachers, excellent principals, and excellent schools; it also laments our failure to reach that goal.

Public education may be in danger. In the last decade politicians have called for more control and accountability, more standards, and more testing. Parents have opted for more vouchers, charter schools, magnet programs, and home schooling. These choices signal their dissatisfaction. Our institutions, critics say, cannot compare with those of our competitors. They cannot provide consistent, high quality education for all children all of the time. They need to be replaced.

Educational leaders are perpetually challenged by the gap between promise and reality. In this current era of continuous scrutiny, much-heralded dismay, and competing reforms, what can they do? Where should they focus their energies? What genuinely makes a difference for children?

"Those who have worked to improve schools over the past decade have found that every aspect of school reform depends on highly skilled teachers," Linda Darling-Hammond (1999) notes. We agree. Growing evidence links skilled teaching and student learning and challenges our deep-seated assumptions about who can achieve. We know what good teachers are able to do and the difference they can make in the lives of children. We also know when teaching is not good enough to help children learn yet not poor enough to trigger a dismissal. Finally, we can identify organizational beliefs and practices that erode commitment to excellence and sustain "good enough" and "getting by." Now we need to act on our knowledge and convictions.

Written for professors of education, superintendents, principals, supervisors, staff developers, school board members, professional union heads, and mentors, this book is a tool kit to help leaders recognize and confront institional and individual mediocrity. Our goal is to provide an excellent teacher for all students. Earlier works on changing teacher quality have emphasized finding and getting rid of incompetent teachers (Bridges 1992, Andrews 1995, Lawrence 1993, and Jones 1997). Here we focus on on improving, not removing teachers. Field-tested tools and strategies are designed to help leaders do the following:

- Assess their own competence, control, and conviction
- Assess institutional practices and beliefs that support and sustain mediocrity and eliminate these unpromising practices
- Collect data from multiple sources, describe problems, and design effective improvement plans
- Detect early signs of mediocrity in novice teachers
- Develop cultural practices that support the growth of both the novice and experienced teachers
- Assess evaluation contracts and incorporate appropriate legal contract language

This book is organized around different entry points in confronting mediocrity. Chapter 1 "Introduction" helps to clarify behaviors we want to change when we confront mediocrity through "visits" to three different teachers. One is probably incompetent; one is excellent, and one is mediocre. We suggest that mediocre teaching is both created and nourished by supervisory shortcomings and institutional deficiencies, and we present our model of intervention. Sally Friendly, our prototypic mediocre performer is introduced; her case will be revisited throughout the book.

In Chapter 2 "Confronting Institutional Mediocrity" we consider debilitating beliefs that sap conviction and unpromising practices that allow mediocrity to persist. We also examine how school leaders create practices, structures, and norms that support excellence. This chapter is supplemented by three surveys located in the Appendixes: one for assessing individual leader's competence, conviction and control; a second, "Unpromising Practices," that allows leaders to analyze institutional practices that support mediocre teaching; and a third survey "Grading your Evaluation Procedures and Practices."

School leaders need competence in defining and intervening in cases of mediocrity. Nine profiles are presented in Chapter 3 "Profiles of Mediocrity." These are organized according to three causes of substandard performance: lack of expertise, limiting beliefs, and external influences. Effective and ineffective supervisory responses to these cases are detailed.

In Chapters 4, 5, and 6 we provide field-tested tools to help supervisors identify, intervene, and improve mediocre teaching.

In Chapter 4 "Selecting Data Sources" we focus on the multiple sources of data that can be used for those who want all teacher evaluation to move to more broad-based assessment.

Chapter 5 "Describing Strengths and Problems" provides a comprehensive series of framing questions to help the evaluator isolate the performance strengths and weaknesses. Adapted from *The Skillful Teacher* (Saphier and Gower 1997), the framework is organized around five major roles of the teacher including: classroom teaching, professional growth, performance of administrative duties, communication with parents, and contribution to the staff. Using the Sally Friendly case, we provide examplars for an observation report and a summary evaluation report.

Chapter 6 "Designing an Improvement Plan" details the exact steps and strategies for designing improvement plans where the responsibility for change rests with the teacher. We examine a problem-based model for plan development as contrasted with an activity-based plan, using the Sally Friendly case.

Chapter 7 "Model Contract Language" is an annotated model that gives leaders the enabling legal contract language to confront mediocrity.

Chapter 8 "A Principal Confronts Mediocre Teaching" highlights the importance of personal conviction. A principal tells his own story of evolving into a principal who advocates primarily on behalf of students rather than teachers. In the story of Brenda, he details how tenacity and planning, together with institutional support, helped to raise one teacher's performance.

In Chapter 9 "Preventing and Detecting Mediocrity in New Teachers," we present strategies to hire, nourish, and retain new teachers. We will also provide leaders with criteria for detecting early signs of mediocrity and provide guidelines for nonrenewal.

In Chapter 10 "Evaluation in the Early 2000s," we look at promising trends such as peer review, standards-based learning, the use of teacher portfolios, and the use of tests as a source of data to evaluate teachers.

The Epilogue "Voices of the Students" reminds us that students have much to say about their teachers. Listening to them allows us to share our conviction about why we wrote this book.

The Appendixes contain surveys to help practitioners assess individual and institutional stances and competencies, a sample improvement plan worksheet, and a final evaluation form and supporting materials on the performances expected of teachers.

Acknowledgments

We would like to thank Dr. Jon Saphier for his support and encouragement and for writing *The Skillful Teacher* with Bob Gower, which is the pedagogical basis for our work. For our past and present colleagues at Research for Better Teaching who have contributed generously to this project: Marcia Booth, Mary Ann Haley, and Gayla Moilanen gave us helpful critiques. Sandra Spooner and Roberta Spang provided invaluable assistance in advancing this project. Special thanks to Greg Ciardi for contributing material on peer assistance and to Ken Chapman who enriched our profiles of mediocrity. Louise Thompson helped us organize our early thinking. Other colleagues have contributed along the way including: Deb Reed, Fran Prolman, Ann Stern, and Paula Rutherford.

We also thank the Massachusetts Association for School Superintendents, especially Paul Andrews, who supported materials testing through the Association's Professional Development program.

There are numerous colleagues who have influenced our thinking. These include: Maryellen Coles, Robert Fried, Barbara Hill, Ron Ivanna, Donna Jemilo, Bruce Labs, John McEwan, Ana Miranda, Susan Piland, Patricia Randall, Bill Ribas, Marianne Rogers, Richard Santeusanio, Barbara Saxton, Paula Sennett, Irene Sherry, Jayne Snarsky, Linda Mederos Stevens, Margaret Strogny. James Warnock from the Burlington, Vermont Public Schools was especially helpful. Michael Fung from Boston contributed wonderful ideas on interviewing new teachers that were incorporated into Chapter 9.

We are especially grateful for the help of over one hundred administrators from Massachusetts school districts who allowed us to pilot ideas and materials. These include the following Massachusetts districts: Andover, Belmont, Boston, Braintree, Franklin, Wellesley, Revere, Whitman Hanson, and Silverlake Regional.

Our teams of reviewers were immensely helpful. Irwin Blumer, Dennis Foreman, and Donald Pierson gave us thorough critiques. We owe special thanks to our content editors and critical colleagues Margaret McMullan and Judith Boroschek who held us to high standards.

We want to thank the Duxbury public schools for being a special field site. Eileen Williams, Ruth Lynch and Joellen Rando, and Ron McCarthy all contributed greatly to the project. Nanci Bourne skillfully managed Wayne during this project as well as contributing secretarial help. We would like to thank all the students we interviewed; they gave us insight about unidentified classroom mediocrity. We thank specifically Becky Stamski for giving us our framing quote.

Our families played supportive and often participating roles. Carolyn Platt did critical reading and gave constant moral support. We thank Betsy and Maggie Ogden for logo design ideas and Patty Fraser and Ray Tripp for their enduring support of our work. Younger family members also contributed as Dana Platt helped design our organizing graphic and Rud Platt was our new-teacher consultant and web page designer. Owen Tripp helped to develop our first data base. Genevieve Saphier helped us with our first literature search.

We are also appreciative of the support of Ed Bridges from Stanford University who blazed the trail for our work with *Managing the Incompetent Teacher*.

You would not be reading this book were it not for our project manager and editor, Merry Post. She stuck with us and was especially rigorous in holding us to high standards for writing.

About the Authors

Alexander D. Platt, Ed.D.

Andy Platt is a Founding and Senior Consultant of Research for Better Teaching, a Massachusetts based consulting firm dedicated to the professionalization of teaching. He has taught at elementary, middle, and high schools and was Assistant Superintendent in a Massachusetts school district. In the last twelve years, he has worked with over 1000 administrators in long-term courses to develop increased skill in supervision and evaluation. He has specialized in helping supervisors identify and improve underperforming teachers. Dr. Platt has been active in the Association for Supervision and Curriculum Development and is a past President of the Massachusetts Association for Supervision and Curriculum Development.

Caroline E. Tripp, Ed.D.

Caroline Tripp is Director of Curriculum at Research for Better Teaching. A teacher of teachers with 30 years of experience in public education, she has been an Assistant Superintendent, K-6 curriculum specialist, K-12 staff developer, and has taught at the college and high school levels. Dr. Tripp has been active in the Association for Supervision and Curriculum Development and is a past President of the Massachusetts Association for Supervision and Curriculum Development. Her special interests include instructional leadership, supervision and evaluation, building professional communities in schools and school systems, and teaching in standards-based classrooms.

Wayne R. Ogden, CAGS

Wayne Ogden is the Principal of Duxbury High School in Massachusetts. Before working in Duxbury he was Principal of Springfield High School in Vermont and a high school social studies teacher in Massachusetts. Wayne served for six years on the Commission on Public Seconday Schools of the New England Association of Schools and Colleges and was on the advisory Boards of the Principal Centers at Harvard University and in Vermont.

Robert G. Fraser, Ed.D., J.D.

Bob Fraser is an attorney and former Assistant Superintendent for Personnel, with more than twenty-five years' experience as a labor negotiator. His primary areas of expertise are personnel administation, labor law, negotiations, and education law, including special education. Dr. Fraser has been an active member of the American Association for School Personnel Administrators. He is currently a partner at Stoneman Chandler and Miller and has been an instructor at Boston University and Harvard University Schools of Education.

1 Introduction

I can teach myself, so I am all set. Some kids need a real math teacher. This teacher can't help them at all. (Becky, high school junior)

Becky's incisive observation is echoed by dozens of other young people we interviewed. We asked them about their excellent teachers. They said such teachers were rare, perhaps one out of every four or five they encountered in their short careers. Then they told us clearly and with great consistency what excellent teachers—"real teachers"—did. The students also told us what less skilled and caring teachers did and the impact "getting by" had on the their learning.

Pressures to Confront Mediocrity

In our work with school leaders, we often ask them to describe the biggest problem they face in trying to raise student achievement. Mediocre instruction—the inability to provide reliable, consistent high quality teaching in every classroom—surfaces quickly on their list of frustrations. They, too, can tell us what excellent teachers do. Pressed to elaborate on what is missing in the classrooms of those who are "just getting by," however, leaders from mentor teachers to superintendents describe a shifting mix of characteristics. Although these characteristics are rarely bad enough to lead to teacher dismissal, they will diminish student learning.

At best, supervisors say, students mark time or hold their ground with mediocre instruction; at worst they fall behind or miss mastering skills and concepts necessary for the next steps of their education. Convinced that they

The standards and accountability movement with its increased emphasis on high stakes, external assessments underscores the link between teacher practice and student achievement.

could do a better job of improving classroom instruction, some leaders report a sense of helplessness. They wonder where and how to invest their effort effectively in order to make a difference for students. Others, equally convinced that consistent high quality teaching is an unattainable goal, report themselves to be resigned to the inevitable: some children will be fortunate and have "real" teachers; many children will be unlucky much of the time.

Becky's criticism, captured above, carries a significant message. This message—that students need "real teachers"—becomes more urgent in light of the pressure arising from declining public confidence in the schools, increased attention to school and teacher accountability, and changing teacher demographics.

Unwilling to be content with the single option of public school education, for example, parents and policy makers are demanding alternatives. Growing numbers of advocates believe options such as vouchers for private education, charter schools, magnet schools, alternative programs within schools, or home schooling offer them a better chance to secure an excellent education for their children. Public schools, some claim, are antiquated institutions whose members are unable to monitor or change their own performance to meet the demands of a changing society.

The standards and accountability movement with its increased emphasis on high stakes, external assessments underscores the link between teacher practice and student achievement. An unprecedented forty-nine of fifty states have moved towards the adoption of state standards and frameworks. Rigorous and demanding in many cases, these frameworks require substantive knowledge of content, an ability to deliver organized curriculum around sophisticated concepts, and a wide pedagogical repertoire.

Moreover, teaching and the outcomes it produces have become increasingly public. If we could once cover up for those teachers who did not perform at high levels, that time is gone. Schools can no longer "choose" the children who will take these tests nor can they select which data about performance will be made public and which will not. Teachers can no longer choose which parts of the curriculum they will teach nor can they expect to "get by" by closing their doors.

To meet standards for student achievement, schools must increasingly pull together; faculty must pool their technical knowledge and skills and hold one another accountable for reinforcing common goals and objectives. Schools that have been successful in raising student achievement, Newmann and Wehlage (1995) note, are marked by strong professional communities where teachers "pursue a clear shared purpose for all students' learning, . . . engage in collaborative activity to achieve the purpose, . . . take collective responsibility for student learning." The good news here is that collaboration both brings inadequate performance to light and "puts more peer pressure and accountability on staff who may not have carried their fair share (Newmann and Wehlage, 1995). The "bad news" is that administrators cannot afford to ignore that performance.

Beyond the pressures from diminished public confidence and increased attention to accountability, schools face a demographic challenge that may further fuel mediocrity or create an historic opportunity to do our work in new and powerful ways. By the year 2006, 200,000 additional teachers will be needed to meet both the anticipated increase of 5 million students over 1995 enrollments and the large attrition of veteran teachers. This figure does not include proposed increases in staffing to achieve class size reduction. Currently there is a shortage of teachers in math, science, bilingual and world languages, and special education, and substitute teachers are increasingly scarce. In order to meet the demand for teachers, undertrained and uncertified novices will have to be hired while we simultaneously lose many of our expert veteran teachers, especially at high school.

We also face difficulty in attracting excellent school leaders. They, too, will be affected by the demographic changes as the baby boomers retire and the school population expands. In well intentioned efforts to raise standards, Massachusetts, North Carolina, Oregon, and Georgia are the first states to pass legislation removing tenure for principals. Administrative salaries have risen far more slowly than teachers' salaries, despite a longer working year for administrative staff. Prospective administrators are already looking at the greater responsibilities with few compensating benefits and decide to stay in the classroom.

At this turn of the century, then, external forces—well publicized alternatives to public education, mandated standards and assessments, and changing demographics—provide a convincing opening salvo for confronting mediocrity. Real, day-to-day leadership for change, however, means working from the inside to influence the culture of the organization and the behavior of its members.

Who Owns the Problem?

We began this book because *we believe all children deserve real teachers,* people who believe in them, who have the skills to help them learn and perform at high levels, and who are passionate and knowledgeable about what they teach. Furthermore, we have clear evidence that

- Good teaching makes a genuine difference in the lives of students.
- There are many fine teachers to serve as models.
- There is research available to tell us almost everything that we need to know in order to provide competent, caring instruction for all children.
- Some educators have built and sustained cultures of high achievement even under the most difficult of circumstances.

If the public and private hunger for capable, high quality teaching is compelling and if we have clear evidence there are many places where such teaching happens, why doesn't it happen in every school and classroom? Why does mediocre instruction survive in communities ranging from affluent suburbs to the poorest urban schools?

As we look closely at the roles we, and others, play in supporting and sustaining mediocrity in schools, the picture that emerges is complex. For example, we could easily blame

- Teacher unions for the protectionism that leads them to defend substandard performance and to fight for narrow contract language that restricts the rights of evaluators
- Administrators who have historically avoided confrontation by inflating the evaluation ratings of teachers whose performance they know to be well below standard
- School boards and administrators who abandon demands for administrator and teacher performance in return for concessions on salaries and benefits

- States that allow lifetime certification or establish mechanical recertification procedures in which "seat time" rather than demonstrated competence is what counts
- Politicians who use the schools to pay back political favors for friends and relatives
- Teachers who stop challenging themselves to be constant learners
- Parents who demand or accept inflated grades for minimum work or who routinely share complaints privately or outside of school but refuse to put such complaints in writing

What about the students who work after school and have little time for homework or who watch hours of TV and make no effort to complete their work? Don't they and their families share some of the responsibility? It's easy to find candidates for blame, and school-bashing books are amply represented on the shelves. Mere blaming, however, serves no useful purpose. It seems clear to us that all the participants cited above contribute to a culture that supports and sustains mediocrity. Correspondingly, all these groups can help to change that culture. As school leaders we might be tempted to point the finger of blame elsewhere, but let's choose to start with ourselves and some of the variables we control and could change first. Let us look at how our own beliefs, our supervisory shortcomings, and the limitations and deficiencies that have been "institutionalized" in our school systems have prevented us from effectively confronting and improving mediocre teaching.

 # What Do We Mean by Mediocre Teaching?

To begin confronting mediocrity, we need to recognize its existence, be convinced that it is a problem, and believe we can make improvements. There is no easy, clean definition to guide us in doing so. Mediocrity is most often understood as a relative term. It is variously defined as "not quite good enough" or "of middling quality" or "second-rate." Thus it helps to begin our discussion by establishing distinctions between what skilled assessors might call incompetent instruction and what they would deem excellent. Three benchmark cases give us an opportunity to look at the differences between the clear ends of the continuum and what we would deem second-rate:

Doug Noyes, whose performance is so far below standard as to be considered incompetent

Nancy Kerr, whose performance is high quality because what she knows and is able to do enables her students to learn and to achieve at high levels

Sally Friendly, whose knowledge and/or performance is neither substantive and skilled enough to help most children learn nor poor enough to warrant a move toward dismissal

To establish what the low end of the performance continuum looks like, we begin with Doug Noyes.

Profile of Incompetent Teaching: Doug Noyes

Mr. Noyes has taught social studies for 22 years at Eastville High School. Let's visit one of his classes in March. It is 11:30 a.m., and 25 Modern European History (general level) students are spilling through the door. They slide their desks into cluster formation so they can be close to their friends and as far from the teacher as the space permits. Less than a third of the students have their textbooks and notebooks. Shuffling through some well worn lecture notes, Mr. Noyes neither greets nor acknowledges students as he gets ready for the class. The bell rings; students are still entering. He does not ask them why they are late or why they are unprepared for class but says to one of them simply "You are late." The blackboard is clean.

Mr. Noyes's expectations for the work procedures are unclear and unenforced. There are few personal connections being made. Teachers like Noyes rarely develop rapport with or earn respect from their students. There are no signs that he has planned for this class beyond writing down the topic if keeping a plan book is required by the school.

Two minutes after the bell rings, Mr. Noyes says "Okay, today we are going to cover the four causes of World War II. Take out your notebooks while I take attendance." Five students respond by taking out their 3-ring binders with unpunched ditto handouts spilling out. Most students ignore the request and continue talking. "Okay, let's simmer down while I take attendance." He calls the roll and checks off his attendance log. Students "simmer down" but do not take out notebooks, which are either crumpled in their locker or lost. He takes three minutes to complete the attendance routine, "Ackerman, Baer. . . ." Then he passes out some paper for those without notebooks. "Who needs paper today?"

Incompetent teachers burn valuable learning time using routines as a cover. Attendance-taking occupies minutes when it should take 20 seconds. The start of class signals that nothing much of importance will be taking place, and neither focus nor engagement are expected or called for. There is no framing of the objectives—that is, what students should know, or be able to do, or the purpose of the lesson.

Mr. Noyes goes to the blackboard "Okay, we can start now." He writes "Four Causes," followed by the numbers 1 through 4. Jamie in the back of the room curses audibly. Mr. Noyes ignores him. Mary yawns, and Brian puts his head down preparing for his daily nap. "I *hope* you had a chance to read the homework assignment" Noyes says in a voice clearly implying his belief that they will not have had a chance. Four kids say "What homework assignment?" and Mr. Noyes responds, "I put it on the board at the end of the class yesterday. You know, two pages about the causes of World War II. If you didn't have a chance to do it, I will go over the material now. You had better listen up. There is a quiz tomorrow." There is no attempt to check who did the reading. Mr. Noyes opens up with the same lecture he has used for years.

Teachers like Noyes focus on covering content, not on students learning significant ideas. Threat of a quiz is an effort to buy compliance, if not interest. They have a very limited repertoire of explanatory devices, relying mainly on the blackboard and sometimes an overhead projector. There is no clear standard for homework completion, much less for its quality.

Fifteen minutes into the class, 80 percent of the students are disengaged or disruptive. Two students are spending time copying their Spanish homework from a classmate in order to be prepared for the next period. That teacher checks homework. Three boys are out of their seats and playing "push lite," a game of friendly poking. Two girls are applying make-up and chatting quietly about a recent date with Chad. Two other students are quietly playing a math game, and one girl is quietly doing her French homework due the next period. The students have tested the limits and know exactly how much they can get away with. Mr. Noyes punctuates his presentation with refrains "Okay, knock it off," "Enough of that." "Come on, this will be on your quiz. You won't learn it if you don't pay attention. One more thing from you, Jack, and you will have a suspension."

Noyes's attention-engaging techniques are virtually absent. He ignores all but the most flagrantly inappropriate behavior. There is no attempt to refocus students, much less to involve students in the discussion or check their understanding. Rather, he resorts to grade threats to try to motivate them. Even the better students have written this course off.

This process continues for the entire class. The bell rings, and students stream out the door as Mr. Noyes calls out: "Be sure to read the next section in the text for tomorrow, and don't forget the test." Students head out for lunch without being dismissed. There is no summary or wrap-up, and the homework will likely be ignored. When he is asked about the class in the post-observation conference, Mr. Noyes says: "These kids are in the average group because they don't care much; they never do their work. I can't really teach them. They have no interest in the material." The fact that this may be partially true masks the underlying problem.

Teachers like Noyes blame the students for not behaving and not learning and refuse to be held accountable for their failure to learn. They will not take any responsibility.

A check of his grade book shows very few entries, but all term grades are A's and B's.

Low-performing teachers like Noyes often buy students' acquiescence with high grades. This practice is referred to as "Horace's Compromise" in the book of the same name by Ted Sizer.

If this sample is representative of Mr. Noyes's daily teaching, the skillful evaluator should rate his performance as incompetent. He lacks adequate skills, capacities, or qualities needed to meet a reasonable set of standards. In all areas of performance, he falls well below standard. Using Bridges'(1993) descriptions, he fails to:

- Maintain discipline
- Manage the routines of the classroom
- Set a climate of discipline and respect
- Clearly communicate objectives
- Use a variety of explanatory devices to reach various learners
- Impart subject matter effectively
- Communicate and enforce high standards and expectations
- Involve the students in their own learning
- Set and assess standards for quality student work
- Produce intended or desirable results

> **LEGAL NOTE**
>
> **Incompetence:** "Incompetent means lacking the requisite or adequate abilities, capacities or qualities needed to reach a reasonable set of standards." (Lexington Public Schools, AAA Case #11-390-00571-94 Bruce Fraser)

Evaluators usually, but not always, respond to teaching that is this poor. If the impact on student learning is not immediately obvious or there is no crisis to force action, Noyes may survive. In fact Bridges (1993 p. 19) notes that "Only the most flagrantly inept in any organization or profession is apt to be fired or to be disciplined."[1] Unless they are induced to consider the broader impact of allowing Noyes to continue and begin to advocate for students, Noyes's supervisors may say "He has been that way forever; he cannot change" and choose not to confront him on his poor performance.

Doug Noyes represents one end of the performance continuum. The focus of this book, however, is neither on the "flagrantly inept" nor on the incompetent performer. He or she usually gets the supervisor's attention. Principal Jack Wyatt neatly sums up our purpose and the frustration he and many of his colleagues feel when he notes "If the teacher is totally screwing up I can better deal with that than I can deal with a teacher who is just 'doing the job.'"

To address mediocrity, we need to capture what "just doing the job" looks like. We need to somehow get at the essence of mediocre performance, to put it in its position between incompetence and excellence. In order to do so, let's next develop a vision of excellence by visiting Nancy Kerr's 5th grade classroom. Let's see what she is doing to help students learn and achieve at high levels.

Profile of Excellent Teaching: Nancy Kerr

"Good Morning, Jeff. I had a great talk with your mother last night. She is so proud of the hard work you have done on this essay unit and the way your persuasive writing has improved with each draft. This time you *really* did what you've been wanting to do. Your beginning and your closing paragraphs are both great attention-getters."

Excellent teachers make personal contact. They also give immediate focused academic feedback to their students and attribute success to effort as well as to acquired skill/ability.

---

[1] Bridges (1993 p. 2), basing his estimates on two other researchers, believes that about 5 percent of the teaching force could be described as incompetent. Using this figure he states the impact in these terms: "The total number of students taught by these teachers exceeds the total combined public school enrollments of fourteen states."

As they enter, students go to their portfolio cubby without any prompting, pick up their materials, sharpen pencils, put homework into the homework bin, and consult the board for the sponge activity. Today Bus 4 is late, so three students will come 10 minutes late. "Please work on your journals while we wait for Mary, Ben, and Raoul," Mrs. Kerr says. Students are all on task, some conferring quietly with each other, while Mrs. Kerr circulates. "John where is your journal?" (He took it home.) "That is not an excuse. You know what the expectations are. I know you will come through on this tomorrow, right?"

Mrs. Kerr is typical of excellent teachers who have their management routines well oiled and are prepared so that students are meaningfully engaged and can function without constant direction during transition times. In her class students are expected to work well independently and to take considerable responsibility for learning. There is also a sense of community; students respect and help each other. These teachers also monitor students and swoop in to communicate positive "You can do it" messages regarding an expected work procedure.

"Okay, by next week we will wrap up our study of the American Revolution. We will end this unit with a debate where you will be asked on the spot to defend either the American or British perspective on what happened on Lexington Green. To prepare you for this we need to do two things. First you need to be really clear about the chronology, the events, and the major organizing concepts. This builds on the work we did last week when we read the textbook account that students in Britain use. This week we are going to be looking at primary sources to help understand different perspectives."

Mrs. Kerr skillfully frames the learning for the students and connects to things they have already learned. Furthermore she shows that she has a deep knowledge of the subject matter and the importance of building concepts before having students debate.

"I am excited about this unit for two reasons. I've never done it in this way, so it is new to me—and also I really think it is important to be able to take different perspectives to help us to become better thinkers about history. You know I *love* a good disagreement in history—and especially this part of American History. I'm looking forward to hearing you talk about which accounts you find most persuasive and why. I'm wondering if you'll have new insights as a result of having to take someone else's point of view.

Excellent teachers are passionate about what they do. They take risks by experimenting with new ideas and model constant learning. They view learning as a joint pursuit.

"I have read your journal entries from last week and the paragraph summaries you completed on Concord and Lexington. From what I saw, I'd say I need to find a way to help you better organize information. You did not do as well as I had hoped on the open-ended question that you had to do cold. One of the reasons I am trying this new approach is that this is a hard concept, and I need to give you a tool to use independently in the future. This cause-effect graphic organizer will help improve your analysis skills and help you next week to prepare to analyze the war from the two perspectives."

Excellent teachers modify their curriculum based on data collected on student learning. These teachers use student work as a springboard to modify instruction. They are focused on teaching transferable skills that students can use independent of the teacher in the future. Excellent teachers take responsibility for failed student performance.

"You know how sometimes you have trouble seeing a problem from someone else's perspective. For example, when you are having an argument with your brother or sister, this skill will help you to sort out and analyze other people's perspectives to help you deal better with conflict." So learning this skill will be useful in your life as well as in this class!

Great teachers excel both at connecting personally to their students and connecting their teaching to the student's lives. Her objectives are made relevant to the students, and they are crafted to foster real-life applications.

Observing Nancy's classroom, we see rich evidence of student work. On the bulletin board are social studies projects with carefully completed rubrics and statements of self-evaluation. In talking with students, we note they feel stretched and challenged.

Excellent teachers have carefully embedded the criteria for success into their assignments. The work is important, and students are pushed to perform at high levels.

Nancy Kerr's teaching establishes a standard, what Grant Wiggins (1998) calls "a desirable degree or level of exemplary performance—a worthwhile target irrespective of whether most people can or cannot meet it at the moment."[2] We do not label Nancy's teaching excellent because she "does all the right moves" or because she exactly fits a particular pattern that someone somewhere has designated as "the way to be effective." Were we to continue to watch what Nancy Kerr does and to examine the processes her students use, the products they create, and the progress they make in their learning, we would be able to amass significant data about her repertoire. We would also be able to make judgments about her capacity to reach into that repertoire for what different children in her classroom need in order to learn. We would see that she holds high standards and expectations for all of her students and that she has many ways to help students successfully meet her standards. In fact, if we looked at longitudinal data about student performance, we would find a consistent pattern: most—if not all—students in Nancy's classes make significant academic progress during the course of the year. If we interviewed young people and their parents, we would hear that Mrs. Kerr does not give up on students, that she "loves what she does" and "is always learning something new and bringing it in to the class." If we examined her unit plans we would see a curriculum carefully crafted to develop understanding about important concepts, to assess student's learning, and to push them to think about complex ideas and express themselves clearly and articulately. Finally, we could look beyond classroom teaching. Nancy Kerr is good at all aspects of her job from being a helpful colleague to performing routine duties and to communicating effectively with parents.

---

[2] Grant Wiggins, *Educative Assessment: Designing Assessments to Inform and Improve Student Performance*, San Francisco: Jossey-Bass Publishers, 1998, pp. 104–105.

Hereafter we will use Nancy Kerr as a kind of shorthand reference for many ideas; we will use her to personify the kind of "real teacher" and skillful instruction we think all children need. There, are, therefore, four points to remember about Nancy Kerr:

1. What Nancy does should not be attributed *solely* to innate ability; she has invested, and continues to invest, significant effort, and she has acquired teaching and learning strategies purposefully and incrementally over time.

2. Nancy is not a "unique" phenomenon; her performance can be replicated; what she knows and is able to do can be captured, analyzed, and taught to others.

3. Nancy is not a "superstar"; she is an excellent teacher, not because she is the most entertaining, dramatic, innovative faculty member in town, but because year in and year out, students in her classroom feel welcome, take risks, learn, and perform at high levels, and make significant academic gains from their personal starting points.

4. Nancy's knowledge and skill mean she can make maximum use of every opportunity for children to learn; children neither "mark time" nor settle for doing less than their best work during the time they are with her.

Finally, let us visit the classroom of a teacher who certainly is more effective than Doug Noyes but does not approach the performance of a Nancy Kerr.

Profile of Mediocre Teaching: Sally Friendly

Each day 26 students enter Mrs. Friendly's 5th grade class at Center Elementary School in Springfield. She greets the students with "Hi, John. You look nice today Bill, and you too Kamisha."

Mediocre performers are not always unpleasant. Sally appears to care about the students.

She is well organized. The schedule for the day is on the board and the worksheets are arranged in neat folders on the shelf. As she goes over the day she says with some enthusiasm "Today is science day. You are going to have a fun science experiment activity on batteries and bulbs." Kids like the science program because it provides a change of pace from frequent seat work.

Mediocre performers are often organized. Their classrooms can be repositories of transient enthusiasm. But there is a superficiality to their curriculum planning. Plans may be organized, but tend to be anchored in activities rather than on important student learning outcomes.

"Okay, I have put the experiment sheet and materials on your desks. I am going to give you 10 minutes to complete Part 1 in pairs. Go to it."

Mediocre classrooms are characterized by missed opportunities and narrow repertoires. It is what is not done that speaks loudly. No context was set. The teacher fails to find out what students already know about batteries and bulbs. No objectives were communicated; no confusions anticipated; no connections made to the past or the future. There is no reason given for the activity, perhaps because the activity is the objective.

Mrs. Friendly has been teaching 12 years at grade 5. The children are not unhappy in her class. "She is nice." "She lets us have free time on Friday afternoon." "She is not as tough as Mr. Octane." The parents, in general, are not displeased. They describe Mrs. Friendly as "Okay," "nice to the kids, not as challenging as the 4th grade teacher, Mr. Octane." One parent says: "She doesn't stretch them, but they don't lose much ground." "The kids are occupied." There are very few parent complaints, perhaps because parents recognize the Mr. Octanes of the world are rare; they can't expect them every year, and Mrs. Friendly is a nice person.

So there is an air of neutral support with occasional complaints. Once every few years a parent of an "A" student will tell the principal that Mrs. Friendly's standards and expectations are unclear. Last year one father who was sending his son to a private school in grade 6 mentioned to the principal that son Frankie had done very little writing during the year and thought he might want to "look into the standards."

Unlike Mr. Noyes's class, there is order and on-task behavior by students. But unlike Mrs. Kerr, there are no opportunities for high-level thinking, and standards and expectations for students are set at a minimum. "Sally Friendly" teachers expect little and get little from students. She is warm and treats students well. But in terms of instruction, she is performing at a mediocre level in the classroom, and so are most of her students.

But Sally does contribute to the school. Sally frequently organizes social events. When staff are sick she is the first to circulate a card. She makes a genuine contribution to the school. The principal constantly muses, "What would we do without Sally?"

Frequently in cases of mediocre teaching, performance outside the classroom gets magnified. Something not central to teaching allows the evaluator to boost the overall appraisal. Measurement people refer to this as an observer error, such as a "leniency effect" or "halo error." (See Chapter 4 for a discussion of error sources.) One positive area of performance can become an escape hatch. Often great high school coaches with poor classroom performance get high evaluation appraisals (see Chapter 3 Frank Steele).

As a result, Sally Friendly has received good to excellent evaluations from Principal Smith for the past four years and before that from Mrs. Henry. Before new evaluation procedures were phased in recently (see Chapter 5), on a checklist format she had received the highest rating in everything except a "very good" in "instructional variety" and "meeting individual needs."

Mrs. Friendly is typical of teachers who can control their students, keep them generally on task, and are generally organized. They are not the *regular* focus of parent complaint. They do not draw the attention of the administrator even though their instruction is mediocre.

LEGAL NOTE

Marginal is another term frequently used to describe substandard performance that is not as bad as incompetent. Marginal is a good term to describe
performance that is just above or just below what is acceptable for an individual.
Inefficiency is a first cousin of incompetence but may be the closest legal term to
the term *mediocrity*. "'Inefficient' in the context of teacher performance means not
producing the effect intended or desired within a reasonable period of time
whether or not the teacher has knowledge or capability." (Lexington Public
Schools, AAA Case #11-390-00571-94 Bruce Fraser)

The Leadership Challenge

Sally Friendly represents the crux of the dilemma that sent us looking for clues
about what constitutes skillful leadership. Sally Friendly and Nancy Kerr have
received the same performance ratings. If put on the spot and asked to compare the two individuals, evaluators would most likely agree that Nancy's ratings are accurate, not inflated. However, few would be likely to describe Sally as
excellent.[3] Correspondingly few, if any, would say Sally should be dismissed.
*She is not totally incompetent or inefficient. Given appropriate interventions,
feedback, and opportunities to learn, Sally can grow.* However, Sally's students
need an advocate. And Sally needs someone with conviction to reject the idea
that she is "good enough to get by" so that she can get on with the business of
improvement.

Under current conditions in most schools, only a crisis or a significant
increase in parental complaints is likely to attract the attention of a supervisor
beset by what s/he perceives to be more pressing problems. Without the presence of skillful leadership, Sally's students will be shortchanged. *They will lose
opportunities to learn what they would have learned in Nancy Kerr's class.*
Should they suffer a second year of mediocre instruction, the long-term effects
of such lost opportunities will be magnified. We will consider Sally Friendly's
case again in more detail in Chapter 3. Throughout the rest of this book, her
case will help us think about what skillful leaders can do.

Confronting Mediocre Teaching: A Focus for Our Efforts

The problem of mediocre teaching, represented here in the contrast between
Mrs. Kerr and Mrs. Friendly, is a nested or multi-layered one. We cannot simply point to individual teacher performance issues and say we understand

---

[3] In several informal studies we found that over 90 percent of teachers in the sampled districts
were rated as excellent in their evaluations. But when supervisors were asked how many were really
excellent, the number dropped to about 20 percent.

either the cause or the cure. As Figure 1-1 shows, the problem is caused and exacerbated by

- Supervisors and teachers with skill deficiencies
- Supervisors and teachers who hold and act on limiting beliefs about their own or others' ability to learn
- Institutional norms and practices that support and sustain mediocrity
- Leaders who fail to build the institutional culture and professional community necessary to support excellence

Consider our cases. Certainly Mr. Noyes and Mrs. Friendly must bear part of the responsibility for their own performance. They need certain skills and capabilities that they either do not have currently or are not choosing to use. On a second level, however, the substandard performance of these teachers persists because of mediocre supervision. No one in authority has called attention to the fact that students are not learning or that performance is inadequate; no one has required changes. Finally, an organization whose practices and norms make it possible for Mr. Noyes or Ms. Friendly to receive positive performance appraisals year after year is equally at fault. Standards for acceptable performance are often set by the lowest quality performance that will be tolerated in the organization. Thus, in this environment Nancy Kerr becomes the exception. What she does is not expected of all teachers and consequently not available to all students.

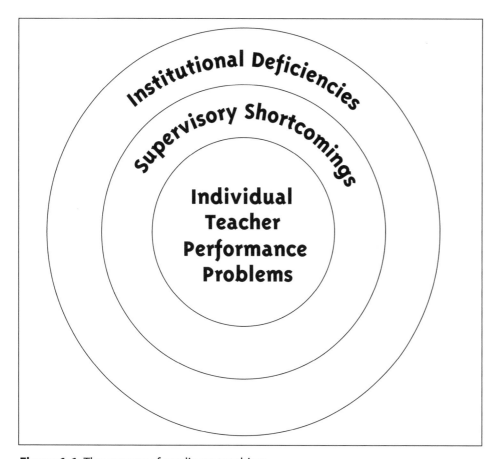

Figure 1-1 The sources of mediocre teaching.

So what do skillful leaders do? In Figure 1-2 we add three conditions that generate the energy and focus for confronting mediocre teaching and building norms that support and sustain excellence. Our "3 C" conditions are:

Conviction: a widely shared institutional belief that every child deserves and can have expert instruction and that supervisors and evaluators must be advocates for students

Competence: increased technical capacity to select data, describe the problem, and design a plan at either the individual or institutional level

Control: adequate structures, processes, and resources to support the evaluators and supervisors who are charged with confronting mediocre performance

Applying all the 3 C's, leaders must systematically attack institutional deficiencies, supervisory shortcomings, and teacher performance problems.

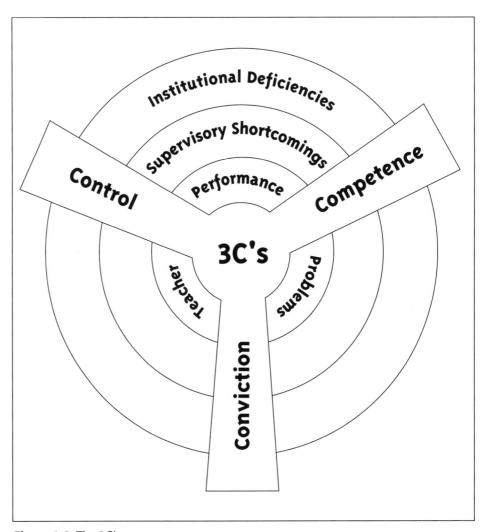

Figure 1-2 The 3C's.

2 Confronting Institutional Mediocrity

When students are pressed to name the one change that would be the most important in helping them learn more, "having more good teachers" easily tops the list.[1]

Evidence now abounds that ordinary teachers can do extraordinary things—or at least realize incremental improvement with all kinds of [students]."[2]

Helping large numbers of teachers to do extraordinary things seems to define our challenge. To have lasting impact, the work of changing mediocre performance cannot simply take place in a single location or on a case-by-case basis. Whole school systems and entire education communities must invest effective effort to get this work done. To work wisely and strategically, skillful leaders need what Peter Senge calls "true proactiveness," the capacity to see "how we contribute to our own problems" (1990 p. 21). Seeing what we control also lets us see what we can change.

In this chapter, then, we consider how the behavior of organizations, with their complex systems, unexamined beliefs and assumptions, and routine decisions, can create or sustain mediocre performance. We also consider the ways in which skillful leaders use the problem-solving prerequisites of conviction, competence, and control (Figure 1-2) for two distinct purposes:

1. To identify and "wipe out" debilitating beliefs and unpromising practices that foster or protect mediocre performance

2. To build common purpose and vision, strong and skilled professional communities, and the structural capacity to support excellence

[1] *Getting By: What American Teenagers Really Think About Their Schools*, Public Agenda, 1997, p.22.
[2] Mike Schmoker, *Results: The Key to Continuous Improvement*, ASCD, 1996, p.41.

We begin with the question of institutional conviction, defined as the shared belief that *every child deserves and can have expert instruction* and that the primary role of supervisors and evaluators is to monitor and to advocate for student learning. Without widespread institutional conviction, evaluators are unlikely to tackle mediocre performance even when they recognize its existence and have the contractual authority to address it.

Shaking Debilitating Beliefs

Debilitating beliefs are deeply rooted assumptions and shared myths that shape the ways in which members of an organization tackle their work. Often buried, unrecognized, and unchallenged, debilitating beliefs can sap institutional conviction. Skillful leaders must expose these controlling assumptions. They must think about themselves and their work in new ways and adopt new patterns of behavior. As we have worked with whole school systems, we have noted four broad categories of beliefs that create or feed institutional deficiencies:

- Diminished expectations for adult learning
- Diminished aspirations for achievement and opportunity
- Inappropriate problem definition and goal setting
- Negative assumptions about costs and benefits

Diminished Expectations for Adult Learning

Sometimes the words or actions of evaluators suggest that they do not believe in the following:

- Their own ability to learn or change
- The capacity of other adults to learn or change
- Their own ability to help, support, or have an impact on others

Their behavior reveals that people at all levels of the school district have given up on one another. The giving up can be blatantly obvious or subtle and insidious. Teachers sort and label students into those whom they can teach and those for whom they believe no amount of teaching will make a difference. Administrators sort and label teachers into those who are "just naturally wonderful" like Nancy Kerr and those "who can only do so much" like Sally Friendly. Superintendents do not believe their administrators have conviction or competence and thus do not hold those administrators accountable for careful work with teachers. Conversations in such places are laced with the language of hopelessness:

"What can you expect? She's been like that for 20 years."

"He has relatives in high places. We're just going to have to find ways to get around him because all hell will break loose if we try to do anything."

"He's two years (or five years) from retirement; I can't start asking him to learn this now."

"There's no way that the union and parents will back me if I expect her to do what a superstar does. That's just totally unrealistic."

"Nothing I could say or do will produce any difference in what he does."

"You can't teach an old dog new tricks."

"You can't make a silk purse out of a sow's ear."

Sometimes these assertions are supported by data or the prior experiences of the speaker. More often they are not; they are simply statements that have been made by so many different people over so many different years that they have taken on a ring of truth. Echoed from administrator to administrator across the organization, they become part of the unexamined "guidelines" that excuse evaluators from naming and taking on mediocre performance.

Building Conviction about Adult Learning

When members of an organization talk about what they can and cannot reasonably expect of each other, they reveal the visions that shape their behavior. Shared visions that give humans a sense of what they could create, Senge notes, "compel courage so naturally that people don't even realize the extent of their courage. Courage is simply doing whatever is needed in pursuit of the vision" (1990, p. 208). Later in this chapter, we examine concrete strategies that skillful leaders use to build cultures that have high expectations for teaching and learning and to create teams that can count on one another for high levels of technical competence. No matter what other initiatives they undertake, however, leaders must be forceful and articulate about their belief that all members of the organization can learn and perform at high levels. They must present new data to help build conviction. They must collect, and encourage others to collect, new stories featuring people who can collaborate, solve teaching and learning problems, and do "extraordinary things." In effect they must supply substitute visions and substitute mythology. Finally, they must set up the structures and provide training in the strategies that help people experience what it means to be successful (Schmoker 1996).

Diminished Aspirations for Achievement and Opportunity

A companion to diminished expectations for adult learning is the notion that some schools, some towns, some clusters or grades simply cannot have what others may take for granted. When school personnel are acting on such a belief, they do not ask for top quality performance because of some belief they have about the setting in which they work. Perhaps they assume teachers in their town would not be able to meet a particular standard; perhaps they assume that asking for a certain standard of performance would somehow be unfair given socioeconomic or environmental limitations students face. This diminished aspiration manifests itself in statements such as:

> "Remember this is Lowtown. We can't pay the kind of salaries that attract good teaching. If you want that kind of thing you should move to . . . "

> "We're not Richtown. Our teachers don't go to Harvard. They haven't had the kind of training you'd have to have to do _____."

> "That stuff is all right for school X. They have all that parent support (or money, or a new building, or some other wonderful resource.)"

> "Look, Teacher X is one of a kind; you certainly can't expect everyone to perform at that level."

> "S/he won't stay here. As soon as there's a chance, s/he'll be gone, and the fancy program will go too."

In some cases the norm of not asking, not daring, and not dreaming becomes deeply ingrained. Both teachers and supervisors subscribe to the notion that so-called "second-rate places" get (and deserve) second-rate teaching.

Building Organizational Capability

Skillful leaders understand that organizational capability is neither dictated by characteristics of the setting nor limited by characteristics of a student body. Schools, they believe, cannot depend solely upon the efforts of a few superstar performers to raise student achievement. Schools must rely on a team made up of many heroes and heroines working productively together, and teams must be able to count on the competence of all of their members. In their landmark study of school restructuring, Newmann and Wehlage (1995 p. 29) note

> When schools are unable to coordinate teachers' diverse aims for students into a curricular mission focused on high quality student learning, when teachers have few opportunities to work together to devise approaches suited to the school's student body, or when schools pursue multiple innovations without sustained, long-term consistency, it is difficult for even the most gifted teachers to make a positive difference for students.

To confront mediocrity, then, we need to create cultures of excellence. We need to tap into the moral purpose and desire to make a difference that pulled individuals into teaching in the first place. Creating new dreams and articulating clear shared purposes, Senge notes, provides the spark and sense of excitement "that lifts an organization out of the mundane" (1990 p. 208). Confronting mediocrity by daring to ask more and by providing the necessary time and structures to help teachers work together to rise to those expectations, allows organizations to increase the overall technical competence of their members. Over time, collaborative planning, curriculum development, and problem-solving create a richer set of resources for all faculty members to draw upon. Moreover, clear shared visions and teamwork generate what Newmann and Wehlage call collective responsibility. All teachers see themselves as people who are accountable for student achievement. As this culture builds, it both strengthens institutional conviction and exerts peer pressure on those who are not meeting the standards (1995 p. 31).

In some cases the norm of not asking, not daring, and not dreaming becomes deeply ingrained.

Inappropriate Problem Definition and Goal Setting

Debilitating beliefs also reveal themselves when groups decide there is only one way to solve a problem and that one way is too difficult to do. Sometimes supervisors define the challenge of raising overall levels of instruction in a school district as "How can we fire mediocre performers?" That problem definition is very different from asking "How we can help those whose performance needs to improve to meet the high minimum standards of the school district?" or "What are the different ways in which we can make it clear that every child deserves and will have expert instruction?"

Describing the Problem and Designing the Plan

Guaranteed to tie up district resources, drain emotions, and spread paranoia, firing is an inappropriate and unrealistic first response to dealing with mediocre performance. To combat the effects of this "we'll never be able to do it" belief, the skillful leader must focus attention away from the notions of punishment and onto what students need—highly skilled, caring teachers bonded together in effective professional communities. In Chapters 4, 5, and 6 we examine the processes by which skillful leaders use multiple sources of data and carefully structured improvement plans to help individuals either make their performance more effective or make the choice to move on. At the institutional level, leaders need to use multiple sources of data to expose organizational deficiencies ranging from poor contracts to ineffective evaluation procedures to a failure to give negative feedback or poor performance ratings no matter how egregious the performance. Once leaders have used data to find new problem definitions, teams of supervisors and evaluators can work on realistic, attainable goals and the strategies to reach them. Administrative teams and school boards then see firing as a last resort along a continuum of potential solutions, all of which the key players in the district are capable of carrying out.

Negative Assumptions about Costs and Benefits

When groups of supervisors talk frankly about the costs of confronting mediocre performance, four basic categories of fears generally surface. All are linked to the common belief that asking for improvements will fracture relationships and endanger collegiality. Many supervisors worry, for example, that their staff members will be "devastated" or "destroyed" by information about areas requiring improvement, no matter how humanely the data are presented and the request for change is made. Others assume that they will lose long-time social and professional friendships they value because the recipients will be so angry. Still others are concerned that they will lose the good will of the school or credibility with their staff because they will be perceived as being too demanding. Finally, there is the fear that staff members will respond with anger and acting out, thus disrupting the positive and productive climate of the school and drawing the administrator into a battle. This fear of emotional pain and inevitable conflict, sometimes accompanied by the belief that they have neither the skills nor backing to get the job done, becomes debilitating when it leads an evaluator to back away or look away.

Understandings about Gains

The moral certainty that children need advocates helps overcome perceived costs. Being part of a professional community that holds itself accountable for achievement and whose members collaborate to solve problems and support one another helps. Developing competence at collecting and presenting data in ways that are fair, humane, consistent for all evaluators, and linked to student learning (the focus of Chapters 4 and 5) also builds courage.

Michael Fullan notes that "People behave their way into new beliefs, not just think their way into them" (1993 p. 15). Later in this chapter we examine a sampling of practical activities skillful leaders use to help supervisors develop new attitudes and approaches. In Chapter 8 we tell the story of one individual's decision to become "a kid's principal." Skillful leaders collect such concrete illustrations of risk, tenacity, and incremental progress to help build courage and conviction, not only about the importance of the work, but also about the evaluator's ability to bring about positive changes for children without destroying adults in the process. Leaders chant "This work is important; we can do it and do it well; we won't give up on one another." They exhort, comfort, and stand beside those who are asking for excellence. They also look for sources of confusion about what is important and for the ways in which the institution may be undermining its own best efforts and resolves. These we have called unpromising practices.

Unpromising Practices

Beliefs lurk under the surface of day-to-day actions; unpromising practices are the standard operating procedures that reveal or reinforce these beliefs. It is unlikely that a single practice can be identified as a key institutional deficiency. To confront mediocrity at a system-wide or organizational level, therefore, we need to look for patterns. We need to look for a series of choices or reactions that together make a supervisor afraid to take on mediocrity and block an institution's ability to develop competence and control. Because they are so widespread and so rarely examined, a half dozen of these unpromising practices merit closer attention. (See Appendix B "Unpromising Institutional Practices Survey.")

Practice One: Transferring Problems

Almost all administrators can describe a time when they recognized that children assigned to a particular teacher were getting "a raw deal," that is missing critical learning opportunities available in other classrooms. Parent or student complaints, patterns of test scores over time, or classroom observation may reveal the problem. The institution's response to that recognition signals whether it believes that adults can learn and must be expected to perform at high levels or whether it has fallen into a habit of protecting mediocrity.

Tailoring Classes

Transferring the problem by tailoring classes is one popular response to weak teaching. Rather than expecting all teachers on a faculty to work successfully with a broad range of students, administrators routinely hand pick and assign groups whose parents will not complain or who think of themselves as average and have learned to expect less of a teacher. Depending upon their perceived weakness, mediocre performers may also automatically be given smaller classes, or only honors groups, or only so-called low achievers, or they may be "protected" from children with special needs. In each case the assumption is the same; the teacher cannot be changed, so we will solve the problem by changing the children. Oftentimes, this practice shifts most of the burden to the most disenfranchised students in a school system and further compounds the negative impact on achievement.

Moving "High Maintenance" Children

Transferring one child to solve one year's issue does not institutionalize mediocrity. Routinely transferring students because a teacher cannot cope with high profile children, or because of legitimate parental requests, or because students themselves present evidence that they are not getting what other classes are getting is an unpromising practice. When information about the underlying reasons for such transfers is not shared with the teacher, data about such transfer requests are not part of the evaluation process, and teachers are not asked to respond and grow, the district sends key messages about its beliefs and expectations. These messages signal that the mediocre performer can keep on doing whatever s/he is doing with impunity. They may also suggest to outsiders that the school is unable to monitor the quality of its own professionals, thus triggering further rounds of transfer requests in self-defense.

Transferring Staff

When a staff member hears that she or he must improve performance, the staff member can face the issue head on or become a moving target. Particularly in large districts with numerous options for placement, transferring staff who are "weak links" to a new site holds great appeal. Either openly promoted or tacitly condoned by district leadership, the practice is sometimes cynically called "the dance of the lemons."[3]

What Bridges calls the "escape hatch" of transfer within or between schools survives as standard practice because the script people use to explain such actions is filled with the language of good intentions: Teacher X is being sent to a different school in order to "give her a new lease on life, a second chance, a new perspective." Moreover, Teacher X is going to this new place without an evaluation history, with his or her "slate wiped clean" because the "kind and fair" way to give a person a second chance is to banish the record of past performance. Perhaps, the administrator thinks, the fit will be better, or a new supervisor will be more capable of dealing with the mediocre performance. If so, that supervisor can start the data collecting process anew without all the old baggage. Perhaps, after all, confrontation will not be necessary, and the staff member will somehow "catch" through osmosis the higher standards of the

[3]Edwin M. Bridges, Philadelphia: Falmer Press, 1986, p. 31.

Allowing certain staff members to teach the same subject or grade year in and year out while others are asked to stretch and change is another practice that supports mediocrity.

receiving school. Perhaps, the staff member thinks, this new administrator will understand me better or not be so "unreasonable" in his or her demands. Perhaps the workload at this new school will be less, or the union will be stronger, or the teachers won't be involved in all these new programs and committees. In this script, neither teachers nor administrators appear to take responsibility for fixing the pattern of mediocre performance. Their job is to shift the problem elsewhere while avoiding controversy and hard feelings.

By adopting various mixes of transfer solutions, administrators seek to balance the school's assets and liabilities and to solve immediate problems without creating obvious new ones for themselves. Norms of practice in the school system, moreover, encourage them to find the solution that will "do the least damage to the smallest number of children" or that will "isolate and minimize the impact of mediocre performance."

Inevitably, such short-term solutions carry long-term consequences. First, certain groups of children and sometimes certain schools are disproportionately affected because teachers are being protected from being asked to improve. Second, the institution is left with a pool of people who have been labeled on the grapevine as substandard performers but for whom there is no documentation. Each year there is a delay potentially magnifies the amount of time and energy required to make change. Third, because evidence continues to be swept under the rug or sent away, neither the supervisor nor the teacher develops competence. The supervisor neither builds nor acts on his/her conviction about the importance of good teaching.

Practice Two: Enabling Mediocrity through Work Assignments

When principals routinely accommodate low levels of teacher performance and school districts routinely accommodate low levels of administrator performance by assigning less challenging work to those who do not meet standards, they enable mediocrity. The enabling manifests itself in a variety of ways depending upon the institution. Tailoring classes to accommodate for teacher weaknesses has already been mentioned above. Other practices include agreeing that teachers with seniority should always "get the best classes" regardless of merit or preparation and agreeing that teachers with seniority should not be asked to take their turn at dealing with the most challenging children in the school. Making novice practitioners "pay their dues" with a schedule composed of classes or students no one else wants allows mediocre practitioners to get by without dealing with difficult students. It places the neediest children with teachers who are the least likely to have a broad range of skills and sends the message that there are no consequences for failing to perform at high levels. Allowing certain staff members to teach the same subject or grade year in and year out while others are asked to stretch and change is another practice that supports mediocrity. Finally, reducing the academic workload of mediocre performers so that their schedules are laden with "duties," small groups, and make-work sends the message that there are no consequences for failing to perform at high levels.

Explanations of work assignments often reveal the performance expectations administrators have internalized by following the standard operating procedures of the district: not all teachers can or should be asked to stretch or to change and arranging for some teachers to have easier jobs is a kind way to respond to their perceived limitations. The practice allows those who "can do" many opportunities to expand their skills. Those who are shaky become stuck in that mode because they are not put into situations that would require them to improve.

Practice Three: Basing Evaluations on Sparse or Nonexistent Data

In Chapter 7 we discuss contract language and the limitations of certain evaluation systems in greater detail. Here, however, we need to consider a series of expedient practices that cause evaluation to become an empty exercise. Institutions create conditions in which mediocrity can thrive when they do the following:

1. Rely extensively on "quick and dirty" checklist approaches to performance evaluation that allow evaluators to make judgments without providing extensive, substantive evidence in support of such judgments

2. Overload supervisors and evaluators so that the individuals in charge of documenting performance and pushing for improvement are unable to collect the necessary data to do so

3. Limit the kind or amount of data upon which an evaluation is based to one small part of the teacher's roles and responsibilities

4. Allow administrators to produce yearly evaluations full of sweeping generalities and phrases that are equally interchangeable from one write-up to another

All of these practices fail to recognize the critical role of data in effective supervision and evaluation.

As profiles in later chapters reveal, mediocre performance is most often characterized by patterns of behavior rather than by discrete, easily identified actions. For example, planning may be nonexistent or ineffectual; standards for student work may be low or inconsistent, as indicated by assignments given, feedback provided, and grading. The professional may use the same limited repertoire of ways to explain and help students understand concepts regardless of the changing demands of the curriculum or the needs of particular students. In the classrooms of mediocre performers, children may consistently, although unintentionally, be deprived of opportunities to analyze, synthesize, evaluate, or make decisions. The negative impact on student learning often arises because of missed opportunities, because of what did not happen that could, and should, have happened. Thus, finding and interpreting the patterns of choices or nonchoices in a classroom becomes the critical role of the evaluator.

Documenting a pattern of response requires substantive data that have been collected over time and from multiple sources. Low standards for student work, for example, show up in homework assignments, in testing, and in the kind of written responses students are asked to make in class. Yet these sources of information rarely find their way into the evaluation process. While we know intellectually that all aspects of a professional's performance must be assumed to contribute to how well he or she provides opportunities for students to learn, it is hard to put that knowledge into practice. Pressed for time and laboring under unchallenged assumptions about what is fair or appropri-

Low standards for student work show up in homework assignments, in testing, and in the kind of written responses students are asked to make in class.

Almost inevitably, teachers whose classroom performance is mediocre but who sustain the extracurricular or social life of the school will have received good to excellent evaluations.

ate, too many school systems rely on simple checklists. They use rating systems unsupported by artifacts or written evidence, and make judgments after one or two announced visits to a classroom. Teachers become accustomed to evaluations that are based on limited data, on the evaluator's impressions, or on such unexamined norms as "anyone who keeps a classroom in order and does not send problems to the office is a good teacher."

Compounding the problems presented by evaluation systems that do not require adequate data collection is the practice of assigning evaluations. Generally, administrators in American schools supervise and evaluate too many people annually to be able to do a creditable job. Often, they perform their supervisory and evaluative roles in isolation from colleagues and without benefit either of extended training or of clearly articulated standards of performance that have been adopted by all evaluators in the district. Because the act of evaluating staff consists primarily of rushing to do the minimum required by contract and of crushing final reporting into the smallest amount of space and time possible, both teachers and evaluators come to accept the premise that it would be "impossible to capture or document what it is a teacher does." Taken a step further, the practice leads the players also to assume that it will be impossible to document what it is someone does not do.

Practice Four: Assigning Inappropriate Weight to Data Unrelated to Student Learning

Elevating other kinds of contributions to the life of the school above the ability to generate high levels of student academic performance is also an unpromising practice. As our profiles in Chapter 3 illustrate, the mediocre performer wears many faces. There are enthusiastic, kind people like Sally Friendly who are not particularly effective at helping children learn but who have numerous redeeming qualities as human beings. They run after-school programs, clubs, field trips, and fund raisers; they volunteer for the PTO and the school council. There are also individuals like Frank Steele (see Chapter 3) who have been "getting by" doing less than their best work in the classroom but fulfilling some other need of the school district: coaching, ordering supplies, providing a safe haven for difficult adolescents, directing the school musical.

Almost inevitably, teachers whose classroom performance is mediocre but who sustain the extracurricular or social life of the school will have received good to excellent evaluations. The practice of ignoring substandard classroom performance and basing a teacher's evaluation largely on extracurricular contributions may reflect the supervisor's belief that the individual in question cannot learn or cannot be asked to do more. Over time it is easy for such teachers to rationalize shortcomings in instruction and/or content knowledge because they legitimately see themselves as making important contributions to children's overall development. Both the institution and the teacher thus evolve a pattern of settling for less than the teacher might reasonably be expected to produce.

To check for the existence of this practice, leaders need to read evaluations and tune in to conversations that present either-or scenarios: that is, "Either I put up with X's less than stellar performance for the sake of all the good she does in other areas of school life, or I run the risk of alienating her and having no one else to do that job." Vehement denials that the academic performance of students should be taken into account when determining an individual teacher's evaluation are also warning signs. If such denials are accompanied by an explanation that some teachers simply cannot teach certain material or children, they signal the presence of debilitating beliefs about who can learn and what the institution has a right to expect.

Practice Five: Allowing Written Evaluations That Contain Mixed Messages and/or Inflated Performance Ratings

Evaluators who want to be kind or who are afraid of "destroying the self esteem" of someone, may choose to couch their observations and recommendations for change in tentative or ambiguous language. They may further compound the problem by tacking together statements that praise and approve and statements that give evidence of problems in the same sentence. Thus a supervisor who has noticed that the teacher rarely requires students to go beyond single-word responses to questions, never asks students to give evidence to support their oral responses, and rarely asks students to explain their thinking in writing when they have been assigned a problem, will write in the evaluation:

> *Your fast pace and rapid-fire response create a lively momentum. Perhaps you might want to think about exploring ways in which you could introduce children to the idea of giving reasons for their answers.*

or

> *The teacher's warm rapport and quickness to praise made for a happy environment. While they love being called on, it would seem that children are somewhat reluctant to give reasons for their answers and may need to be stretched. It is suggested that you try popsicle sticks and maybe rewards for thinking, which would be entirely consistent with the delightful way in which you motivate youngsters.*

Teachers reading the selections above would be hard pressed to recognize that the supervisor has found a worrisome pattern that s/he wishes the teacher to change. It would be quite easy, for example, for a reader like Sally Friendly who is especially proud of her ability to give "warm fuzzies" to focus on the beginning and ending of paragraph two and screen out the rest. Teachers reading these selections would also be unable to determine exactly what practices they needed to stop and what they needed to start doing. Finally, the recommendations above are written to sound as if they are teacher options: that is, the teacher may or may not choose to make any changes in her practice, and either outcome will be perfectly acceptable to the supervisor. It is highly unlikely, then, that any of these recommendations will bring about the kind of change the supervisor wanted in the first place.

Mediocrity is protected by poor or tentative writing and mixed messages. It is also encouraged in places where there has been little attempt to develop shared high standards and expectations for teacher performance. If the definition of excellence is not widely understood among evaluators, they can easily fall into the trap of elevating practices that might be considered a normal and expected part of a competent teacher's work. Excellence then has no real meaning in practice because everyone on a faculty is "excellent" no matter what choices they have made or what results they have produced. Since all staff are excellent, there is no more to learn and no more that can be done. All suggestions to the contrary become threats in such a scenario. Failures in student performance must be attributed to the students because they have not responded. This unpromising practice can easily occur in districts with high socioeconomic levels and with high levels of student performance that may have little connection to how they were taught.

Institutions that condone either mixed messages in evaluation write-ups or a regular pattern of inflated performance ratings, set up situations that limit both teacher and student learning.

Practice Six: Low Standards for Hiring New Teachers and for Renewing the Contracts of Novices

Districts create a form of institutionalized mediocrity if they routinely hire and retain teachers for reasons other than that teacher's performance in his/her professional role. When school systems hire or retain teachers in order to do favors or build political capital, administrators often find themselves saddled with individuals who cannot perform at the high levels required to produce student achievement. In addition, they may find themselves trying to confront individuals whom the grapevine has labeled as untouchable either because of their "connections" or because they have some real or imagined rights to jobs that make them different from others in the school district. In either instance, children may suffer because of the perceived paralysis, and the culture of the school may be affected by the real or imagined favoritism.

The job of evaluating and supervising new teachers presents special challenges that Chapter 9 addresses in greater detail. New teachers present a school system with a clean slate and a chance to "get it right." Institutions become their own worst enemies when they fail to be concrete and forthright with novice practitioners about areas requiring improvement or assume they need to make allowances and excuses for beginners even after extensive support has been provided. Allowing new teachers to be mentored or co-opted by marginal cultures or mediocre performers can undermine a district's efforts to improve student achievement by hiring bright new teachers. Novice practitioners who have not made substantive improvement after two years of good quality support should be let go. Continuing to support them signals that the district has lowered its standards or lost its conviction.

 # Creating Conviction, Competence, and Control

Establishing norms of excellence means doing more than identifying and reacting to unpromising practices. On the following pages we offer a series of broad recommendations and sample strategies to help build institutional conviction and competence and the structural capability to support excellence.

Recommendation One: Get data, ask hard questions, and pay attention to the answers.

Using multiple sources of data to describe present patterns and identify gaps is as important to confronting institutional mediocrity as it is to taking on individual cases. Specific facts and unanswered questions based on the data allow teams to focus on something other than vague fears and perceptions of hopelessness. Data can prevent random finger-pointing. Data can help teams of people to set clear, attainable goals and pursue those goals with initiative and tenacity.

The Appendix offers several self-assessment tools that can serve as starting points for thoughtful discussion and as guides to identify practices that may need to be changed. The "3C's Supervisors' Survey on Competence, Conviction, and Control" in Appendix A is meant to be a practical tool that individual administrators and administrative teams can use to take stock of the barriers and limitations they perceive in their own settings. Appendix B "Unpromising Institutional Practices Survey" can be used by leaders and administrative teams to diagnose the health of the institutional practices and identify goals for improvement. Appendix C "Grading Your Evaluation Procedures" allows school systems to conduct an informal check on the degree to which supervisors and evaluators have the structures and processes they need to take on mediocre performance. The box that follows offers other sample strategies for obtaining instructive data about beliefs and practices as revealed in evaluation patterns.

Recommendation Two: Assume that all members of the organization must perform at high levels. Make the norm of excellence non-negotiable, and act on it in many different arenas.

Skillful leaders are driven by a powerful vision of performance and the belief that many people can learn to function in that way. They engage the attention and commitment of others both through the choices they make in a variety of regularly recurring situations or "arenas" and through the ways in which they

---

Collecting Data about Present Evaluation Patterns

- Examine evaluation procedures to determine whether they allow the use of multiple sources of data to get information about what a teacher does to help students learn and whether anyone in the system actually uses multiple sources of data.

- Analyze three to five years' worth of final evaluations to determine whether they effectively discriminate between good and bad performance or whether all teachers are commendable all of the time.

- Assess final recommendations and the contents of improvement plans to determine whether there is any connection between data presented in evaluations and subsequent recommendations and suggestions, check whether recommendations and suggestions are limited to "glow and grow" generalities or include specific, measurable goals.

- Randomly sample a variety of different evaluators' written work over an extended period to determine the degree to which they continually set forth improvement challenges and/or document substandard performance.

- Examine the match between teacher performance ratings over a five-year period and a variety of measures of student achievement for that same period; use the patterns uncovered to raise a series of questions for future study.

explain those choices. Hiring, assigning resources like professional development time and money, promoting and transferring staff, working with committees, responding to grievances, and examining student achievement are all examples of arenas in which norms of excellence can be created.

Establishing Norms of Excellence

- Make everyone a contributor. When hiring, resist the urge to replicate organizational strengths. Recruit new faculty who fill holes in the collective expertise, e.g., strong math and science teachers for elementary school and people who can teach content reading and writing skills for high school.

- Expect excellence of new faculty. If possible, observe teachers before hiring them. If not possible, act swiftly and humanely to weed out those who do not meet high minimum standards within two years. Do not look the other way when young teachers have poor work habits, poor communication skills, or weak content background.

- Openly battle complaints and grievances about what veteran faculty can be asked to do. Expect experienced faculty to learn and be able to use the best of what newly trained professionals are bringing into the district. Set timelines for learning, establish criteria for successful performance, provide choices and support, follow contract guidelines, and confront the professional honestly if the work is not done.

- Make sure responsibility for continuous improvement is shared. Establish a "50% from the organization and 50% from the professional" formula for distributing training time, energy, and resources. Hold those who do not choose to participate in the organization's professional development equally responsible for demonstrating competence as those who have participated.

- Reject or require changes in principals' evaluations, teacher goal statements, curriculum project descriptions, grant applications, and school improvement plans if the product does not meet high standards. Teach all individuals the strategies they need to improve their written and oral work rather than relying on the voices and pens of a few selected role models.

- Change dominant assumptions about the sanctity of teacher autonomy. Structure multiple opportunities for collaborative problem solving and hold all members accountable for carrying out agreed upon solutions.

Skillful leaders create cultures that reject "good enough" and "getting by." They seek worthy challenges to care about and pursue. By paying attention to a collection of "gaps" between present and desired student and adult performance, leaders signal that *the work of excellent teachers is never done.* In public and private speech, leaders make it clear that children's needs are driving the push for instructional improvement. They establish, in effect, the moral imperative that helps to give an entire organization conviction.

When they pursue this strategy of finding worthy problems before the problems find them, skillful leaders honor and facilitate teacher collaboration and teacher-designed solutions. Teams indicate how they will choose to pursue improvement goals. Leaders then announce that *all* members of the community will ultimately be held accountable for narrowing the student performance gap by solving the identified problem. Evaluation focuses on gathering

> ## Substituting Collective Responsibility for Individual Autonomy
>
> Skillful leaders use the levers provided by outside forces ranging from state and national testing to public interest in charter schools to chip away at the notion that teachers have the right to be left alone to do less than their very best work on a regular basis. Such forces, leaders are heard to claim, demand that all members of the professional community rigorously examine their own practices, set forth improvement goals, and pull their own weight in collective endeavors.

data about the impact of strategies, unit plans, assessment practices, etc. that have been selected by teachers to close the gap. This approach helps to deal with the mediocre practitioner who goes through the motions, has all of the moves, yet misses the essential content questions and organizing ideas that students must learn. It emphasizes outcomes as well as activities.

Building norms of excellence and deep commitments to student learning requires that faculty members give up a certain amount of individual autonomy in service of agreed upon goals. The longer teachers are left in isolation to solidify their beliefs and practices, the more difficult it becomes for them to admit to difficulty and to ask for help (Schmoker, p. 20). In *Renewing America's Schools*, Carl Glickman presents an interesting finding: "Faculty in successful schools are less satisfied with regard to their teaching than are faculty in the less successful schools" (1993, p. 16). This finding has relevance for leaders because a large proportion of those whose practice is labeled as mediocre are not dissatisfied or displeased by what they are doing. Moreover, if schools have subscribed to the well worn tradition of celebrating teacher autonomy and claiming collective excellence without sufficient evidence, individuals have considerable ammunition to resist supervisory efforts for change. Whenever possible, teachers need the exposure to shared goals and visions, useful data about the success of their efforts, and peer collaboration to see the gaps in their own performance for themselves and to be part of the group that designs the solution.

> ## Strategy for Building Professional Community: SOS Meetings
>
> **What:** Brief, intensely structured meetings to study and learn from 12 to 25 real cases going on in the school system during a particular year.
>
> **Who:** Convened by district-level leadership responsible for teaching and learning and/or for personnel; attendance is mandatory for all building level and central office staff assigned to a study group.
>
> **Why:** To build conviction, competence, and a common voice among team members; reveal inconsistencies and lack of clarity about standards and expectations, procedural problems, etc.
>
> **How:** Groups of 6 to 20 administrators plus appropriate district level staff who will support them meet for 1.5 to 2.0 hours every 4 to 6 weeks.
> Each administrator identifies two cases, one of which must involve mediocre performance, that raise important questions or challenge the understanding of the group and the capacity of the system.
>
> Sessions are brief and intensely structured; team members formulate the questions presented by the case, make recommendations and agreements, and learn about the impact of the work during follow-up reporting and next-step planning.

Recommendation Three: Invest significant time and energy developing professional community and technical competence among supervisors and evaluators.

While much has been written about the negative impact of teacher isolation, administrative isolation can also be problematic because evaluators do not get the social and emotional support that they need, evaluators are not able to learn from one another, and individual interpretations of standards and procedures lead to uneven or inequitable practices within the same evaluation system. In order to help administrative teams develop the shared conviction and technical competence they need to confront mediocre performance, skillful leaders employ a number of different promising practices. These strategies are matched to the needs of their school systems and to the problems uncovered during their data gathering expeditions. Many strategies, such as the examples that follow, offer evaluators a chance to behave their way into new beliefs as they collaborate with colleagues.

Approaches like the SOS[4] sessions outlined use a case study format and collegial problem solving to offset the isolation experienced by evaluators and to identify the presence of debilitating beliefs. Meant to be productive work sessions, SOS meetings require a good facilitator who can both focus the discussion on evaluation's connection to improved teaching and learning and help the group surface new understandings and agreements generated from case studies. Participation by staff who can give procedural and/or legal support and by individuals who have the authority to reconcile conflicts and make decisions sends a key signal. Because one of the two cases a supervisor reports

---

Strategy for Building Professional Community: Grand Rounds

What: Joint, unannounced classroom observations or artifact examinations and debriefing sessions conducted by teams.

Who: Any combination of teachers and administrators whose responsibilities involve instructional leadership; should be led by a skilled evaluator with acknowledged expertise in seeing and analyzing the impact of teaching decisions; may also include outside partners from universities, consultants, individuals from other schools, etc.

Why: Breaks down administrator isolation; fosters the development of shared vision; provides quality checks and lets individuals sharpen their skills by collaborating and by observing expert evaluators.

How: Clusters of 2 to 5 observers jointly visit and script the several 25 to 40 minute instructional segments or review and analyze the same collection of artifacts (e.g., samples of student work, teacher tests, teacher assignments and feedback on assignments, etc.)

Teams jointly analyze their findings, determine what they would write about and what they would talk about with the teacher, assign a rating in relation to state or local standards, identify the issues revealed by the visit, and reflect on their implications.

---

[4]Judy Boroschek, Assistant Superintendent of the Wellesley (Massachusetts) Public Schools, to whom we are indebted for this idea, initiated Supervisor of Supervisors meetings as a way for district level leadership to develop competence in supporting and monitoring the work of principals. Others use the SOS title to signal conviction about taking on mediocrity or to symbolize a commitment to help one another and to learn from one another.

on regularly must involve confronting mediocre performance, group members have an opportunity to reflect on their own standards and expectations. Second cases, that is those not involving mediocre performance, often evolve from work done in a prior year, from unanticipated crises, or from a "stress point" in the system such as the need to make decisions about the competence of beginners. Oftentimes, the moral support provided by the group problem-solving and by the opportunities to rehearse language and sharpen thinking helps counteract the emotional drain of a difficult case.

In his study of the way in which New York City's Community District 2 goes about instructional improvement, Richard Ellmore (1996) notes that both central office staff and principals routinely conduct joint visits to schools and classrooms to signal that nothing is more important than instructional improvement. The visits are both part of the formal evaluation process and part of the essential work of learning about teaching and providing feedback and coaching to teachers. The underlying belief, Ellmore says, is that "shared expertise is more likely to produce change than individuals working in isola-tion"(1996 p. 10).

Institutions have long used the concept of visiting teams for purposes of program evaluation and school accreditation, and professional development schools have used such approaches with beginning teachers. Grand rounds work on the same principal of shared expertise. Data gathered by the teams is used to improve the overall competence and effectiveness of the evaluation system as well as to develop clear, concrete definitions of problems to be solved. Participants often report themselves much better able to discriminate between levels of performance in relation to a standard after they have partic-ipated in one or two series of grand rounds with colleagues.

Strategy for Developing Technical Competence: Checks of Inter-Rater Reliablilty

What: Regular practice sessions and performance tests to determine whether evaluators are using common standards for diagnosing and rating performance.

Who: All primary and secondary evaluators; may also involve individuals charged with giving feedback, supporting assistance plans, mentoring, etc.

Why: Designed to make certain that evaluators and those who give feedback are fair, consistent, and hold high standards and expectations for all practitioners.

To reveal inconsistencies, lack of clarity or agreement about standards and expecta-tions, procedural problems, etc. and to provide practice in skills such as conferencing and writing about standards.

How: Sessions can be led by an outside facilitator or consultant or by acknowl-edged experts within the school district and can take place in short bursts as part of regular administrative meetings or professional development activities. Participants share, evaluate, and rate a common experience, e.g., simulations, joint observations, video clips, examination of sample artifacts, that helps them compare where they stand in relation to others.

Interventions such as the three we have outlined above are intended to build strong professional communities among evaluators, to increase a team's collective responsibility for confronting mediocrity and to provide individual members with the social, emotional, and technical support they need to do the job well. Several other concrete strategies are worth noting under this recom-mendation.

> ## Strategies for Building Conviction and Competence
>
> ■ Have evaluators read and critique one another's observation and final reports for their clarity in discriminating between levels of performance and identifying what makes a difference for student achievement.
>
> ■ Pair novice and expert evaluators and ask them to conduct a minimum number of joint observations.
>
> ■ Hold routine problem-solving sessions in which administrators come to agreement on the way in which they will all deal with challenges presented by some of the classic profiles of mediocrity (see Chapter 3).
>
> ■ Establish evaluator study or book groups or encourage evaluators to take a course together.
>
> ■ Have administrators participate on improvement planning teams (see Chapter 6) for other schools and/or act as a second evaluator or another pair of eyes for a difficult case in order to gain experience and insight about how the work is done.

Recommendation Four: Conduct extensive training and open discussions among all members of the school community about what excellent teaching looks like and what it means for a teacher or administrator to meet a high standard.

Two of our essential conditions, competence and conviction, are nurtured by this recommendation. If we are to have the kind of inter-rater reliability necessary to deal with mediocre performance fairly and humanely, this step must take place. Almost without exception, our work in school districts has taught us that administrators have wide-ranging definitions of what constitutes acceptable and excellent teaching. Thus the grade or ranking a teacher gets depends on who the evaluator is and what the evaluator believes. Some evaluators have very high standards and expectations; others reward lavishly what their colleagues might call simply doing the job. Teachers unions rightfully point to the discrepancies and complain that the system is unfair.

Focusing on developing images and standards for high performing teaching gives us more clarity in recognizing mediocre performance by its absence. By public discussions of excellence, we do not mean holding one open forum on standards and asking for community input. Here we refer to an ongoing, multi-year project in which many different procedures and practices are aligned in the service of excellence. In such a project, all those who evaluate in a school district are required to assess the impact of their decisions in the following situations:

■ Analyses and judgments of teachers' work

■ Decisions about hiring, raises, and reappointments

■ Recommendations for transfers and procedures for assigning teachers to classes, grades, etc.

■ Responses to formal and informal data about student achievement

Unless considerable time is spent on defining the desirable targets, supervisors and evaluators are unlikely either to internalize standards or to develop the courage to push for better performance in their schools. To create coherence and consistency, however, administrators will require sustained practice with colleagues. Including mentor teachers, resource teachers, union representatives, and teachers who serve on improvement teams as coaches or critical friends in the conversation helps to spread understanding and increase collective responsibility.

Recommendation Five: Establish evaluation agreements that allow identification and separate treatment of substandard performers.

This step gives supervisors the authority or control they need to get the job done. Although the recommendation seems to be eminently sensible, many school systems attempt to confront mediocre performance in systematic ways only to find themselves hampered by antiquated procedures or obscure restrictions. Chapters 4, 5, and 6 describe a process of identifying data sources, describing a problem, and designing a plan to help mediocre performers improve. A good evaluation system needs to provide the structural supports for each of these steps. Chapter 7 discusses contract language specifically. Before new contract agreements can be negotiated, however, school boards or their designated negotiators must agree that there is a need to find fair and humane procedures for dealing with substandard performance. District administrators must be articulate and tenacious in communicating what present language allows them to do as opposed to what actually needs to be accomplished.

Summary

In Chapter 8 you will read one principal's account of how he came to be what he describes as a kid's principal. "I'm here for the children" is a line that many of us have memorized; it slips easily from our lips, and we have stopped examining whether our behaviors actually support such a claim. In fact, many unpromising practices have that label because they do not help either adults or children to learn and grow. Laying the groundwork for this genuine transformation of focus and reinforcing a commitment to children first is one of the most powerful contributions a leader can make. When institutions have fallen into the habit either of ignoring mediocrity or of actively protecting it in a variety of ways, leaders must pointedly signal an end to business as usual. Promoting excellence means proactively looking for mediocrity in all the right places. Finally, messages about what the institution can accomplish need to be couched in the same powerful terms that excellent teachers use with students: "This work is important. We can all do it, and do it well. Supervisors and evaluators will not give up on you even if you give up on yourself."

3 Profiles of Mediocrity

T here are no incompetent teachers here. There's no one who is bad enough to fire" many school leaders will tell us. "My problem is some people just aren't doing a very good job. Their work is mediocre; they are really just getting by; for example, I have one individual who. . . ." A story will follow. Each tale will be different; sometimes the variations are distinct, at other times subtle. Each case will illustrate how challenging the work of pursuing excellence can be. As the leader tells the story, however, common themes emerge. There are themes about what holds the teacher back, about extenuating circumstances and tradeoffs, about institutional barriers to change, about why the supervisor, or perhaps even the supervisor's supervisor, believes "It will never get better; nothing can be done."

These stories from the field have helped us to see that no single definition or easy checklist captures the inherent complexity of this issue. Mediocrity is both a multifaceted and a nested problem. It reveals itself in a variety of ways, happens for different reasons, and persists because individuals and institutions do not always know how to change. The nine vignettes in this chapter are composites drawn from our own experiences and from dozens of stories we have heard in detail. In each composite we attempt to capture a different "profile" of mediocrity and to examine some of the conditions that allow it to persist. Each provides enough detail so that the reader can recognize common patterns. The nine vignettes fall into three categories: lack of expertise, limiting beliefs or attitudes, and problems from external influences.

Confronting mediocrity requires three essential conditions: (1) supervisory competence, (2) authority or control granted through both the contract and through clear support from key members of the organization, and (3) the conviction that taking steps to improve performance will make a difference in students' opportunities to learn. Supervisors, armed with the powerful belief that both the institution and individuals within it are capable of doing a better job for students, become a key part of the equation that makes improvement possible. Ineffective supervisory or leadership responses, on the other hand, tend to magnify the effects of mediocre performance.

In the vignettes that follow, therefore, we examine both ineffective responses—those that do not display competence, control, or conviction and are therefore most likely to perpetuate the mediocre performance—and skillful responses—those most likely to help a practitioner either change or make the decision to leave the profession. Each profile comprises several parts.

Profile Summary The profile summary describes the key characteristics of the case and allows you to determine the relevance of a particular case to your own supervisory situation.

Profile The profile is organized as follows:

Background
Student Experience
Outside the Classroom
Challenges for Supervision
Ineffective Supervisory Responses
Skillful Supervisory Responses

The cases are organized into three groups based on the major cause of mediocrity:

Group 1: Lack of Expertise

1. Sally Friendly: agreeable but superficial
2. Whim Winger: lacks expertise in subject matter and planning

Group 2: Limiting Beliefs about Teaching, Learning, or Schools

3. Frank Steel: coach with an attitude
4. Donna D. Limits: differential expectations, PR expert
5. Peter Passable: union activist, competent but resistant
6. John Whiner Collabnot: complainer and noncollaborator

Group 3: External Influences

7. Mary Pity: unending personal problems
8. Louise Biere: substance abuser
9. Hank Frail: physically failing

This chapter can be used in several ways. Actual cases can be matched to the ones in this chapter using the Profile Summary. Supervisors can then analyze their responses using the Ineffective and Skillful Supervisory Response lists. A second application could be to present a profile case during an administrative workshop or course on leadership, without supplying the implications or responses. Supervisors could be asked to describe what they think would be ineffective responses and what would be skillful responses.

Group 1: Lack of Expertise

The cause of mediocre performance in the first group is lack of expertise. Both Sally Friendly and Whim Whinger lack skill in planning and/or knowledge of subject area. But both of them also have pleasant personalities and can manage their classrooms, which has tended to be weighted heavily in their performance evaluations.

Profile 1: Sally Friendly—Agreeable but Superficial

You may want to refer back to Chapter 1, where we first met Sally Friendly.

Background

Sally Friendly has taught 5th grade for 12 years. When she was hired, her principal was looking for a way to compensate for a 5th grade faculty that parents described as "cold, distant, and not student centered." Although her undergraduate record was unimpressive, Sally was warm, outgoing, positive, and eager to teach. Her principal felt the school and grade level group needed those personality traits more than it needed a record of academic achievement. Sally has been, in fact, a consistently positive and pleasant presence in the school. She is seen as sympathetic to students with learning problems and is organized, although superficial, in her planning. She stays late, works hard, and willingly spends weekend and summer time on school projects.

The decision nine years ago to put Sally on a permanent contract was not easy. She was well liked by other teachers but had mixed reviews from parents and kids. She was described as "nice," "organized," "easy to talk to," "accessible," but also "shallow," "not too sharp," and "undemanding." During Sally's tenure evaluation, Carolyn Pilat, the math coordinator, noted that Sally was superficial in her understanding of the curriculum and was unable to meet the needs of the better students, an assessment echoed informally by some parents of higher performing students. But there were few formal complaints. Her observation by the coordinator also referred to "too many seasonal activities." Despite these shortcomings, most people felt Sally had earned a permanent contract because of her hard work, organization, strong management skills, and her focus on making the classroom a happy place for students.

Over the years she has generally received superior ratings and only occasionally a "needs improvement" rating. Mrs. Pilat has left the district, and the new math coordinator has been focused on a middle school text adoption rather than on the work of an experienced group of 5th grade teachers. Although there are few direct complaints about Sally's teaching, parents with second siblings coming into 5th grade are starting to request Mr. Smith, the other 5th grade teacher, because the students "learn more." Results on the last three years of standardized tests administered in the spring confirm parents' informal sense. There is clear evidence of students slipping in their achievement. The three years of data reveal that students predicted to achieve at certain levels almost all failed to achieve the expected levels of performance (see Chapter 4 for how to use student test results in teacher evaluation).

PROFILE SUMMARY

- Management and routines not a primary problem
- Mediocre undergraduate transcript
- Nice to all
- Motivated and hard worker
- Well liked by faculty
- Contributes to life of school
- Activity level planner, responds to fads
- "Review and celebrate" curriculum
- Is not thoughtful about instructional decisions
- Instruction driven by desire to keep students busy

Student Experience

Students feel comfortable in Sally's class, which is one of her major goals. The climate is warm and welcoming. Students see her as nice and enjoy coming to school. Individuals with low self-esteem are nurtured, if not intellectually challenged. Because Sally thinks of her objectives in terms of "doing activities," learners experience the year with her as a series of disconnected events whose purpose is often unclear. Rarely does Sally either make intellectual connections between different activities to let students see "the big picture" or push students to try harder or to move their work to the next level of performance. Her admirable energy is directed towards splashy projects, and her curriculum could be characterized as "review and celebration." Students spend the first six weeks of the fall reviewing 4th grade material, then make a transition into the celebration curriculum, beginning with Columbus Day and ending around Easter. She even celebrates St. Patrick's Day.

Sally is guilty of "assumptive teaching." This means that she assumes that students know things. "They should know this by 4th grade," she is often heard to say. She does little to assess where students are rather than where they should be. Carolyn Pilat once described her as instruction as "teaching by mentioning things." Once subjects are mentioned, she assumes her students understand and moves on.

Much of Sally's practice seems driven by the need to keep kids settled down, occupied, and happy. When students are not involved in projects, they do many worksheets—some would say busy work. She has them playing many games such as "Jeopardy History," "Trivial Math," or "Hangman."

There is a lot of teaching by direct telling to "get the major points across," as she puts it. In three observations, Sally did about 75 percent of the talking. Rarely does she teach important concepts and skills. Significant student learning objectives are not clear. There is a bulletin board with student papers, each with a smiley face sticker. Feedback is rarely specific, and she is generically positive. Assessment is vague. Criteria for grades are unclear. Most youngsters describe the work she gives as "pretty easy" and report that, as long as they turn in the work, Mrs. F. is happy.

In addition to much telling, there is some yelling. She does lose her temper when frustrated by kids who are resistant or bored, but, for the most part, being nice is enough to control the class. Basically, Sally has few management problems that might cause a supervisor concern.

Outside the Classroom

Sally attends courses and workshops regularly. Last year she took a course offered by Collaboration Associates where she studied expectations and cooperative learning. She was an eager participant but did not seem to "get it" at times. For example, in a discussion about minority achievement, Sally spoke sympathetically about the obstacles children faced and said she believed pressure to meet standards and expectations from teachers would "lower their self-esteem." (For a detailed case of low expectations see Donna D. Limits.) Her written work was superficial, but she did complete the requirements and finished the course with a B.

She does not seem to be reflective about her practice and views things in black and white. Sally is a fad teacher and lurches from one approach to another depending on which workshop she last attended. She has given up and re-adopted whole language techniques three times. She immediately "switched" to cooperative learning after attending the course mentioned above. This meant kids did all their work in groups without the rigorous checks and balances of individual accountability presented in the course. She is organized but not always able to explain her instructional decisions. When asked in a conference about why she presented certain information about explorers in a social studies unit, she spoke about "getting things across until they sink in" and "keeping the students in check." She does not focus on important ideas and key understandings.

As a member of the staff, Sally is a very high participator. She serves on the Sunshine Committee as well as the School Council. She contributes little in terms of ideas but is a warm presence and is always willing to "bring the brownies." Recently she helped the principal host the "Annual Pitch and Putt Barbecue" at the principal's house.

Challenges for Supervision

Sally's profile comes to light in an era of increasingly demanding public scrutiny of student performance. While some might say she should never have been given tenure, she is an example of a teacher who was granted professional status because she filled a perceived need or because of supervisory default. Sally presents a challenge (1) because her effort is enormous but not effective, (2) because she genuinely believes she is doing what is right for students, and (3) because the school system has failed to give her the feedback she needs. Over a long period of time, the school system has valued and rewarded her nurturing presence and ignored her shortcomings in teaching concepts and skills. She is far from incompetent and has a long career ahead of her. Sally falls into a category that "nice is no longer good enough." She further illustrates a generation of educators who have focused more on what teachers teach rather than what students learn. The challenge is to help her grow in intellectual rigor while still validating her strengths. Sally needs to believe that she can still be warm and nurturing and yet become a teacher who holds children accountable for high standards and expectations.

LEGAL NOTE

Most states set a probationary period before a teacher can be granted tenure or permanent status. It normally ranges from two to five years of employment with a valid teaching certificate or credential. The best time to release a mediocre or inefficient teacher is before the teacher is granted tenure or permanent status. If, at the end of the first year of employment, the supervisor is not convinced that a teacher holds a high probability of being excellent by the end of the second probationary year, the teacher's contract should not be renewed. If, at the end of the second year, the supervisor is not convinced to a reasonable degree of certainty that the teacher is excellent, the teacher should not be granted a third probationary year. Although tenure is generally a creature of state law and the law generally authorizes the nonrenewal of the contract of a nontenured teacher without requiring a statement of reasons, teacher unions have in many school districts negotiated complex teacher evaluation procedures with numerous traps for the evaluator. Additionally, contracts will incorporate the so-called "just cause" standard that, as a practical matter, will empower a labor arbitrator to substitute his or her own judgment about a teacher's competence for that of school administrators. Therefore, the best time to protect students from mediocre teaching is during the probationary period, when the highest standards of excellence should be applied to decisions on the renewal of teaching contracts. Once a teacher has obtained tenure or permanent status, for all practical purposes you have entered a "marriage in a religion that does not recognize the legitimacy of divorce."

Ineffective Supervisory Responses

Ineffective supervisors will:

- Buy into the debilitating belief in diminished expectations for adult learning (see Chapter 2). Accept Sally for what she is—a nice staff member with limited abilities who contributes to the life of the school, is nice to the students, and does little harm.

- Give up on Sally and expect little, just as teachers accept nice C students.

- Follow Unpromising Practice Five and allow written evaluations that contain mixed messages or inflated performance ratings (see Chapter 2). Inflate performance ratings "Not everybody can be a super star" is code language for the expectation that "Sally will never be very good and can never improve." Therefore, ineffective supervisors will:

  - Use extensive, positive "edubabble" environmental praise in her evaluations: "comfortable environment," "creates a nice atmosphere," "sets a warm climate." See Figure 5-1.

  - Overemphasize her personality traits ("warm and friendly").

  - Overweight her contributions to the school ("always willing to help out").

  - De-emphasize or ignore any instructional weaknesses.

- Not share the test results from the past three years with her.

- Maintain the deal that avoids direct feedback that would rock the boat. (Clear delineation of weaknesses would upset her and endanger her willingness to carry out tasks for the school.)

- Use nonspecific recommendations of the "improvement" or "needs to " variety ("Sally needs to improve her wait time" "Sally needs to expect more from her students").

- Use too little direction, relying on a nondirective supervisory relationship.

- React only if parent complaints arise.

Skillful Supervisory Responses

Skillful supervisors know that Sally is not measuring up in the classroom and that, though she has some limitations, she can perform at a higher level. These leaders do not accept the mediocrity as "the most that can be expected." These supervisors know that there are probably limits to growth, but there is room for incremental improvement.

Skillful supervisors will:

- Believe that Sally can stretch and get better. She is the C or D student who with coaching and effective effort could be a B, although she might never be a gifted teacher.

- Build on Sally's two strengths: being positive and receptive to learning.

- Give clear feedback in a structured, collegial context with exemplars and models of the kind of practices to be substituted for what she is currently doing.

- Use a coaching model that emphasizes high direction and high support. Sally should be encouraged to offer alternative ideas, but the supervisor should make the final decision as to what happens until she proves herself over time.

- Be directive and establish clear benchmarks for improvement.

- Put Sally in a team with highly reflective teachers.

- Be willing to invest time and resources over a two-year period and be realistic about expectations for progress.

- Focus on curriculum planning as part of an entire school priority so that addressing Sally's issues becomes partly individual intervention and partly institutional intervention. (For more detail on dealing with planning issues, see Profile 2 Whim Winger.)

Skillful supervisors know that Sally has a long career and that even a small improvement will affect hundreds of student lives. They are willing to tackle the problem and remember that if resources and time have not yielded results within two years that termination will never get easier. These supervisors firmly believe that a teacher who is not getting better is getting worse; they make it clear that failure to improve is not an option.

Profile 2: **Whim Winger—Lacks Expertise in Subject Matter and Planning**

Background

Whim Winger is a seasoned, middle school science teacher in his early 40s who is most often described by his supervisors as "competent and fun, a good guy." He likes and relates well to his 8th grade students and has an established repertoire of instructional strategies and activities that students find engaging.

An organized person, Whim puts a premium on order and efficiency. He has developed a formula for keeping his workload down that includes keeping lesson plans and planning time to a minimum. Good experienced teachers who've "been around for a while," Winger believes, should know what they are doing and "not mess with what works." His plan book entries, therefore, are characterized by brief listings of activity and chapter names, perhaps interspersed with a note to remind the students of an upcoming test or to pass out a study sheet. He "plans" on the fly, in his car or in the hall, and has been known to assert that his spontaneous, unstructured lessons are often his best.

Genuinely believing that one of the characteristics of an effective teacher is the capacity to "wing it," he is whimsical and spontaneous. Whim resents the principal's requirements that he prepare detailed plans for his annual observation, write out his thinking and mastery objectives, and identify his major cognitive transitions. In fact, partly because he has had so little experience doing so and partly because he sees little value to analyzing and reflecting on his

PROFILE SUMMARY
- Has a reasonable repertoire of instructional techniques
- Is well organized in management tasks
- Plans lessons on the fly; rarely creates or uses unit plans
- Curriculum delivered has no organizing themes, questions, or objectives
- Assesses sporadically; assessments not linked to state or local curriculum frameworks. No clear check points to see how kids are progressing
- Holds "grandfathered" certificate but knowledge of subject matter is limited and superficial or he is teaching out of field

objectives and ways to reach them, Winger has a great deal of difficulty in getting any kind of detailed plan on paper.

The lack of planning manifests itself in the classroom in a variety of ways: questioning sequences are often random or laden with requests for single-word recall; comprehension questions are garbled or inexplicit and need to be rephrased or repeated before students can answer; students are rarely told why they are doing something, what they will learn at the end of the lesson, or how ideas are connected to one another; students can pull Winger into off-task discussions that take up large amounts of time, but they are discouraged from trying to pursue speculations or messy questions about the content. He calls this "being spontaneous."

Finally, Whim is text- and workbook-bound. Unless someone else has developed it and required him to use it, he almost never provides a detailed visual, an alternative way of explaining something, or an overview of key themes or essential questions that goes beyond the book and workbook. Students lacking strong auditory skills are at a disadvantage in his classes.

Whim's problems are exacerbated by a second issue: his limited knowledge of the subject area he has to teach. Undergraduate coursework in life science served him reasonably well until the district realigned its 8th grade curriculum to match state testing requirements. Winger's certification as a K-8 general science teacher allowed him to remain in his position when the curriculum shifted to earth science, although he had had no formal coursework and had done little reading in the field. Initially the district sent him to a three-day institute to "tool him up" for the new focus and invested in a variety of "teacher-proof" curriculum kits and books to help Whim and his colleagues make the transition. Since that time, Whim has learned what is in the textbook but has neither developed a grasp of the structure of the discipline and its organizing questions nor acquired any depth or substance to his content knowledge. Thus he does not see complexities or interesting questions, does not mention new areas of scientific discovery, and seems unable to stimulate much curiosity in students. Because he has not actively pursued further study in the field, his information is sometimes inaccurate or out of date. Students catch him in mistakes, and, from time to time, parents send in corrections or supplementary material. He shrugs off such encounters as minor or picky.

Student Experience

Students think earth science is "fun but sort of weak." They like the days when Whim does activities such as "neat stuff with rocks" or building volcanoes out on the playground but have difficulty expressing what they have learned. Most become anxious when they have to deal with the alternative assessments or essay questions the curriculum specialist assigns once every six weeks, because these assessments require them to apply concepts learned in one setting to a new situation. Whim simply requires them to memorize facts or label drawings. Youngsters who have a fair amount of prior knowledge and curiosity about earth science say that Whim isn't interested in their thinking and doesn't want them to disrupt the class by raising additional points or questions. These students perceive that Whim "likes kids who don't know very much better than kids who know a lot" and that he becomes angry if they point out either confusing information or something they believe to be inaccurate.

Outside the Classroom

Winger has little use for what he sees as endless rounds of curriculum tinkering and complains bitterly about having to give up lots of things in his teaching because of pressure to teach to a test. He has not read the state frameworks or even his district's curriculum documents in any detail. Without significant lead time to prepare, he would be unable to tell a parent or visitor how what he was doing in class fulfilled the district's learning goals for students. He hates the idea of essential questions, themes, or commonly prepared unit plans, all of which he describes as "ambiguous, time-consuming and unhelpful." Thus he finds himself feeling resentful and resistant when he is forced to attend curriculum meetings. He does not like to be put in the role of a difficult person and feels a strong sense of lost identity as the district defines quality teaching in ways that seem to leave him out.

Challenges for Supervision

Like Sally Friendly, Whim Winger emerges as a profile of mediocrity only when the institution begins to focus on whether students are being given maximum opportunities to learn. Whim needs to do significant intellectual work on his own and to see the value of that work. Caught by surprise as standards for teaching and learning became more rigorous, Winger could justifiably claim that his supervisors have "never found fault with" his performance before and that the ground rules have been changed unfairly. It is likely that the institutional response has, in fact, not given him any reason to question either his beliefs about what constitutes good practice or his stance on how much knowledge he needs in order to teach earth science.

Ineffective Supervisory Responses

Ineffective supervisors will:

- Miss the planning problem because they do not require and examine unit plans (as opposed to lesson plans) as part of their data collection for formative or summative evaluation.

- Miss the content knowledge problem because they do not require evidence of ongoing learning in a content area.

- Label Winger as someone who is either too set in his ways or too limited to learn how to design an effective unit and will require him to strictly adhere to a plan developed by an expert, e.g., a textbook publisher, consultant, or curriculum specialist.

- Dodge the planning problem by focusing the evaluation on all the aspects of teaching in which they perceive that Winger does well, like personal relationship building, student involvement, and active participation.

- Treat the planning problem lightly by using words such as "consider improving your plans to be better aligned with the frameworks."

- Agree with and give credence to Winger's assertion that he cannot be expected to learn about new developments in his field or implement new curriculum unless the district gives him time, training, and materials.

- Avoid presenting Winger with concrete data about how his choices (or lack thereof) affect student performance.

Skillful Supervisory Responses

Skillful supervisors will:

- Regularly require teachers to present unit plans tied to state and/or district frameworks and standards as evidence of their understanding of subject matter and their competence in planning.

- Discuss and practice using planning questions and/or templates (see Figure 4-2) with the entire faculty and routinely evaluate teachers for evidence of such planning.

- Routinely sample and analyze tests and assessments to determine what kinds of learning goals are being valued.

- Expect teachers to present evidence of the way in which they keep themselves current in the field they are teaching, above and beyond district training.

- Interview randomly selected students and/or collect samples of student work to determine how well they understand key concepts and are able to display essential competencies identified in the curriculum.

LEGAL NOTE

The use of test scores as an indicator of a teacher's effectiveness in the classroom is obviously very controversial. Nonetheless, some courts have been willing to sustain the use of test results when employers have relied upon them as a factor in decisions to dismiss tenured personnel. "It is possible that the discretion of a Board may, at times, to those more generously endowed, seem to have been exercised with a lack of wisdom. But the Board's decisions in the exercise of its discretion are not vulnerable to our correction merely if they are "wrong," sustainable only if they are "right." . . . It is our holding that the administration of the internal affairs of the school district before us has not passed by judicial fiat from the local Board, where it was lodged by statute, to the federal court. Such matters as the competence of teachers, and the standards of its measurement are not, without more, matters of constitutional dimensions. They are peculiarly appropriate to state and local administration." *Scheelhaase v. Woodbury Central Community School District*, 488 F.2d 237, (Iowa, 1973).

Group 2: **Limiting Beliefs about Teaching, Learning, or Schools**

Some teachers hold limiting beliefs about teaching and learning or about the purpose of schooling. These beliefs are played out every day in schools and classrooms. (For a full discussion on limiting beliefs, see Chapter 2 "Teacher Beliefs" in *The Skillful Teacher*, Saphier and Gower 1997.) The following four cases describe different kinds of limiting beliefs. Frank Steel believes that control and discipline is the best measure of good teaching. Donna D. Limits has differential expectations for different students while Peter Passable equates good teaching with drill and practice. Finally, John Whiner Collabnot values only his classroom teaching and is not a participating member of the school community.

Profile 3: **Frank Steel—Coach with an Attitude**

Background

Frank Steel is 55 and has taught social studies for 26 years at Valley High School. Over that period he applied twice for assistant principal and once for department head, but all three times the interviewing committees felt Frank had an "edge" that might not make him a good administrative team player. He has been a very successful boys' basketball coach. His record in this small high school is one of the best in the division for the past 20 years. He pushes his athletes and creates a tough, winning attitude. He concentrates his efforts on winners, and the results have paid off in the record. He loses several athletes every year who feel he is insensitive, but his success, as measured by wins and losses, is indisputable. He has some strong community support from the athletic boosters.

The same organizational qualities that make him a good coach are present in the classroom. His grade book is clear and organized, almost like a gamebook. The Friday multiple choice quiz grades are neatly recorded with the terms tests in red. His lesson plans are clear in terms of what is to be covered: "HW pp. 34–36" "Go over Chapter 3 Revolutionary War."

But the enthusiasm evident on the field does not translate into the classroom. He gets no joy out of teaching and is certainly not a learner within his discipline. He does not feel valued for his teaching, which is an accurate perception, and his defensiveness springs partly from feelings of insecurity. He lacks commitment either to his students or his subject matter.

Student Experience

Students enter a traditional classroom. The classroom is orderly. Walls are sparsely decorated with a historical time line and a few maps yellowed by time and chalk. Student work is not in evidence. The left side of the blackboard says "World History read pp. 60–68" with each of his four sections listed in chalk-framed boxes below. The rest of the board is empty.

Students sit in rows and spend a lot of time answering quick questions— almost like a basketball drill. "From your reading last night, give me the date of

---

PROFILE SUMMARY
- 25-year veteran
- Excellent coach, mediocre teacher
- No management problems
- Teaching driven by control, not by passion
- Resistant to change
- Hostile
- Frustrated and stuck
- Three R's—Routine, Ritual, and Resignation

Paul Revere's famous ride. Tell me three facts you know about the drafting of the constitution." Students are asked few comprehension questions and are given little wait time. They are kept alert and on their toes. There is a respect for Mr. Steel's authority. All the kids call him "coach." But students are not being intellectually challenged, and students rarely move beyond this drill and practice. The class is predictable but not boring because it does not drag. Male athletes fare pretty well. He knows their names and gives them small breaks in terms of grades and incomplete work. It is not blatant but known! He rarely knows the names of the other students. They say, "He doesn't really know me." Most kids think that the class is okay and it is—just okay! His strengths as a coach translate only in terms of control and management; he has less commitment to the classroom.

Outside the Classroom

We have already discussed Mr. Steel's successful coaching, which certainly deserves recognition. At faculty meetings, Mr. Steel sits in the back of the library, facing sideways. Sometimes he corrects the multiple choice quizzes; at other times he leafs through a textbook or swaps golfing tips with Bill, his golfing buddy. Steel attends the minimum number of courses, just enough to maintain his certification status. He prefers workshops with few if any requirements. He has taught the same courses for several years and feels he does not need new ideas. Steel is tight with the old boys. Ten years ago he would have been called sexist, but he has made an effort to modify his language, only occasionally slipping now by calling the new female teachers "girls." He participates in and originates much of the faculty room complaining. (For a case that deals specifically with the complaining teacher, see Profile 7 John Whiner Collabnot.)

Challenges for Supervision

Steel represents a subset of male teachers who entered education 25 to 30 years ago. Many were athletes in high school, went to the local colleges, and counted on teaching as an interim step on their path to becoming administrators. There is an underlying frustration from Steel's unfulfilled expectation that he would become a school administrator by his mid-30s. He receives little satisfaction from his classroom teaching, and he puts little investment there. He derives most of his satisfaction from coaching. Significantly, Steel has been rewarded by previous administrators for his classroom management. Any classroom praise he has received has been related to the control he establishes, especially with some "tough" kids. The challenge is for the supervisor to work around his defensiveness to help him grow into a more rounded professional.

Ineffective Supervisory Responses

Ineffective supervisors will:

- Not give direct feedback about the low standards of teaching because they know that Frank is resistant to change and is quite defensive about any negative feedback or suggestions.

- Ignore Frank as much as possible. He is dismissed as "having problems with authority."

- Inflate his appraisal, emphasizing Frank's success as a coach and his classroom management but not confronting the poor classroom teaching. They will accept the fact that "Frank's heart and mind are on the field," thus absolving the supervisor from any need to intervene.

- Endorse the concept that "success is measured in averages." That is, if you are good enough in one area of performance (in this case coaching), it can compensate for poor teaching. It is a statement of values by the supervisor.

Skillful Supervisory Responses

The skillful supervisor sees the same profile of behavior as the mediocre supervisor but decides not to look the other way. Skillful supervisors realize that Frank has built a shell around himself and that behind his demeanor is the fear of looking bad and being exposed as "behind the times." Any hope of reaching Frank depends on making him feel valued rather than hunted.

Skillful supervisors will:

- Realize that Frank will never be bad enough to get rid of nor will he improve without attention.

- Have a "career coaching" interview not tied to a specific observation and try to get Frank to project ahead five years (see Career Coaching Interview in Chapter 4).

- Build on Frank's strength, organization, and try to refocus some of his energy into the classroom, not through confrontation but through enlisting him.

- Provide Frank with opportunities to lead subgroups or committees to tap his frustrated desire for leadership. Seed the committee with positive role models.

- Give Frank direct feedback and use goal setting to help him create a plan with short-term and long-term objectives, then provide direct feedback on goals with Frank providing self-evaluation. (The supervisor here is building on a strategy that Frank uses in his coaching. All his athletes have goal charts and are asked to evaluate their progress regularly.)

- Make frequent informal visits to let Frank know accountability is not just the formal observation, that the supervisor is not looking the other way, and also to convey that she/he values Frank as a person and as a professional.

- Frequently engage Frank in short hallway conversations about teaching, not coaching.

The skillful supervisor will not ignore or give up on Frank nor allocate large amounts of time to his improvement.

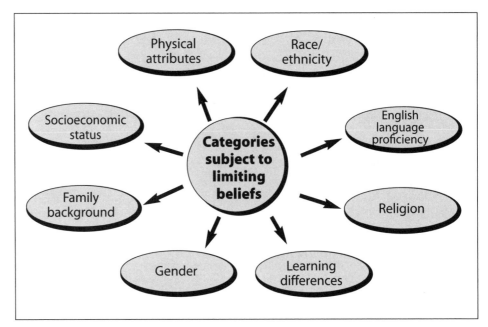

Figure 3-1 Limiting beliefs. The case of Donna D. Limits focuses on the effects of low expectations for students of low socioeconomic background. You can substitute any of the categories in this figure to match your particular situation.

Profile 4: Donna D. Limits—Differential Expectations, PR Expert

Background

Donna has taught 7th grade English for 14 years. She is seen as a well prepared individual who is an enthusiastic and popular teacher. She is an integral part of the social fabric of the town. Social status is important to Donna. She lives on "the Heights" in the upscale section and is connected to the town's power structure through her husband. Because she invests considerable energy on her public image, she has excellent relations with parents, especially her neighbors on the Heights.

Mrs. Limits describes herself as a person who both likes and cares about "children at risk," defined in her view as students who come from families with low socioeconomic status. She shows her understanding first by sorting and labeling such students with phrases such as "my low ability kids, the youngsters from the River Apartments, my inclusion kids" and then differentiating expectations in ways that she believes will "help" each group. Donna often talks about giving students an opportunity to decompress before they start class because their lives are so stressful they cannot be expected to get right down to work, about reducing her standards for reading because children's home lives are too chaotic to make reading possible, and about not making students uncomfortable by giving them back unsatisfactory work to do again.

Although she does not recognize it, a foundation of low expectations for performance linked to external factors such as students' home lives and their parents' education underlies Donna D's pleasant demeanor and enthusiasm. A revealing quote from the faculty room tells the story: "I set different standards for different students. I know some of them cannot be expected to perform as well as others. They come from broken families. They have no support at home. That's the way it is." As a result, there are two calls she does not make. She does not call on students in class, to avoid embarrassing them, and she rarely calls home if the student in one of her labeled groups is doing poorly. She will, however, call the parents of a student whose background she finds a good predictor of potential success. (This vignette is adapted from material from *The Skillful Teacher*, Saphier and Gower 1997, p. 302.)

"There are certain kids who really don't have the ability. I will give them a little nudge in their grade if they show some effort. Some people call this watering down the standards. I call it reality." No matter what Donna's intention, the acceptance of lower standards is a quiet but potent performance-limiting belief. Finally, Donna does not see herself as biased or class conscious because she would never engage in overt slurs or insults. With all the best intentions, Donna limits potential achievement because she believes that intelligence is fixed. She believes that her efforts will not make a difference. In fact, the sorting and the limited expectations effectively liberate Donna from assuming too much accountability for the academic success of the labeled groups.

Student Experience

Students are aware of the differences in the way Donna treats them although few if any ever confront her with those discrepancies or raise the issue with any other adult in the school. Most youngsters internalize the experience and tend to believe that in some way they deserve the lower expectations, so they do not push back against the sometimes condescending "niceness." Witness the experience of Mark, a "jock" who lives on the poor side of town:

Donna: "Good Morning, Mark. How did the hockey game go?"

Mark: "We won."

Donna: "That's great! I guess that means you were not able to get to the writing homework."

Mark: "Right, I was really tired, you know."

Donna: "That's okay, we'll pick you up."

The problem is that Mark rarely does homework, and Limits never demands it or provides an alternative structure to make it up. At the end of the marking period, Mark gets a C when he earned a D. When his mother calls to ask Mrs. Limits what she can do to help, Donna says "Don't be upset; C's are OK during the hockey season." What she is really saying is that C's are the best Mark can do—with a little grading help from his teacher.

Donna can be tough with and challenge students from the affluent sections of town whose work is not high quality. Students whom she is "protecting and supporting," however, become accustomed to lots of praise regardless of the effort they invest. She puts smiley faces on all their work but fails to state criteria for success so that these individuals have little sense of what they did that earned the praise. In fact, Donna tells students that they are doing well when they are not. Students entering her classroom with poor writing skills feel accepted but make very little progress. Her students' standardized test scores show a small difference from other 7th grade teachers, although statistical significance is hard to prove.

Outside the Classroom

Donna attends many courses and workshops and prides herself on being at the forefront of the faculty in collecting great new activities that will be fun for her classes. She and her students often have their pictures in the local paper or are mentioned in the district newsletter. Although Donna regularly tells her principal that she appreciates suggestions and feedback, she most often responds to suggestions with a series of elaborate disclaimers about why various segments of her population would be unable to handle whatever the principal is requesting she try. Two years ago she agreed to teach the process writing program, which was part of the new 7th grade curriculum. When the curriculum coordinator commented on her failure to implement the new approach, she said, "Oh, I had to give it up. My low groups were so frustrated. They had nothing to write about because their parents can't afford to take them places, their vocabularies were so limited, and so many of them come from single families where Mom or Dad is too busy to help. I just didn't want to put those children on the spot and make them feel uncomfortable."

Challenge for Supervision

Dealing with this type of mediocrity is very difficult because the problems are not easily defined. Differential expectations are not easily detected, particularly when there is widespread acceptance for such distinctions within the broader institutional culture. First, the supervisor must be aware of and able to capture a subtle pattern of limiting choices both within the teacher's classroom and within the broader school culture. Moreover, the supervisor must be willing to present Donna with convincing data that may be upsetting both to her and to her political connections. Second, the institution must create cultural conditions that help Donna face up to her own unexamined assumptions. Donna's comments about having to lower her standards and about what students cannot do are not always made where an administrator could overhear and address them. Fellow faculty members in her audience who hear the remarks may not necessarily agree but may be reluctant to "take Donna on." In fact, unless many members of the faculty are engaged in examining their own beliefs about ability and achievement, colleagues may not even recognize the implications of Donna's statements.

Donna does not recognize her own behavior. Because she is entertaining and often innovative in her activities, she garners outside attention and frequent praise. Those who might legitimately complain about Donna, that is the parents of the children for whom she holds such low expectations, rarely do so. When she receives disaggregated data about the achievement of groups of students within her classes and suggestions about what to do, Donna's initial responses sound agreeable. However, she routinely avoids making the requested improvements and often explains such failure by citing her students' "disadvantages." She has a plausible excuse for every occasion, and her past experiences have taught her that busy administrators have compelling, more overt problems to divert them. She also counts on her political leverage and personal charm to soften recommendations and to inflate her performance ratings. Donna resembles Sally Friendly because few supervisors would single her out as a "difficult" or "incompetent" faculty member. Sally 's effectiveness is compromised by her lack of teaching expertise. Donna's effectiveness, by contrast, is not limited by her lack of technical repertoire but rather by a system of buried beliefs, a subconscious mindset, that causes her to shortchange groups of children.

Ineffective Supervisory Responses

Ineffective supervisors will:

- Not realize that the problem of low expectations is an institutional problem, one reflective of larger societal values, and will treat it as an individual problem.

- Not raise issues of differential treatment of kids either individually or during meetings and professional development.

- Decide either that the most important thing is to have Donna on their side or that attacking Donna personally is a way to get her to listen.

- Overemphasize the positives in the appraisal write-ups. Not raise student progress as an issue, even informally.

- Give most feedback orally; little is written down.

- Avoid following up after recommendations.

- Act as though there is little urgency, even in the face of problematic data, because "no one is complaining, so it can't be that bad."

Skillful Supervisory Responses

Skillful supervisors will:

- Realize that Donna is part of a bigger institutional problem. Thus they will deal both individually with Donna and collectively with the faculty because diminished expectations are often held by many teachers.

- Establish a facultywide focus on the effects of diminished expectations using, for example, attribution theory and defining what is meant by effective effort (Saphier and Gower 1997, p. 317).

- Involve the entire faculty in reaching out to parents and in having parents help to identify what best helps their children to learn and to perform at high levels.

- Plan professional development that focuses on examining biases associated with socioeconomic differences within the community.

- Evaluate Donna and her colleagues, using an array of measures, including student achievement data.

- Realize that being nice is not enough and be willing to confront the poor teaching by a structured response that moves from a suggestion to a recommendation.[1]

- Realize the power of the written recommendations with benchmarks for assessment.

- Structure responsibility through goal-setting and self-evaluation measured by student progress.

---

[1] A colleague of ours, Kenneth Chapman, makes a very interesting distinction between suggestions, recommendations, and expectations (directives) and believes that supervisors do not often make distinctions. A **suggestion** is optional; the teacher can implement it if he/she wants. It implies that present performance is okay, and that there is no damage to students. A **recommendation** signals that the teacher must change what he/she is doing and that the supervisor will follow up to be sure. How the change is made is up for discussion, and the teacher can choose. An **expectation** signals that the teacher must change what he or she is doing, and the supervisor will stipulate how it must be done and in what time period.

Profile 5: Peter Passable—Union Activist, Competent, but Resistant

Background

Peter Passable has taught 4th grade for 24 years and at age 48 is at midcareer. He has good relationships with students. He is one of only three males in the elementary school, so Peter relates especially well to certain boys; for many students he is the first male teacher they encounter. He has a traditional, well organized style and really believes in the importance of mathematics, especially computation. He spends 70 percent of the time allocated to math on drill and practice, and his students have done exceptionally on computation. But more recent testing has revealed shortcomings in open-ended problems and in some areas of geometry. Peter's type of mediocrity is difficult to address because he does have a narrow domain of legitimate success and is supported by parents more familiar with traditional instruction. Parents are not demanding higher level problem solving and are quite content that students know their multiplication tables through 12 fluently. Because of parent support, there has been little motivation to change. He lacks interest in learning new things or in reflecting on his teaching.

Passable has been with five principals and expects three to four more before he retires at 61. He has been known to say that "Reflection is for mirrors. I teach, I don't reflect." He is rather satisfied with his performance and considers the three observations and conference cycles to be a biannual ritual without much meaning. In addition, Peter is very active in the union and in recent years has become a contract monitor and a clock watcher. He is on time, but barely, and leaves at the contracted time. He views all requests from the principal through the contract and does not hesitate to call for a grievance.

Student Experience

Students always sit in rows and almost always interact with the teacher in a traditional, tripartite recitation model. The teacher asks a question, the student responds, the teacher responds and asks another question. Expectations for work procedures are very clear, and there is frequent drill and practice. There is a certain satisfaction in being able to subtract 6,799,557 from 7,574,993, and students can brag to their parents about this feat. Parents are delighted to hear old, familiar terms such as "borrowing," having heard some reference a few years ago to "regrouping." Because he spends so much time on computation, he never gets to geometry and statistics, which are tested on the new standards-based state tests.

Outside the Classroom

Peter Passable contributes occasionally in faculty committees, attends meetings punctually, and is very task oriented. He makes an excellent timekeeper. Professional development for Passable is another hurdle. He is very "risk averse" and selects short-term offerings. He is respected by the faculty for his role as guardian of the contract and has a slightly cynical sense of humor much appreciated by the "old guard." He played an important role last year in contract negotiations where the association was able to narrow the data sources used for evaluation to two observations every two years and to avoid the use of student performance data, which was desired by the School Board. He is aggressive about using the grievance process and has effectively gotten several principals to back down even on reasonable requests so that they can, as one principal put it, "maintain harmony with the union."

Challenges for Supervision

Peter Passable's form of mediocrity is embedded in his name. He is a passable teacher, but he is considered successful by many parents, whom he uses as a shield to avoid change. This form of mediocrity is especially difficult because Passable does have a legitimate area of success, so there has been little incentive for him to change. Passable's protective union cloak provides an extra supervisory challenge. Taking on Peter directly means you are taking on test scores, parents, as well as a certain volley of grievances. What complicates the supervision further is that Peter is caught in the changing definition of what makes good math teaching. What was okay a few years ago is now considered mediocre. As Steel was rewarded for control, Passable was rewarded for his strong teaching of computation. This served him well on the old norm-referenced tests such as the Iowa Test of Basic Skills. But scores on recent standards-based tests have been disaggregated, revealing that Passable's students have lower test scores on geometry and statistics subtests than on computation. But the supervisor does not want to publicly embarrass Passable. The supervisor needs to realize that potential grievances should not be a reason to back away from confrontation but needs to take a skillful approach to this supervisory challenge.

Ineffective Supervisory Responses

Ineffective supervisors will:

- Not hold Passable to the same standard as other teachers.
- Go after the Passable because of his union behavior, using the test score to embarrass him.
- Praise Peter for computation test results but not confront Peter with the other gaps in achievement.
- Practice the 3 A's: Accept, Avoid, and Accommodate.
- Allow leadership initiatives to be constantly compromised to ensure harmony.

Skillful Supervisory Responses

Skillful supervisors will:

- Create a motivation for change by presenting data regarding math achievement in areas beyond computation.
- Create a goal-setting plan focused on specific and concrete benchmarks for improvement.
- Clearly distinguish union dealing from classroom performance.
- Announce that they are paying attention and give notice to Peter that, despite years of positive ratings, the supervisor expects him to grow in certain identified and agreed-upon areas.

- In some cases, stay "off the record" about performance in the initial confrontation to remove the grievance mindset. This only works if the supervisor is willing to follow through, with the implication that if changes do not occur that performance problems will be documented. Staying "off the record" should be for only short periods of time—three to four months.

PROFILE SUMMARY
■ Acceptable classroom performance
■ Does not share or collaborate with colleagues
■ Constant complainer in faculty room and meetings
■ Does not have a sense of community and shared responsibility
■ Values only classroom teaching role

Profile 6: John W. Collabnot—Complainer and Noncollaborator[2]

Background

John Whiner Collabnot is widely considered to be a good high school English teacher. He has taught seven years, is passionate about his subject, is well prepared, and challenges his students. He sees himself more as a college professor than a high school teacher and has completed everything but his dissertation for a doctoral degree in English. All his classroom observations have been positive. He has grown as a teacher during these seven years but views his job very narrowly. Collabnot believes that anything other than classroom teaching is an inappropriate demand on his time and detracts from his academic work with his students. He has developed several interesting approaches to "uncovering" literature but is both reluctant to share with colleagues and unwillingly to be part of curriculum committees whose charge is to revise and upgrade the program of literature and language studies for the entire school.

---

[2] Thanks to Ruth Lynch and the administrators of the Duxbury Public Schools (Massachusetts) for assistance in the development of this case.

Student Experience

Students who invest even minimal effort in school are generally positive about Mr. Collabnot. He is especially successful with, and prefers, higher achieving and highly motivated students, but can reach many different types of learners who are attracted to his passion for his subject. His advanced literature classes are challenging and similar to college seminars. After a year when he complained about the "low quality" students he had been "sent," the department head granted Mr. Collabnot's request to teach only honors. The department head told the principal that "Collabnot is much better with the higher level students." Collabnot insists that he will not chase students who are doing poorly, but he is always available after school for anyone who wants to learn. Although Collabnot has little patience for students who are afraid or defiant, he is willing to spend lengthy periods of time with students who take advantage of extra help. He routinely excuses himself from late arrival at staff meetings because he has "been with his kids."

Outside the Classroom

Collabnot believes that his job is limited to classroom responsibilities. Performance of routine duties is a very low priority. Paperwork is incomplete or misplaced, deadlines are ignored, communication with parents is minimal. He has isolated himself. He is not part of a broader community of teachers and students and feels no sense of collective responsibility. For example, if a group of 9th graders whom he does not teach are shouting in the hall outside his room, he will complain to the 9th grade team leader about "your kids making noise" rather than solving the problem or saying something to the students himself.

John also feels little responsibility to participate in school and department deliberations. He is a constant complainer and regularly portrays himself as a victim. Administrators are always "theys" and "thems": "They're always adding new things for us to do. How do they expect us to do all of this? Why didn't they tell us about this sooner? Whose idea was it? They just want us to do their work for them. They're not treating us as professionals. Why do they get the new copier and we get the 1950s Xerox? They don't appreciate us."

John does not contribute to department discussions. If he does speak, it is to convey his disapproval of anything he has not suggested himself: "This is a really bad idea. We tried this five years ago. I don't have time to modify the curriculum for that student." John is not a team player and has no suggestions for improvement.

Challenges for Supervision

Supervisors may or may not want to equate the importance of collaboration and being a member of a community with the importance of proficient classroom teaching. These competencies, however, are usually on paper as components of an overall appraisal and need to be addressed. New research indicates that having a healthy professional community is correlated with high-performing schools (Neuman and Wehlage 1995). Collabnot's behavior, if unaddressed, can affect the entire culture of the school. Capturing useful data can be problematic. Sometimes the behaviors are subtle and difficult to detect because they occur outside the view of the supervisor, for example in the faculty lunch room or in a parking lot conversation with a parent. Sometimes they are more overt and may be on public display, for example, in a faculty or committee meeting. In either case, John's failure to collaborate and his constant complaining detract from the strong professional community of learners associated with high-performing schools. Because John is unwilling to collaborate or to share materials, only his students—a very small part of the total school population—have the opportunity to benefit from this teacher's knowledge and expertise.

Interestingly, while classroom mediocrity may be less visible to other teachers, failure to collaborate affects all the staff. Some teachers know it is happening and are watching and waiting to see if supervisors will do anything. Others just ignore it. A few diligent souls may attempt "for the good of the students" to pick up the pieces that Collabnot is dropping. Certainly, after a period of time in which they carry several loads, they are likely to resent the inequities that cause them to contribute more than he does. Finally, even if the Collabnots are few in number, they have a disproportionately large, negative effect on efforts to build a growth-oriented school culture. Supervisors need to realize that other teachers assess both an administrator's and an institution's commitment to certain principles by scrutinizing responses to these individuals. Finally, it is important to recognize that John is a younger teacher who may be suffering from "hardening of the categories" in terms of what constitutes a full professional role. Only those who do not believe he can acquire other skills and stretch his own thinking would allow him to become entrenched as a culture killer.

Ineffective Supervisory Responses

Ineffective supervisors will:

- Make yearly mild recommendations of the "needs to" or "should work to" variety (e.g.,"John needs to share more of his curriculum ideas" or "John should work to become a more contributing member of his department") without identifying follow-up.

- Enable the behavior by not assigning John to duties or by not asking John to serve on any committees.

- Accept John as a maverick and not hold him accountable for being a member of the school community.

- Allow John to be marginalized as a one-dimensional teacher, e.g., "John's heart is in his classroom; he doesn't do . . ." (the implication is that the other areas are not important).

- Criticize Collabnot publicly without giving him any vent time, which may be necessary to enlist his tacit cooperation.

- Punish him by assigning him low-level classes or giving him a position on the School Spirit Committee.

Skillful Supervisory Responses

Skillful supervisors will:

- Clearly communicate to the whole staff the importance of all categories and standards of the professional role and that the supervisors will comment on all areas.

- Enlist faculties to support a positive culture through developing a shared mission statement focusing on being a "community of learners."

- Request that teachers provide sources of data to assist the evaluator in assessing nonclassroom areas of performance, thus forcing the teacher to reflect on his or her performance outside of classroom teaching.

- Enlist Collabnot in helping with the design and implementation of his curriculum, perhaps with a new teacher.

- Involve him in taking responsibility for identifying and developing plans to resolve issues he complains about. (Some complaints may be legitimate.)

- Form teams of administrators who meet to share and discuss strategies for dealing with noncollegial complainers as a school or district. (Since Collabnots can cause adverse cultural impact, the solution needs a systemic response in addition to an individual response.)

- Acknowledge John's good classroom performance but clearly communicate the importance of collegiality and collaboration as a school value and a professional responsibility.

- Ask " Is there are anything I can do to help you achieve your goals?"

- Invite Collabnot to team teach a course with some inclusion students.

- Set the standard, use goal setting around these issues with self-evaluation benchmarks and follow-up conferences.

- Share results of the reference: *Successful School Restructuring: A Report to the Public and Educators,* from the Center on Organization and Restructuring of Schools (Newmann and Wehlage 1995).[3]

Group 3: External Influences

Cases in this category have problems external to school that adversely affect their teaching. Mary Pity suffers from personal problems that have reduced her effectiveness. Louise Biere has become a substance abuser, and Hank Frail's physical condition has undermined his ability to teach. These are tough cases because of the sensitive issues involved and because school leaders do not always have the therapeutic competence that is often needed.

---

[3]"Overall, if we compared two 'average' students, one in a school with low professional community and the other in a school with high professional community, the students in the high community school would score about 27 points higher on a SRS measure. This difference would represent a gain of 31 percentile points" (Newmann and Wehlage 1995, p. 32). "Attaining these conditions of professional community is a daunting task but well worth the effort. We found that students in schools with higher levels of professional community learn more, whether learning is measured as authentic performance or in more conventional terms" (Neumann and Wehlage 1995, p. 51).

Profile 7: **Mary Pity—Unending Personal Problems**[4]

Background

Mary Pity's first seven years of teaching were very good. She was a cheerful teacher full of humor and wit. She actively took courses, eventually getting her masters degree. She served on systemwide committees, showed up at sporting events, and even volunteered to stay over with students at the annual 7th grade overnight lock-in. During these years she brought energy to her classroom. She was a skillful teacher. The next three years were a plateau for Mary. One of her children began to have difficulties at school. She began to cut back on her extracurricular involvement although no one criticized her classroom teaching. The principal began to notice the plateau but decided that she was going through a rough patch with her daughter and therefore opted not to mention any areas of concern. She believed the plateau would end and Mary would once again continue her growth as a teacher if the principal was supportive and positive.

Mary Pity's teaching has been declining for five years. Her personal problems are clearly impeding her school and classroom performance. First, her husband of 17 years walked out; she has had to deal with being a single parent and raising two children. Her child that caused her concern is now 16 and has major learning problems and is a rebel. In addition, last year Mary's mother developed cancer and needs attention. Mary comes to school fatigued. She has gone from very good teaching to what can best be described as less than ordinary. She is not staying abreast of current techniques in her field. At best, she is living on her reputation. She has become an expert at playing on the "sympathy orchestra." The faculty lunch room is a support group helping Mary through each day.

Student Experience

Parents report slow return of work and boredom by students. She does have many activities organized and keeps students busy. Kids call her the "worksheet queen." She does many drill and practice activities and focuses most of her energy on grammar and spelling. Students learn rules, but some parents wonder whether any learning transfers to their writing. Mary Pity has little energy to put into her teaching and is constantly overwhelmed, so she rarely assigns or corrects longer writing assignments. Students, however, receive high grades for completing work. She puts much importance on punctuality and neatness. She has a funny sense of humor. But over the last few years this humor has turned more to regret and bitterness. Students get a large dose of personal stories. Because she is on a team, there are relatively few complaints from parents. She is accepted as the "weak link" on a strong team. Some parents even like her constant grammar and spelling drills because that was what they had in school.

---

[4]Thanks to William Ribas, Assistant Superintendant of the Brookline Massachusetts School District, for his assistance on this case.

Outside the Classroom

Mary Pity has no time to grow professionally and has taken no courses in five years. Her relations with the faculty are based on sympathy for all the issues she is dealing with ("poor Mary" is a constant refrain), but her team is beginning to feel that she is not pulling her own weight and that other faculty members bounce back after personal difficulties. One faculty member commented "I have not heard Mary talk about students in six years though she used to be so focused on them." But in public the "poor Mary" support symphony is loud and clear.

Challenges for Supervision

This profile of slipping into mediocrity because of personal problems is not to be confused with an individual whose performance is adversely affected by temporary "speed bumps." Supervisors need to be very understanding and supportive during those times of personal difficulty.[5] The Mary Pity profile, however, describes people who have been sound performers but have entered into a long-term decline due to a pattern of chronic, ongoing personal problems. These are individuals who have lost control of their personal lives, to the detriment of their performance in the classroom. For these teachers there appears little likelihood that there will be improvement without intervention. This type of case is the supreme test of the supervisor's conviction. Empathy for the teacher needs to be a consideration that is secondary to concern for students who are losing out. Any pressure on Mary to perform at a higher level will be met with stiff staff and union resistance since the sympathy factor is so high.

Ineffective Supervisory Responses

Ineffective supervisors will:

- Enable the behavior by being very sympathetic, giving light loads, constant permission for early departure, smaller classes, and fewer "difficult students."
- Accept all excuses.
- Emphasize in performance appraisals the difficult conditions under which the teacher has worked, essentially praising her for showing up and ignoring the difficult conditions the students experience.
- Continue to side with the teacher rather than being an advocate of students who are losing out.
- Act alone and seek no assistance from the district.

Skillful Supervisory Responses

This profile of Mary Pity's mediocrity is a challenge even to the best supervisors because of the potential effect on the collegiality of the school. Anything

[5]Our colleague Ken Chapman reminds us that quick supportive intervention (granting extended sick leave) with initial personal problems can receive strokes from the sympathy orchestra as well as a quick response from the individual. This can help build a bank of trust and fairness when having to deal with long-term cases like Mary Pity.

that smacks of insensitivity will be met with anger by other members of the staff. Even the most positive teachers can turn against the most respected administrators. So the skillful supervisor wades carefully into this minefield!

Skillful supervisors will:

- Be sympathetic to the teacher while still being primarily an advocate for students.

- Acknowledge personal problems but not accept them as an ongoing excuse for poor performance. "I understand you have been going through a rough patch in your personal life, however, I really need you to return to the quality of teaching you exhibited a few years ago. How can I help you make a plan to do that?"

- Develop an improvement plan that:

  ‣ Calculates a reasonable accommodation schedule with a timetable for incremental improvement.

  ‣ Focuses on identifying performance gaps and setting reasonable goals based on firm expectations.

  ‣ Establishes clear reasonable expectations with benchmarks for assessment and documentation.

  ‣ Sends the message that "whatever has happened is in the past, but things have to improve in the future."

  ‣ Include in the plan outside assistance including, counseling, a support group, or other therapeutic support.

PROFILE SUMMARY
■ Probably an alcoholic
■ Teaching performance declining
■ Non–school-related arrest

Profile 8: Louise Biere—Substance Abuser

Background

Louise Biere is a 45-year-old, experienced, middle school French teacher. In her 18 years she has been a respected, hard-working teacher, never an earthshaker, but always reliable and consistent. Things began to break down two years ago. At back to school night, two sets of parents told the principal there was alcohol on her breath. Later that fall two parents complained that their sons who had been disciplined after school complained about the smell of alcohol on Mme. Biere's breath. This year there have been several more complaints. Several students in her 6th period French class told the principal that she was slurring her vowels. Yesterday Mme. Biere fell down in the hall two hours after school was over and could not stand up. She was not hurt badly, but when the principal arrived to help there was alcohol on her breath. To add to this, Mme. Biere was arrested for drunken driving over the weekend.

Student Experience

Louise historically has been a good teacher. She is enthusiastic about the French culture and language. Her room is decorated with bright posters of Paris. In the past her students have tended to be motivated and responsive. But in the last two years her posters haven't changed and she has seemed disorganized and forgetful. She will assign composition for homework then, the following day, ask the students to submit an exercise vocabulaire. Announced tests will be suddenly postponed because she has not prepared them. It takes her weeks to return papers. One student complained that Mme. Biere lost her major project on Mary Cassatt. Recently, Mme. Biere fell asleep during class while correcting a dictée. In other years she was always available for help three days a week after school. Students now report that, on the occasional day when she is available, Biere seems befuddled and students leave even more confused. There is no doubt that students are getting a lower quality learning experience than in years past; Mme. Biere's teaching is mediocre at best.

Outside the Classroom

Mme. Biere's contribution to the school is narrowing. She no longer runs the French club nor does she attend the regional foreign language teacher meetings that she chaired for years. She has isolated herself from other faculty members, except Mlle. Gerard, with whom she chats frequently in French. Some faculty have questioned whether she is a good role model to be teaching kids.

Challenges for Supervision

Any substance abuse situation that involves legal drugs such as alcohol requires action that stays within the boundaries of the Americans with Disabilities Act (ADA). Alcoholism is generally considered a disease and does not justify discipline in and of itself. An employer needs to determine how the employee's conduct or work performance (which may or may not result from alcoholism) is the basis for the need of discipline.

Ineffective Supervisory Responses

Ineffective supervisors will:

- Not be aware of the Americans with Disabilities Act or its implication to the pertinent state statute.
- Try to force employees into voluntary programs for treatment.
- Will not involve central office, the union, or seek consultation from colleagues or legal assistance.
- Conclude the smell of alcohol alone is sufficient to prove intoxication.
- Focus on condition of alcoholism rather than its effect on the teacher's classroom performance and on students, who view teachers as role models.
- Not anticipate that because alcoholism is not a permissible basis for employee discipline or discharge that alcoholism usually comes up as a defense by a teacher seeking to avoid discipline.
- May be aware of ADA but feel helpless because of the difficulty in suspending teachers affected by the act and therefore:
  - Avoid confronting the issue and hide behind the law.
  - Are unaware of the concept of progressive discipline and its application to cases such as Mme. Biere's.
  - Are afraid to ask for help, fearing a poor reflection on their own management of the problem or misapplying the need to handle problems discreetly.

Skillful Supervisory Responses

The skillful supervisor would avoid most of the traps the unsuspecting, ineffective supervisor encounters.

Skillful supervisors will:

- Realize that there are students who are losing out and that intervention is critical.

- Know about the ADA (Americans with Disabilities Act) and realize that alcoholism is considered a disease. Alcoholism per se does not justify discipline and does not constitute just cause for discipline in and of itself. Currently alcoholics are considered disabled under the antidiscrimination provisions of the ADA.

- Know alcoholics can be held to the same job performance standards as any other employee and that focus on job performance rather than alcoholic condition is appropriate.

- Know that use of alcohol off site is different from use of alcohol on site.

- As part of the intervention plan, provide reasonable accommodation with restructuring of the job that does not impose an undue hardship on the employer. For example, extra duties could be relieved for a period of time or the employer could bend the rules on departure hours.

- Immediately consult collective bargaining agreements and seek central office involvement and/or legal assistance before taking steps.

- Be aware of the need to balance the interests of the employee in seeking help and of the employer in maintaining a proper workplace setting.

- Notify and involve the union early in the process when there is strong evidence in hand.

- Document all interventions.

- Interview the teacher "at the first whiff," attempting to determine whether a problem really exists and the extent to which Mme. Biere recognizes the problem.

- Try to orchestrate a leave (perhaps using sick days) for the teacher to attend a supervised rehabilitation program before the problem becomes worse.

- Know that because alcoholism in itself is not a permissible basis for employee discipline or discharge, alcoholism usually comes up as a defense by an employee seeking to avoid discipline. Therefore, the skillful supervisor focuses the conference on teaching performance.

- Institute a progressive series of warnings and seek to encourage Mme. Biere to enroll in a treatment program.

Profile 9: Hank Frail—Physically Failing

Background

The following case highlights the problem of mediocrity that results from physical disability and deteriorating health. These are people whose life is teaching. Because there is usually no mandatory retirement age, these teachers can remain for years with declining performance. Their previous performance, which in this case was superlative, is really not relevant. Some of these teachers have been terrific, and others have been average, but the problem is current performance. What makes this problem different from many of the other cases is that there is little hope of performance improvement and much likelihood of further deterioration.

Hank has taught high school history for over 35 years. He is a legend and has enthralled students with his knowledge of the Middle Ages. In recent years his health has slipped. First he suffered a mild heart attack from which he recovered three years ago, then more recently a slight stroke. He has resisted invitations to retire with dignity, indicating that he had a few more "good years." It is known that money is not his primary motivation for continuing. Teaching is his life.

Student Experience

Many students have signed up for his class on the recommendation of older siblings, only to be disappointed. Hank Frail can no longer move around the room and sits at his desk. His stories, which used to delight, now are repeated several times, and he talks incessantly about his grown-up children and grandchildren. Poignantly, but sadly, students can now recite the names of all the dogs he has had over the years and how many students were in his rural Minnesota graduating class. Hank's wife has passed away, so school is "all he has." Students are very protective and do not complain but know that it is a wasted year. But this year, three parents have called to complain that Mr. Frail has little energy and is repeating himself.

Outside the Classroom

Hank is a noncontributing member of the staff but is the sentimental favorite of the older faculty. He forgets duties, and other teachers cover for him. He falls asleep during meetings, and teachers shield him so the principal can't see him nodding off. At departmental meetings, he makes an occasional wry crack that gives the old-timers a flashback of the "old Frail," while new teachers in their 20s hope they won't become future Frails. All would say he no longer contributes much to the school.

Challenges for Supervision

Like Mary Pity, Hank is a sympathy grabber and a "damned if you do, damned if you don't" supervisory problem even for the most skillful supervisor. There are two ineffective response patterns. They both stem from good intentions.

Ineffective Supervisory Responses

Ineffective supervisors will:

- Exert unprepared pressure for resignation. This comes about because the supervisor has decided that it is time to go. This immediately serves to unite everyone behind Hank because of his years of loyal service. Comments are heard such as "Sure he is not at his best, but he is still doing a good job." "He deserves to receive the support of the administration during his golden years." "The principal should back off; he still contributes a lot." "He should receive respect for what he has done." "The district needs to treat its senior members with respect." Teachers may also be viewing Hank's treatment as a forecast of how they will be treated. Supervisors need to realize that reactions are very personal.

- Ignore the problem and "buy time." Buying time can work if there is an agreement relative to a retirement date even a few years away. But to ignore the problem is to side with the teacher and not with the students. A teachers' advocate supervisor would likely ignore the situation. A students' advocate principal could not ignore it!

Skillful Supervisory Responses

The skillful supervisor realizes that there is a humane but direct response. This supervisor realizes that perceived mistreatment of this valued employee will result in years of stories of supervisor insensitivity. But to look the other way is to ignore the fact that students are losing out.

Skillful supervisors will:

- Feel responsible to supervise and evaluate with empathy but no "leniency factor" (see Chapter 4).
- Use much wait time and active listening.
- Allow an opportunity for face saving.
- Clearly communicate what is expected, including observable outcomes.

LEGAL NOTE

One of the most fundamental requirements of "due process," "just cause," and basic standards of fairness is that, with respect to performance evaluation, teachers are entitled to know the standards to which they will be held accountable in advance of their application. "Evaluation ... means at least a reasoned and objective measuring of Plaintiff's skills against previously selected recognized and recognizable standards.... Teaching, like any other art, does not lend itself to quantification. But an absence of precision in data-gathering does not warrant vagueness in criteria.... Defendants, in short, must be prepared to express concretely, in advance of its application, every criterion they propose to employ." *Freel v. Mulready*, Middlesex Superior Court No. 77-4322, slip op. (Mass. 1980). (Note: This is a Superior Court decision, as such, it is not binding precedent with respect to other courts; nonetheless, it is an interesting expression of what this judge expected in evaluative criteria.)

- Encourage solicitation of feedback from students and parents.
- Involve another trusted administrator to increase credibility.
- Plan a series of meetings:
  - Invite participation by teacher's colleague at the discretion of the teacher.
  - Retest the teacher's resistance to retirement in persistent but low-key ways.
  - Inform the teacher that there have been some complaints and that they have responded to them by scheduling some additional observations. This assumes the teacher is not on a summative cycle. Otherwise, supervisors just announce the beginning of the observation cycle.
- Not accept the promise of retirement unless it is in writing. Many administrators report that oral promises are withdrawn the following spring.
- Conduct a series of observations. Announce the first observation in respect for seniority and the need to assess "current potential." After a series of observations (perhaps three), a feedback conference is planned, perhaps with a trusted colleague of the teacher sitting in. The conference deals only with the teaching observed, and there are multiple observers, if possible.
- Tell Hank (depending on observations) that an improvement plan is under consideration for the current year.
- Include some reasonable accommodation for reduction in nonteaching duties but not compromise the standards expected for any professional in terms of classroom performance.

The implied message is that Hank cannot receive dispensation from normal standards to which he has been held in the past. The teacher should be invited to help construct the plan. Not surprisingly, this may ratchet up the teacher's anxiety. Readers may interpret the development of an improvement plan as humiliating. However, remember the skillful supervisor always thinks first of students and second of teachers' feelings. We are looking at Hank's performance because we know it affects student learning and that students lose

LEGAL NOTE

Providing teachers with a reasonable opportunity to remediate substandard performance using improvement plans is an essential aspect of progressive discipline and a fundamental requirement of the "just cause" standard. "The teacher, by statute, must be given a reasonable time in which to correct the deficiencies outlined. Considering this teacher's 17 years of service in the district, in addition to 8 years of teaching elsewhere, it seems harsh and unreasonable to accord her only 5 weeks after the notice of deficiency before the first observation and 8 weeks before the notice of termination to remedy 25 years of teaching practice which was now labeled deficient for the first time." *Joy Ganyo v. Independent School District*, No. 832, 311 N.W. 2d 497 (1981). While the facts in each case may lead to a different result, the general rule is that the longer teachers have been employed by a school district, the more time they must be given to remediate unacceptable performance.

out with mediocre teaching. Current performance is not evaluated by averaging with past success. By not identifying Hank for an improvement plan, we have effectively abandoned our student advocate role. However, being respectful and helping the teacher maintain dignity is critical. The tone should be supportive, not vindictive.

 Summary

Mediocre performance is caused by many factors and takes many forms. Classroom and schoolwide performance is affected by teachers' and supervisors' expertise, beliefs, and attitudes and by external influences. Confronting the lack of expertise of a "Friendly" or the poor attitude of a "Steel" or dealing with the chronic, performance-depressing, personal problems of a "Pity" requires different sets of skills and knowledge. But in all these cases, except Frail, improvement is within the control of the teacher and the supervisor.

Each case presents an opportunity for a supervisor to make a difference in the lives of students and teachers. None of these individuals is clearly incompetent or a clear candidate for dismissal. However, without supervisory intervention, none of these individuals is likely to improve spontaneously. Achieving real change in performance requires the three essential conditions: the three C's: Competence, Conviction and Control.

Supervisors will need conviction to:

- Pay attention and not look the other way when no one else would notice.
- Stay with the case and see it through to improvement or to a decision to invest energy in dismissal or in other cases.
- Keep their eyes first on the consequences to students without worrying as much about the response of teachers.

Supervisors will need competence in:

- Understanding the unique values, skills, and history of each individual.
- Identifying the problems in their unique contexts.
- Giving credible, specific feedback and context-relevant suggestions.
- Knowing the language of the contract and the law.
- Dealing with the institutional and cultural shortcomings that have contributed to the performance lapse. (The planning problem of a Winger and the low expectations problem of a Limits are institutional as well as individual issues.)

Supervisors will need control in:

- Having the human and financial resources needed to support an improvement effort.

- Having a network of supportive peers.
- Having support from the superintendent and school board.

These nine cases do not exhaust the possible ways in which mediocre performance presents itself. They do, however, represent the landscape into which supervisors step. Committed and skillful supervisors make choices. Hypothetically, a K-12 supervisor or the principal of a large building might face all the cases cited in this chapter. Attempting to take on every one at once is a sure recipe for frustration and ineffectiveness. Taking on none simply reinforces institutional mediocrity.

The challenge is awesome. Supervisors are faced not only with the individual shortcomings within and outside the classroom, they must deal with the unique history and personality of each case. Finally, the supervisor is part of a culture that may have debilitating beliefs and unpromising practices. But in taking on individual cases, the supervisor is also affecting these very same cultural beliefs and practices. The supervisor with strong conviction cannot wait for all the institutional factors to be in place.

Which Teacher Should Be Selected First?

1. **Degree of loss of student learning** Select cases where students are losing out. Using this criterion, Collabnot would be a lower priority than a Limits. Hank Frail might be a higher priority than a Passable. Louise Biere might top the list.

2. **Likelihood of success** Supervisory time is an important resource. It is important to pick cases where intervention will have a likely payoff. Using this criterion, a Sally Friendly might be a better investment than Frank Steel.

3. **Impact on an institutional priority or problems shared by many teachers** Some cases invite both institutional and individual interventions. For example, Winger may be an example of several teachers who have planning issues. Limits may fit into a districtwide focus on raising expectations. These might be higher priorities than a Mary Pity with more unique external problems.

In the following chapters, we invite supervisors to build their skills with a set of tools to confront individual cases of mediocre performance in their own schools.

4 Selecting Data Sources

Changing the Nature of Evaluation: The 3-D Cycle

Incompetence and excellence in teaching share one quality; they are easier to capture and to describe than mediocrity. Excellent teaching is a complicated amalgam of technical expertise, subject area knowledge and passion, strong beliefs about learning potential, patience and tenacity, careful planning, and powerful expectations. Because the effects both inside and outside of the classroom are so striking, competent evaluators can generally document and explain what happens and why it works for students. Using widely shared hallmarks like poor management, vagueness and confusion, and harmful relations with students, capable evaluators can also find incompetence with little difficulty. Mediocrity, however, is a moving target, a phenomenon that defies precise portrayal. Caught trying to capture performance that is neither bad enough to be incompetent nor good enough to approve, evaluators too often resort to vague descriptions and generic sets of recommendations.

Leaders who want to confront mediocrity need tools to help them (1) gather accurate data in which they have a measure of confidence, (2) describe precisely the strengths and problems they have recognized, and (3) design improvement plans that really change behavior. Traditional approaches to teacher evaluation have been one-dimensional, both in their ability to describe the nature of the teaching issue and in their ability to identify steps needed for improvement. These models have relied heavily on using what can be observed during classroom visits.

Basing an evaluation on observation data alone is problematic for several reasons. First, the small sample influences the accuracy of the judgment.[1] Second, observations unsupported by other data sources are especially susceptible to the rating errors we discuss later in this chapter. Finally, observation does not even assess all of the areas of classroom performance that may affect student learning, much less areas of professional responsibility outside the classroom.

The limitations of observation for evaluating any teacher are apparent, but those limitations have more impact when supervisors are trying to improve mediocre teaching. As our profiles reveal, classrooms in which mediocre teaching occurs may be orderly, friendly, and safe. Relations with students may be pleasant and positive. Activities may be fun and engaging or suitably structured to help children practice their skills. Children may even be learning something—just not the important skills and concepts they need to help them meet the performance standards to which they will be held accountable. To move an assessment from the vague sense that "something is not happening" to a precise picture of what needs to improve, evaluators need as comprehensive a profile as they can assemble. Classroom observations alone cannot provide such a picture.

Figure 4-1 suggests a framework for evaluation that moves beyond the narrow confines of classroom observation and uses multiple sources of data. We have named this model "the 3-D's" both as a mnemonic to help leaders remember the key jobs they must do—select data sources, describe strengths and problems, and design plans—and as a metaphor for the three-dimensional depth of analysis needed to improve mediocre teaching. Chapters 4, 5, and 6 detail each step of the cycle. In this chapter we present a menu of the data sources an evaluator can use to collect specific, focused information about a teacher's performance. Organized around framing questions from the work of Saphier and Gower (1997), Chapter 5 offers the reader a detailed analytic framework to consider the five roles teachers perform: classroom instructor,

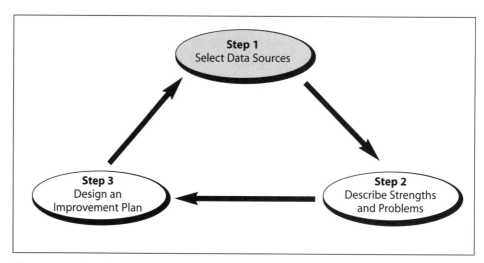

Figure 4-1 The 3-D cycle. (©1999 Ready About Press all rights reserved)

---

[1]A supervisor may use one "full" observation and rarely more than three as the basis for giving a rating that will last several years. Frequently observations are of less than complete lessons. Increasing the number of observations improves the accuracy of the data, but busy supervisors are unlikely to seek this additional work. As a matter of survival, most choose to meet miniumum requirements.

contributing member of the staff, performer of routine administrative duties, communicator with parents and community, and constant learner (Saphier 1993). Chapter 6 suggests ways to build an improvement plan that is problem based and goal focused, rather than merely a list of activities, and shows you how to return to multiple sources of data to assess progress and complete the 3-D evaluation cycle.

The Case for Multiple Sources of Data

The 3-D framework starts with selecting data sources that will develop a comprehensive picture of performance. Because the practice of examining multiple sources of data to build a summative evaluation may differ significantly from many districts' standard operating procedures, we need to examine how moving to multiple sources of data can help improve the accuracy of the judgments. We need first to address errors that are built into any single-source evaluation, and especially one based only on observation.

Reducing Rating Errors

Most evaluation procedures require a supervisor to make a judgment. Acknowledging the problem of rater bias, Stronge (1997) writes, "Like beauty, instructional quality is in the eyes of the beholder. All too frequently whim and caprice color judgments." We have found that without benchmarking practice, training to build inter-rater reliability, and the requirement to look at many dimensions of performance, evaluators select their own rose-colored or narrowly focused lenses through which to view a teacher's skills. That selectivity leads to halo effects and to errors of leniency or severity.

Halo effects occur when an evaluator's ratings of a teacher are unduly influenced by his or her overall impression of the individual. In the case of a mediocre performer such as Sally Friendly, the "good person" perception may insulate the teacher from negative feedback about his or her teaching. A leniency error occurs when an evaluator chooses to "go easy" on a teacher either "to avoid hassles" or because success in one domain is inadvertently overweighted. These two common errors may explain why mediocre performance has historically been inflated. An individual's teaching skills may not be strong, but supervisors find that "She's really good with the hard-to-reach kids" or "He contributes much to school activities," or, like Frank Steele, "He is a great coach." The result is an incomplete or invalid representation of the teacher's overall performance.

The opposite of the leniency error is being unfairly severe in rating a teacher. Severity errors, which are much rarer than leniency errors, occur when an evaluator is "out to get" an individual and therefore ranks the performance consistently low no matter what happens. Severity error is especially noticeable with administrators who develop righteous zeal and a commitment to "take on" an individual. The supervisor tries to avoid giving any positive credit or positive judgments, even though some may be warranted, and writes statements such as "The teacher did check for understanding, but she failed to relate personally to students." In such cases the supervisor should give credit for checking separately and not blur and diminish the positive statement with a "but." In other examples of editorial severity, the supervisor takes unnecessary pokes: "Unfortunately, the teacher chose not to respond to the disrupting students." Here the use of the loaded word *unfortunately* is an unnecessary editorial addition that diverts attention from the central issue. Severity error is especially worrisome as it often indicates a lack of fairness by the evaluator that affects the evaluator's objectivity and so brings into question the accuracy of all judgments.[2]

Expanding the sources of information collected about performance tends to reduce the effect of the sources of error and to increase the accuracy of judgment about the performance.[3] Supervisors are more likely to be lenient, for example, if they do not have adequate data on which to base their judgments. Positive judgments require less support data than negative judgments. Few teachers will question how the supervisor could justify a positive judgment, but most teachers will question the source of data for a negative judgment. *More information, therefore, means more credibility.*

Overcoming Bias and the Limitations of Observation

In a recent observation by one of the authors and three supervisors, the supervisors' assessments were significantly more positive than those of the outsider. The supervisors offered the following explanations for their positive ratings: "She's a hard worker, but not a superstar. You can't have all superstars. It would be unfair to give the lesson a poor rating; she does so much for the school." "What you've got to realize is that she is much nicer than other teachers. The kids really like her." "There is a teacher shortage; I don't want to discourage her. She might leave. Anybody we would find would be less qualified." The supervisors essentially ignored or did not see the poor quality of this lesson.

Evaluators bring their own biases and prior knowledge to each observation. If they have accumulated a deep reservoir of positive impressions, they may not even see problems that are apparent to those who have no "history" to shape their judgments.

In the example in the margin, the teacher's valid strengths in personal-relationship building and contribution to the school created a holistic impression (halo effect) that blinded the evaluators to teaching deficits that directly affected student learning. The halo effect protected the teacher from unfavorable judgments. In fact the observers did not see the problems until the data were cited. The evaluators' choices to opt for leniency also denied the teacher the opportunity to think about her own performance and to make appropriate changes.

In institutional cultures that expect excellence, the use of multiple sources of data sends key messages about continuous growth and learning and about the value placed on demonstrated competence in all areas of performance. "Dog and pony show" lessons handed down from teacher to teacher and trotted out for the yearly evaluation will not suffice. The institution understands that classroom observation

> *leaves out direct systematic evidence about teacher planning, teacher assessment and modification of instructional materials, teacher's choice and adaptation of instructional methods and teacher's working relationship with colleagues, parents and members of the community. (Millman and Darling-Hammond 1990, p.198)*

---

[2]Recipients of poor reports will often accuse an evaluator of being unfair. This is the equivalent of being accused of committing a severity error. If there is a trusted and trained group of supervisors, the teacher could request a second opinion observation with a different qualified evaluator.

[3]"An important feature of effective teacher evaluation is the use of multiple data sources for documenting performance....99.8% of American public school administrators use direct observation as their primary data collection technique. However, primary reliance on formal observation in evaluation presents significant problems (e.g., artificiality, small sample of performance)....The creative use of multiple data sources to measure teacher performance can result in a fuller and more accurate view than is available through more narrowly defined approaches to data collection." (Stronge p. 101)

Analyzing multiple areas of performance, such as those cited by Millman and Darling above, is likely to yield valuable information about both the roots of and remedies for mediocre performance. The process begins with a search for the best sources of data about what a particular teacher knows and is able to do.

The 3-D Cycle Step 1: Selecting Data Sources

Figure 4-2 shows a sample menu of commonly used data sources as well as some used only in special applications. These items are explained on later pages, with implementation tips and anecdotes. You can select from this menu in accordance with your own collective bargaining agreements, the performance descriptors set forth in the next chapter, and the needs of your supervi-

DATA SOURCES CHECKLIST

Observation
- Classroom Observation
  Informal
  Formal
- Outside of Classroom Observation (Professional Meetings)
  Curriculum meetings
  Team meetings
  Department meetings
  Faculty meetings
  Committee work: attendance, quality of participation, etc.
  Special education meetings
- Outside of Classroom Observation (Other)
  Lunchroom
  Hall, recess, bus duty
  Parent conferences
  Back to school night presentation

Conferences
- Conference as interviews (data collecting)
- Career counseling interview conference
- Teacher reporting findings
- Goal-setting conference
- Pre- or post-observation conference (data-sharing conference)

Unobtrusive Artifacts
- Grade distributions
- Student progress reports
- Discipline referrals: quantity and quality

- Student placement referrals by teachers
- Parent/student placement requests
- Newsletters and memos sent home

Other Sources
- Teacher's gradebook
- Supervisor file notes and data
- Teacher's attendance profiles
- Arrival and departure times
- Co-curricular activities and course participation

Student and Teacher Work Artifacts
- Homework assignments, worksheets, and handouts
- Lesson and unit plans
- Tests and quizzes
- Grading criteria and results on specific assignments
- Feedback given on student work
- Student work sample A's, B's, and D's

Surveys and Interviews
- Parent feedback questionnaires
- Student feedback questionnaires
- Student interviews
- Teacher self-evaluation
- Peer review evaluation

Student Achievement Data
- Standardized test score (norm referenced and criterion referenced)
- Performance presentations evaluated by a standard set of criteria
- Portfolio

Figure 4-2 Data sources checklist.

sory situation. Whether the data sources are used as integral parts of the teacher evaluation procedures or as part of the assessment component of an individual's improvement plan, they are offered as a way to increase the precision and accuracy of the effort to confront mediocrity. The comprehensive list of data sources in Figure 4-2 will lay the groundwork for the first of the 3-D's, which is selecting data sources.

Observation Sources

The most common source of information about the quality of teaching is from direct observation. These observations may be formal or informal, **comprehensive**, focusing on many aspects of teaching, or **selective**, focusing on pre-agreed or pre-announced areas of performance.

Classroom Observation[4]

Informal Observations   Frequent, short, unannounced visits give the observer a feel for the class. The evaluator takes few notes and does not do a write-up. Informal observations can be walk-throughs or short sampling observations. They allow the observer to develop impressions that can be examined in more detail during formal observations.

CAUTION   If the informal visits are going to be a source of data, it is important to give immediate feedback with a short, dated note to avoid giving the teacher an unexpected, unpleasant surprise when the final evaluation report is completed. Evaluators should save a copy of this note.

Formal Observations   Either announced or unannounced, formal observations are less frequent and must be in compliance with teacher evaluation agreements. In most cases formal observations are written up with formal narratives and become part of the teacher's permanent record. They become part of the data pool for a final summary evaluation report. They can be comprehensive or selective, depending on the circumstances.

TIPS ON OBSERVATION

- **Start with an announced visit**   It is very important that you see the teacher's "best shot." An announced lesson gives the teacher time to prepare, which may not reveal what the teacher usually does but does say what they can do. Whether it is good or bad, it gives the supervisor a benchmark of performance.

- **Seek out positives**   Observation of substandard teaching should not focus just on deficit identification. It is very important to identify and build on strengths, which is often more successful than remediating weaknesses. Try to catch the teacher doing a few things right. Seek out strengths, but don't invent them!

- **Arrive and begin observation 2 to 3 minutes before the bell**   This is a good time to observe management and personal relationship building. Natural interaction patterns with students are frequently more observable during informal transition times than during class.

[4] These guidelines are relevant to all observations but are especially important to lay the groundwork of fairness for confronting mediocre performance.

- **Consider using the "whole-half sandwich" pattern where you observe one and a half periods over three days** Over three days, observing the last half of a class, a complete class and then half of the third class is very effective at reducing the "dog and pony show" effect and increasing the longitudinal data. It is much more difficult to prolong a show over several days. Some contracts forbid consecutive observations. We recommend that this indefensible restriction be negotiated for elimination during the next round of contract bargaining.

- **Take literal notes** Avoid recording impressions and generalizations. Focus instead on the specifics of what the teacher and students are saying and doing. See *How to Make Supervision and Evaluation Really Work* (Saphier 1993).

- **Don't forget to observe what is on the classroom walls** Annotated student work on bulletin boards, expectation messages, and project artifacts are part of the data for the observation. Keep in mind that traveling teachers and teachers who share rooms sometimes don't control the walls.

- **Consider audio tape or videotape** Audiotape is less intrusive than videotape. Videotape provides a source of data that can be replayed during the conference. However, many teachers, especially mediocre performers, are anxious about the use of video, and it may violate collective bargaining agreements. It probably works better for supervision where the data will not be used for evaluation and is available for the teacher's own scrutiny.

Professional Meetings

Most observations focus on the classroom context. However, there are other opportunities for observation that are especially helpful in collecting data on job performance outside the classroom. Participation in the professional community is an important aspect of a teacher's role, and insight into this participation can be gained by observing the quality of the contributions in professional meetings such as the following:

Curriculum meetings

Team meetings

Department meetings

Faculty meetings

Committee meetings

Special education meetings

While meetings are a rare source of formal data, they become especially useful in cases where teachers are negatively affecting the culture through constant complaining or nonparticipation (see profile on John C. Collabnot in Chapter 3). In such instances, specific evidence of a teacher's noncollaboration, not just hearsay information, is important.

Because the supervisor is usually a participant in meetings, constant note-taking is more difficult and less desirable. However, most supervisors do take recollection notes; these can focus on the contributions and comments (or absence thereof) of all participants, including the target teacher of concern. These could later be included in an interim note to the teacher and become

An experienced teacher was identified as needing an improvement plan. As part of the plan, the teacher was required to work with a coach from outside the district. The teacher agreed to be videotaped and to watch the video with the coach. After 30 minutes, the teacher said "This is really boring." It was a catalyst for some short-term improvement and renewed energy in her teaching. Alas, we must be honest and say that when the principal turned her attention to other matters, the teacher started backsliding—a constant issue confronting supervisors (see Chapters 6 and 7).

part of the data pool for his/her evaluation. Following is an example of a note expressing a supervisor's concern about a teacher's behavior in a meeting.

> *I am concerned by your failure to contribute positively to the professional community of the school. For example, in the faculty meeting of 4/8/99 you sat in the back of the library correcting papers. The only contribution you made was to say "This is another stupid idea. Let's wrap up the meeting. I've got to prepare for tomorrow." This kind of comment undermines the culture of professional support and collaboration and provides a poor model of participation for our three new staff members.*

Outside of Classroom Observation

While supervisors informally observe teachers in the following settings, formal observations would be rare. These sources of data are appropriate in cases when teachers fail to carry out routine administrative duties or where there have been some expressed concerns about the quality of communication with parents:

Lunchroom

Hall, recess, bus duty

The supervisor could observe and make notations in the lunchroom or during hall duty, recess or bus duty. Safety issues and punctuality are the key focus of these observations.

Parent conferences

Back to school nights

The annual back to school night presentation is an underutilized source of information about teachers. Much insight can be gained about a teacher's priorities and his or her skill in communicating with parents.

Supervisory Teacher Conferences

Although observation is a very important source of data, it gives little insight into teacher planning and reflective decision making, both of which are major causes of mediocre instruction. The pre- and post-observation conferences allow the evaluator to clarify the context for the lesson and to give feedback. We suggest that these same conferences also be used as sources of data to assess reflection and decision making.

Conference as Interview

In addition to the traditional use of pre- and post-conferences, think of them as interview opportunities. Most supervisors have participated in hiring and placement interviews where they used a set of questions structured to collect information (data) to help make a hiring or selection decision. In this way, the conference can be used intentionally to assess the teacher's planning and reflection about decision making.

During a data-collecting conference immediately following an observation, the supervisor asked the teacher whether the students knew why they got the

One of the authors attended a back to school night for his high school daughter. The science teacher revealed much about her teaching when she said "Unfortunately, because of AIDS we cannot do the experiments on blood this year. That's too bad because that's the one activity all students found interesting." The message sent to parents was that students were bored with many of the other activities and that the teacher lacked the ingenuity to create alternatives.

grades they did.(Projects had been returned to the students with A and B grades and no comments.) The teacher answered, "Of course they understand; they are now in 10th grade and have been receiving grades since 4th grade." This response (along with others) was added to the write-up to document lack of specificity in giving students precise feedback and communicating the criteria for success.

For teaching, planning takes on the same importance as location in real estate. A prominent Boston area curriculum leader, Judith Boreschek of the Wellesley Public Schools, comments on the importance of planning:

> I have dealt with seasoned teachers who don't see a need for a plan. They have all the classroom routines and management figured out, so they plan by the "seat of the pants." They plan for involvement but don't have a concept of planning for assessment, planning around central concepts and questions, and/or planning to teach challenging and significant skills outside the basics.

Figure 4-3 is a tool supervisors can use to collect data on teachers' thinking about planning. The questions in this planning guide then become the basis for a conference interview. The responses become a source of data about planning. Alternately, the supervisor could share a copy of this organizer and have the teacher use it as a tool to plan a unit or lesson.

Career Counseling Interview Conference

The supervisor needs to assess the long-term growth potential and motivation of the teacher. Every five years all teachers should have a formal career counseling conference with the supervisor and another professional of the teacher's choosing. Career counseling interviews become especially important for substandard performers. In order to focus on career goals and directions, it is important to keep this conference separate from an observation or summary evaluation conference. If there are "personality conflicts" with the supervisor, someone other than the evaluator, such as a guidance counselor, could conduct the conference. It should focus on the individual's aspirations, career goals, and professional achievement and growth goals.

Goal-Setting Conference

The goal-setting conference is more related to planning than to data collection, therefore it is included in Chapter 6, "Design a Plan."

Pre- or Post-Observation Conference (Data-Sharing Conference)

Since our emphasis in this chapter is on data collection, we will not discuss in detail the role of the pre- and post-conference.

TIPS ON CONFERENCES FOR COLLECTING DATA

- Always conduct a post-observation conference before writing up the observations so you can check your data and conclusions and answer questions before formally committing judgments to writing.

- Take notes during the conference.

- Use data-based questions and withhold judgment as much as possible in this data-gathering period. Example: "I noticed that you skipped calling

---

A principal had two 2nd grade teachers in their second year of teaching. He was trying to decide whether to award them a contract for the third year. Both were struggling. He observed each teacher; both lessons presented problems. However, in the post-observation conference, one teacher could articulate exactly what went wrong, and the other one was baffled. Based on the data from the conference, the first teacher received a contract for the following year. The second teacher was let go. It was the power of the conference data that made the difference.

LEGAL NOTE

Consistency is important. Conferences should be used as a source of data for all teachers, not just poor performers. Otherwise, evaluators could open themselves up to harassment charges. We recommend that evaluators regularly include comments from the post-observation conference in their write-ups.

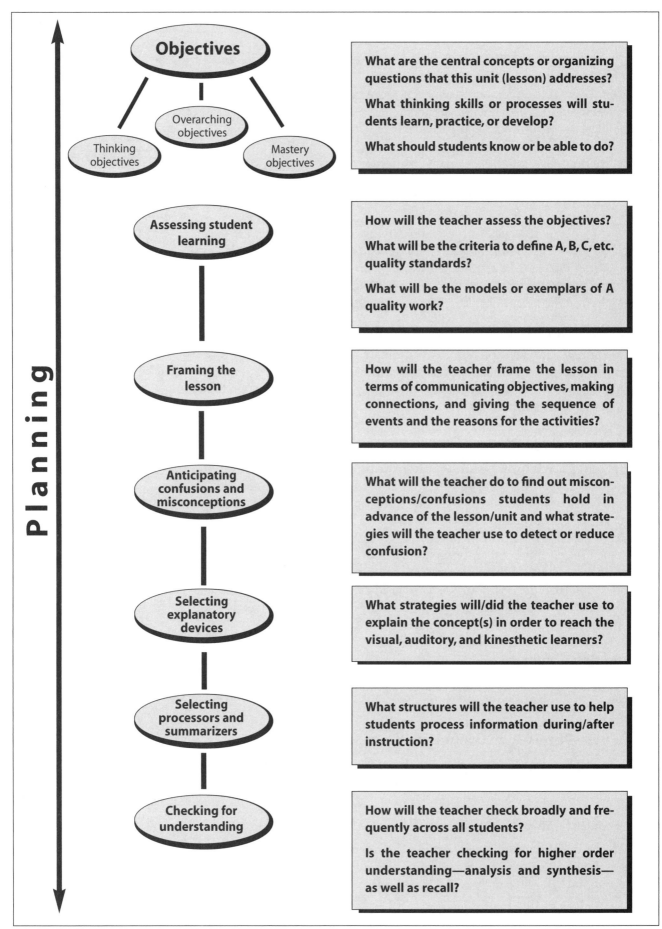

Figure 4-3 Planning Guide. (©1999 Ready About Press all rights reserved, adapted from *The Skillful Teacher*, Research for Better Teaching, 1997.

on Mary. Was there a reason for this?" rather than "Why did you not call on Mary?"

- Read over past evaluation reports and summary write-ups to determine if they are useful sources for conference questions.

Unobtrusive artifacts

Unobtrusive artifacts are data sources that are readily available to the supervisor and do not require gathering time and effort by either the teacher or the supervisors.

Grade distributions

Grade distributions are a ready source of information but need to be used cautiously and put into a context. Supervisors should examine grading patterns when there is concern about fairness or comprehensiveness in the teacher's evaluation of students. Just as supervisors are subject to bias and rating error, teachers too can also fall prey to leniency or severity errors in rating their students.

X Public Schools									
X High School									
Grade Distribution by Teacher									
Sec	Course	Title	A	B	C	D	F	S	I
2	2200	US Hist Pt1	1	1	4	3	12	3	1
4	2200	US Hist Pt1	1	1	4	1	9	3	0
Teacher Totals			2	2	8	4	21	6	1
Percent			4.5	4.5	18.2	9.1	47.7	13.6	2.3

Figure 4-4 The grade distribution pattern of a high school social studies teacher who exhibits severity error.

The grade distribution pattern shown in Figure 4-4 suggests that the teacher is guilty of severity error. Too many students (50%) are getting D's and F's. When asked about the grading pattern, the teacher said that few of the students could "measure up" to his high standards. He had been teaching for over 20 years and felt that the current students, many of whom were immigrants, could "not do the work that students could do in the past." Hence, most of his students got D's and F's, and it was, he said, "not my fault."

CAUTION Grading patterns by themselves are neither good nor bad. A negatively skewed grading pattern (with a high percentage of A and B grades) could either be the result of grade inflation, or it could be that the teacher is successful in moving his or her students to mastery of the identified standards. The result in this case is that many students are achieving at a high level for their grade (mastery learning paradigm). We used to think a bell curve was a nice way to grade. In fact smooth bell curves may be a sign that the teacher is artificially distributing the grades and is not achieving high-level student performance.

A central office personnel administrator told a high school math department chairperson who was receiving a teacher being transferred from another school because of poor performance not to read the past reports. "Give her a fresh start" was the advice. This was poor advice. If we are to be student advocates, all data, including past evaluations, should be available to the supervisor. Withholding information reinforces the "dance of the lemons" pattern described in Chapter 2. Fresh starts and constant transfer without follow-up allows mediocrity to flourish.

A high school teacher in a wealthy Boston suburb complained to the principal that, as the policy permitted, too many parents were overriding teacher recommendations The teacher complained that many students were well over their heads and couldn't do the work. An examination of his grading patterns showed that 80 percent of the grades were A's and B's. This shifted the discussion to grading criteria and standards for assessment.

Student Progress Reports

Quality of teacher feedback to students can be partially assessed by examining quarterly progress reports. Absence of comments or trite refrains such as "a pleasure to have in class," "not working up to potential" can be an indicator of general or inferior feedback to students.

Special notice should be given to midterm warning notices. Failure to notify poor performers in a timely manner is a frequent characteristic of mediocre teaching.

Discipline Referrals: Quantity and Quality

Teachers who have discipline problems often make frequent referrals to the principal. It is important to identify the students who are being removed and make comparisons with their problems in other classes. Evaluators should keep a record of discipline referrals as a source of data. The following anecdote illustrates how referrals can be put into the context of other available data to give fuller meaning.

A teacher wrote a behavioral referral to the assistant principal, "John is destroying the atmosphere in the class. If he does not shape up, I am going to request that he be transferred." The assistant principal pulled out the midterm report forms where "good effort" and "good conduct" had been checked off. In a three-way meeting with the parents, the teacher admitted that he may have sent "mixed messages." Without the data about the midterm report, the teacher might not have assumed responsibility for poor communication.

Teacher placement referrals

Look for patterns emerging, for example, a 4th grade teacher might never recommend special education students to certain 5th grade teachers.

Parent/student placement requests

Collect data on patterns of parent or, in high school, student requests not to have certain teachers or to transfer from an individual teacher's class. Such requests lead to inequalities in class sizes and teacher work loads. For example, there was a high school social studies department where members had student loads ranging between a low of 50 to a high of 150 students because students perceived particular teachers to be less effective. The union raised the fairness issue and exerted pressure on the teacher to get better. The union was the supervisor's ally in this situation.

Newsletters and memos sent home

Written communication that teachers send home to parents or share during back to school night presentations is another source of data. Many teachers send home newsletters. These documents communicate important messages about expectations, performance standards, and the teacher's availability for support, as well as what is taking place in the classroom. Collecting artifacts on parent communication allows the supervisor to assess these key messages as well as the basic level of the teacher's literacy. In one case we know about, the teacher's spelling was so bad the principal asked the teacher to let his secretary proofread any communication leaving the school.

Other Sources

Teacher's Gradebook

Supervisors with conviction to take on mediocrity make this an integral part of their pool of information. It gives them an overview of the teacher's assessment practices for an entire marking period. Scanning a gradebook allows the supervisor to get valuable data such as:

- Number of assignments
- How different types of assignments are graded
- Weighting of assignments (overweighting of trivial True-False quizzes vs. quality writing assignments)
- Completion rate for students
- Extent of make-ups by students
- How many students do the homework
- Extent of grading of homework
- Student turnover in the class

CAUTION Using the gradebook to assess a teacher's priorities fulfills the maxim "you inspect what you expect." That is, what teachers choose to grade is a statement about what they consider important. As with many of the alternative sources of data, you should use gradebooks cautiously and always with other sources of information. You should avoid rushing to superficial judgments about completeness or neatness and instead use the gradebook as an opportunity to probe the teacher's thinking.

Supervisor's File Notes and Data

Parent notes

Letters of complaint or compliment

Notes from parent/student conferences

CAUTION The disposition of parent letters is typically covered in contracts. The best practice is to immediately inform the teacher of a complaint and provide him or her with a copy. All letters of complaint or compliment should be kept on file. Any notes from conferences with parents and/or students should be part of the available pool of data.

Teacher Attendance Profiles

Attendance patterns can be analyzed by checking on the use of allotted sick days, especially Fridays and Mondays.

A new principal noticed the suspicious attendance pattern of a 15-year high school teacher who was out two months due to a serious snowmobile accident. After a week, he needed to call on the sick leave bank because all his sick days had been used up. A curious new principal wondered why a veteran teacher would need to go into the sick leave bank; he should have had almost

300 days to his credit! An examination of the data for the past ten years found that not only had he used up his remarkably generous 20-day allowance each year, there was a 75 percent Monday–Friday pattern. That is, almost all his absences were tagged onto weekends. He felt that he was entitled to these days since they were in the contract. He was dubbed by some cynical supervisor as the 20-game winner. The supervisor discussed the data with the teacher. The attendance pattern improved, and the teacher confined his snowmobiling to weekends.

Arrival and Departure Times

Many supervisors ignore minor contractual breeches repeatedly, and such ignoring becomes part of the tacit institutional agreement that little can be expected. A supervisor with conviction does not look the other way when teachers' arrival and departure patterns violate the contract.

Co-curricular Activities and Course Participation

Supervisors often have teachers submit a survey that includes a list of their participation in co-curricular, sports, and professional development courses.

This is an extract of data provided to the principal by an elementary school teacher as part of the data to assess the "teacher as a constant learner" standard.

Workshops and Conferences 1998–99

So How Is Your Self-esteem?	2.0 hours 9/4
Meteorology	2.5 hours 9/11
Storytelling	2.5 hours 10/8
Costa Rica	1.5 hours 10/15
Nonjudgmental Imagery	6.0 hours 11/8
How to Teach Drawing	2.0 hours 1/9
Box it and Bag it Math	30 hours 2/10–4/9
Inservice Day	4.5 hours 3/7

Looking at this list, the principal concluded that there was a sense of incoherence to the professional development plan. He added this information to other sources of data that indicated that this teacher was not applying anything she was learning in the classroom and was struggling and scattered (perhaps a Sally Friendly type, see Chapter 3).

We recommend that some reflective questions be submitted along with lists of courses and workshops and lists of co-curricular activities. Examples might be "Specifically, how has learning from this session transferred into your classroom?" or "How would you describe the quality of your participation and leadership in the Debate Club?

Student and Teacher Work Artifacts

As teachers move to a more standards-based classrooms aligned with state and districts frameworks, we are seeing great improvement in student assessment techniques (see Wiggins 1998 and Hayes Jacobs 1997 for further information). It is important that supervisors begin to assess the assessments. One way to begin this task is to collect teacher and student work. Here we are focusing on these work samples as accompaniments to other sources of data. In Chapter 9,

"Evaluation in the Next Decade," we will expand the idea to full teacher portfolios.

Homework Assignments, Worksheets, and Handouts

Teachers can be asked to place any material given to students in a box for the supervisor.

Lesson and Unit Plans

Judith Boreschek, Director of Curriculum for the highly respected Wellesley, Massachusetts, Public Schools, believes that far too much focus has been put into single-lesson plans. She believes that unit plans give much more insight into the quality of teaching. All of us know gifted teachers who teach from the plans in their heads without written lesson or unit plans, but written plans are invaluable sources of insight into substandard performance. Written plans are essential for follow-up intervention. Both lesson and unit plans can be keyed to state and district frameworks (see Figure 4-3).

Tests and Quizzes

The supervisor examines artifacts capturing what the teacher is testing to discover the teacher's priorities. This can be combined with the gradebook examination discussed earlier.

Grading Criteria for Specific Assignments

Rubrics and criterion checklists are really helpful in answering the question. "What does it take to get an A?"

Student Work Samples Plus Feedback Given by Teacher

One of the most powerful sources of data is samples of graded and annotated work products by students of different performance levels. The teacher could be invited to bring representative samples showing A, B, and D grades to a post-conference or summary evaluation conference.

CAUTION Any effort to examine student work should be school- or department-based; do not collect samples only from identified poor performers. Teachers can be invited to make a presentation to the supervisor or a group of colleagues and/or to participate in discussions.

Client Surveys of Individual Teachers

Another powerful source of data that adds to the validity of teacher evaluation is structured surveys or interviews of students and parents. The fact that student ratings are used in less than 3 percent and parent ratings in less than 1 percent of schools should not be a deterrent to using them (Stronge 1997, p. 62). They can be designed, analyzed, and reported by teachers and are an important source of information; their use should be expanded.

CAUTION According to James Warnock, Assistant Superintendent of the Burlington Vermont Public Schools, "Surveys are anxiety producers for teachers particularly in the early stages and especially if they are disaggregated by

One principal who was concerned by the quantity and quality of worksheets being passed out requested a four-week collection from all teachers. It gave a rich profile of the work students were asked to complete. There was great variation. Almost all of the samples from mediocre performers consisted of unrelated work papers that, in the principal's opinion, dealt almost exclusively with mechanics and computation.

individual teacher. Their results can certainly be used to validate other data, but be careful about basing too much information on them."

Parent Feedback Questionnaires

In a study involving 77 elementary school teachers, Epstein (1985, cited in Stronge 1997) compared and analyzed ratings from parents and principals and found the following:

> *Principals were more aware of how teachers performed extra duties than of changes in classroom practice; thus doing a good job on noninstructional tasks may have resulted in higher marks from the principal than exemplary teaching. Parents, however, were more knowledgeable about special efforts teachers made to help their children, thus this insight had an impact on parents' ratings of teacher performance.*

This parent perspective certainly should be one piece of data. We believe that all schools and teachers should be seeking regular feedback from parents at all levels

TIPS ON PARENT SURVEYS

- Stronge (1997) suggests that parent surveys may be more successful in elementary schools. There is more regular parent-teacher interaction at those grade levels. We suggest that a "not in a position to evaluate" option on parent surveys is especially relevant when each child has several teachers.

- Parents should be asked to document any ratings they give with specific examples and should be asked to rate only things that they have direct knowledge about.

Student Feedback Questionnaires

How could anyone argue against using group data from students as one source of information about teaching performance? In the words of one high school student, "We are the ones who observe teachers every day. Why don't they ask us for our opinions?" Some people may be concerned that teacher popularity unduly influences ratings, but findings show that students are very accurate in their ratings. Ebmeier, Jenkins and Crawford (1991, cited in Stronge 1997) compared high school ratings of "meritorious and nonmeritorious" teachers and found that students were as accurate as qualified evaluators.

CAUTION Student data should be used carefully by focusing on group responses and patterns rather than individual students. All results should be anonymous. If the district climate or contract does not allow use of this source, the information can be confidentially used by the teacher as data for his/her decision making rather than as evaluation data information. The best teachers already use student data to inform their decisions.

TIPS ON STUDENT SURVEYS

- Student surveys above grade 4 may be more reliable. Manatt (1996) has developed forms for younger students, but many researchers advise using data only from older students.

- Student data are more reliable when collected from a large number of students over long periods of time, which helps establish patterns.

Student Interviews

Even more revealing than surveys are systematic interviews of students. There are two recommended applications.

1. Student interviews to collect specific data around a problem
2. Regular interviews of students not connected to a problem

Student Interview to Collect Specific Data   Supervisors should interview a random selection of students from a class where there have been a significant number of parent or student complaints or where issues have surfaced that need further investigation. Inappropriate behavior by teachers, especially when we are dealing with mediocrity rather than incompetence, is rarely observed directly. Teachers can often edit their behavior in front of an observer. Students will also shed light on patterns of behavior that signal mediocre performance, such as failure to collect, read, critique, grade, and to promptly return work. Students let supervisors know about confusing assignments and about treaties and deals around submission of work.

During a focus group discussion about ways to improve their high school, two young women suggested that the principal establish rules requiring teachers to grade and return tests and papers before the end of the marking period "so that we could learn something from doing the assignments." They pointed out that in one of their classes, work was never returned but that the teacher routinely "got terribly sick" three or four days before grades were due each quarter. She stayed home for several days, the students speculated, to catch up on her correcting. After their grades had been submitted, the teacher would return some of the student papers with a few comments. One or more sets of assignments usually disappeared, but when students complained, the teacher told them to "stay focused on getting into college, and don't sweat the small stuff." They accurately predicted the teacher's next set of days out of school. Examinations of another data source, the teacher's attendance patterns, revealed that she had been following that practice for at least six years; this issue had never been mentioned in her evaluations, which were based solely on classroom observations and self-reported professional development.

TIPS FOR STUDENT INTERVIEWS

- Tell the teacher you will be collecting additional data and explain how you will select the students. Make sure you interview a mix of complaining and noncomplaining students. Include teachers in the selection of students.

- Let the teacher know the questions you will be asking. Make sure the questions are more open-ended than leading. These are examples of questions in response to parent complaints about Mrs. Smith's lack of respect for students.

Poor example: Do you have any complaints about Mrs. Smith?

Better: Do you feel that Mrs. Smith respects you?

Good example: Tell me about your relationship with Mrs. Smith.

When you ask a question, she does not listen to you, she just keeps on going. She does not spend the time to explain to you because she is too busy." (Melinda, 16, interviewed by a principal collecting data on poor teacher performance)

■ Write a summary of the data connected to each question with your conclusions and recommendations.

Regular Interviews of Students Not Related to a Problem The second application is where the skillful supervisor regularly collects data from students and does not focus on one teacher or a single problem. The following anecdote describes this type of data collection.

Principal McEwan of Silver Lake Regional High School in Massachusetts holds weekly breakfasts with his students because he wants to get beyond the perceptions of the student council or eager student volunteers. He feeds and gets feedback on his school. In a parent newsletter (August 1998), Dr. McEwan tells the parents the purpose of the breakfast invitations:

> *The main purpose of the meeting is to discern from the students how the year is going. It is a way to find out their concerns and to address any issues before they become problems. Students have an opportunity to make suggestions and to voice any ideas they might have directly with the principal.*

What is more subtle is that Dr. McEwan is systematically collecting data from a representative sample of students in his school of 1600 students. He learns how students perceive the block scheduling is going, whether teachers are varying the pacing during the 90-minute periods, how the students feel about the homework load, and whether they feel supported in their work. He is not seeking data directly on individual teachers and discourages specific complaints, but he does pick up personnel issues that may need further investigation and intervention.

CAUTION Context is important. This data-collecting strategy works well here because Dr. McEwan has built a culture of respect and trust with the teachers' union. The principal sets the tone. In the words of association building representative Ron Iavanna, "The principal has an open door. He is a people person. We communicate a lot." (Not incidentally, there has been only one formal grievance proceeding in eight years in this school.) It is clear that honest, open communication is an institutional value, so the breakfast meetings are accepted as one more way for the principal to stay in touch with his school and not as a "get the goods on the teachers" meeting.

TIPS FOR STUDENT INTERVIEW MEETINGS

■ Food nurtures participation.

■ If you use a similar set of questions, comparable data can be collected across time.

■ Any data collected should be shared directly with the affected teachers and not held and placed later in a written evaluation. The emphasis is on sharing feedback and problem solving, not a "got you" mentality.

Teacher Self-Evaluation

One of the characteristics of poor performers is that their ratings of their own performance are often significantly higher than those of their supervisor or parents or students. A teacher's rating of his or her own job performance is a crucial piece of information when used in combination with other data. The identification and acceptance of this discrepancy is a crucial first step in moving to improvement. Change will often come from personal commitment rather than a mandated plan from the supervisor. In Chapter 6 we will discuss the importance of teacher ownership of the improvement plan.

TIPS ON TEACHER SELF-EVALUATION[5]

- Ratings should be referenced to the established district evaluation criteria or goals that have been set.

- Self-assessment must always be compared with another source of assessment: peers, supervisor, etc.

- Teachers should predict what ratings and feedback the other sources will show.

- A data-pooling conference should occur where the multiple sources are presented to identify and discuss agreements or discrepancies. A peer who is a friend of the teacher could be invited.

Peer Review Evaluations

There are a few districts in the country (Toledo, Columbus, Cincinnati, and Seattle) that use a highly developed system of peer evaluation and review, focusing on novice teachers and teachers in trouble (Chapter 9 offers further description). We do not recommend adding peer evaluation as a source of evaluation data without making it part of an overall reform effort. Santeusanio (*Educational Leadership* Vol. 55, no. 5, Feb. 1998, pp. 30–32) found that peer ratings were not accurate. Many peer evaluations are based on global impressions (halo error) rather than direct knowledge of performance. Even in the context of direct knowledge, such as collegial interaction, peers are prone to inflate average performance and very reluctant to rate low performance accurately. The leniency error cited earlier in the chapter is common in peer ratings.

TIPS FOR PEER RATINGS

- Use peer ratings, if at all, only for feedback to the individuals and not as part of an evaluation.

- Confidentiality should be assured.

- Instead of asking peers to rate performance, ask for examples of any performance areas they have direct knowledge about. Peers would then provide data only when they have knowledge. They would not rate their colleagues.

Student Achievement

Emerging as a politically popular but controversial question, the role that data on student achievement should play in evaluation is addressed in detail in Chapter 9. Here we cite its importance as an essential diagnostic tool. Identifying mediocre teaching requires the ability to recognize and label sustained, regular recurring patterns of behavior, of decisions or nondecisions, and of outcomes. Good teaching and good teachers should help a child make

---

[5] Adapted from Airasian 1997.

Integrating Several Sources of Feedback: The 360 Degree Evaluation Model

Richard Manatt, the Director of SIM (School Improvement Model) at the University of Iowa, has for several years advocated increasing the validity and reliability of evaluations through using teacher self-evaluation, student, parent, and peer feedback as a 360-degree view of a teacher's performance. He and his colleagues have developed student feedback instruments to be used for students as young as kindergarten through 2nd grade (Manatt 1997).

Richard Santeusanio, Superintendent of the Danvers, Massachusetts Public Schools, has negotiated an agreement with the teacher's union to establish a 360-degree evaluation (Educational Leadership Vol. 55, no. 5, Feb. 1998, p. 30). He modeled the process by being the first to participate. Teachers have the option of electing the traditional clinical supervision and evaluation procedures or the 360-degree evaluation feedback. Teachers participating do a self-assessment and then get data from their immediate supervisor and peers. They have the option of but are not required to receive feedback from parents and students. Dr. Santeusanio reports that the examination of the data from multiple perspectives allows discrepancies to be identified. Everyone participating then develops an action plan.

The jury is still out on the impact of the 360-degree process on teaching performance. Dr. Santeusanio says "I think this process has helped administrators and teachers come up with better action plans, which presumably improves teaching. Still too early to tell. Because we are getting involved in systemwide 'critical friends' training (Annenberg Institute), I think peer feedback will be much better and lead to better teaching performance" (interview February 1999).

---

progress from his starting point each year. At the very least, evaluators and teachers need to ask and answer the following questions when a teacher's summative evaluation is being prepared:

- What credible sources of data about student performance in meeting agreed-upon standards are currently available for us to look at together? How have we done so?

- How has that information from those data sources been used thus far to generate goals for students, to document progress, and to shape instruction?

- What are the planned next steps or changes the teacher will make in order to help each student make gains?

Evaluators should expect to review and reward evidence that teachers are holding themselves accountable for what children know and are able to do both as individuals and as professionals who contribute to the effectiveness of a school.

Summary

Collecting and using evidence drawn from a variety of data sources (1) increases an evaluator's competence and credibility, (2) reduces the impact of bias and judgment errors, (3) allows the evaluator to develop a more complex and precise profile of the teaching performance, (4) eliminates drawbacks associated with using classroom observation alone, and (5) provides clear guidelines for goal setting and improvement plans.

5 Describing Strengths and Problems

Sally Friendly's classroom is under control and she is well organized. . . . She is nice to the students and creates a pleasant climate. In her teaching, her instructional objectives are not as high level as they could be. She should consider attending a workshop on teaching thinking skills. . . . We are fortunate to have such a nice colleague in our midst. (Sample extracts from past Principal Frank Smith's Final Summary Evaluation)

These vague statements, typical of many found in summary evaluations, neither detail Sally's strengths nor define her problems. The "should consider" recommendation is not likely to cause Sally to change her teaching performance. Supervision and evaluation systems need to be structured so that substandard teaching is addressed directly, humanely, and decisively (Saphier 1993). The kind of language represented in

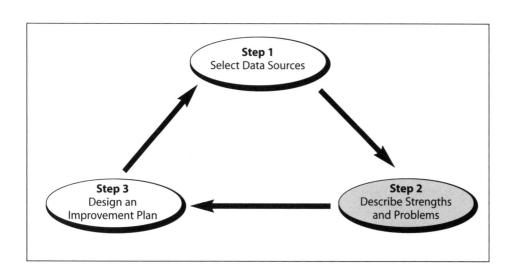

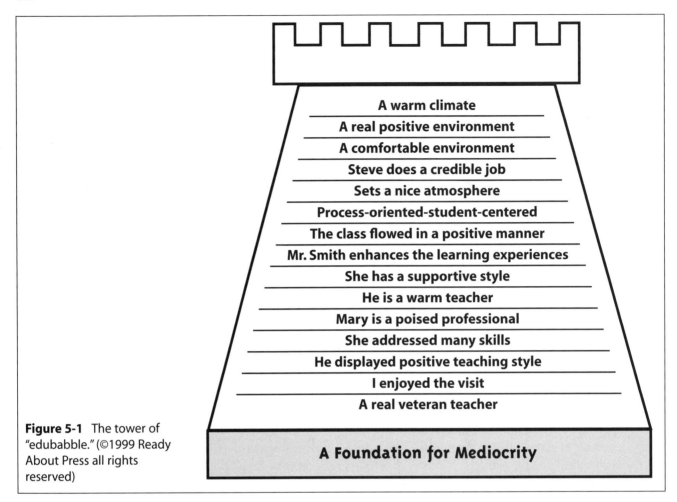

Figure 5-1 The tower of "edubabble." (©1999 Ready About Press all rights reserved)

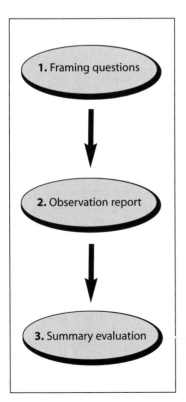

Figure 5-2 Flow of Chapter 5.

the preceding extract and in Figure 5-1, which has been extracted from observation reports, is neither direct, humane, nor helpful if we want to change teacher performance to improve student learning.

To confront mediocre performance, supervisors need instead to clearly identify problems and *describe* strengths, the second "D"and the focus of this chapter. Chapter 4 detailed the menu of possible data sources evaluators can use to examine teaching. This chapter presents an evaluation framework to help the supervisor determine what performance standards need to be evaluated to more fully capture the complexity of a teacher's performance. More detailed description better defines strengths and problems, which prepares the way for designing an improvement plan—the subject of Chapter 6.

Figure 5-2 shows the flow of this chapter. We begin by presenting a comprehensive framework for evaluating teachers, based on the work of Saphier (1993) and Saphier and Gower (1997). Since most districts base their evaluations on observations, we provide a model observation report in the second part of this chapter that uses the categories introduced in the evaluation framework. We have included an annotated list of tips to guide the supervisor in writing up detailed and thorough reports of mediocre lessons. At the end of the chapter, we provide a model final summary evaluation report showing how data from several observation reports and other sources can be integrated into one summary write-up. By the end of Step 2 of the 3-D cycle, strengths should be clearly described and problems should be identified so that a focused improvement plan can be drawn up in the third step, which is to design the plan, presented in Chapter 6.

Introduction to the Evaluation Framework

Leaders need to have the conviction that mediocre teaching, when identified and confronted, can be changed and improved. Leaders should reject the belief that teachers are born skillful and should resist the temptation to accept under-performance as a fixed state. They need to believe, rather, that there is a definable knowledge base on teaching that can be learned. This learning requires that the supervisor give concrete, specific feedback based on multiple areas of performance. Figures 5-3 and 5-4 specify these multiple areas of performance.

The complex roles of professional teachers fall into two broad categories: nonteaching and teaching. A fully developed professional must perform well in both of these domains (Saphier 1993). In the nonteaching role, the teacher needs to contibute to the staff, to be a constant learner, to perform routine administrative duties, and to communicate with parents and the community (Figure 5-3). Classroom performance is the central role, which is analyzed in Figure 5-4. Figure 5-4 defines skillful teaching as a set of performance areas, each of which demands a complex set of teacher decisions (Saphier and Gower 1997). Thus, for example, a teacher makes management decisions about how to keep attention and establish routines and makes instructional decisions about how to frame instruction for clarity. These decisions are based on the teacher's knowledge and repertoire of teaching skills. Mediocre performers lack fully developed skills in identifiable areas. Once identified, these skills can be learned. Viewed in this way, teaching is not a prescriptive set of techniques but rather a set of contextual decisions. Teachers can learn to become more skillful.

How to use the Evaluation Framework

This chapter focuses on giving supervisors more competence in describing and defining individual cases of mediocre performance. As a supervisory tool, we have created a set of framing questions in each area of performance. The supervisor can scan the questions and make a holistic judgment about a teacher's performance. Problem areas can be identified that can be investigated through systematic data collection keyed to certain areas of performance. We are not advocating unfairly focusing on areas of weakness. We are proposing that a complete description requires a base of evidence and a plan to get that evidence.

CAUTION The checklist format should not entice the supervisor to check off areas of performance without citing the supporting data. Supervisors need to provide data to answer these questions in order to make judgments about a teacher's strengths and problem areas.

For example, if the teacher in question is like Sally Friendly (Chapter 3, "Profiles of Mediocrity"), we have sufficient evidence to know that she has positive relationships with her students and manages her class adequately. We would want to focus on collecting more detailed information about her curriculum planning because this is an area of weakness. Thus we would find evidence by collecting student and teacher artifacts. With a noncollaborating

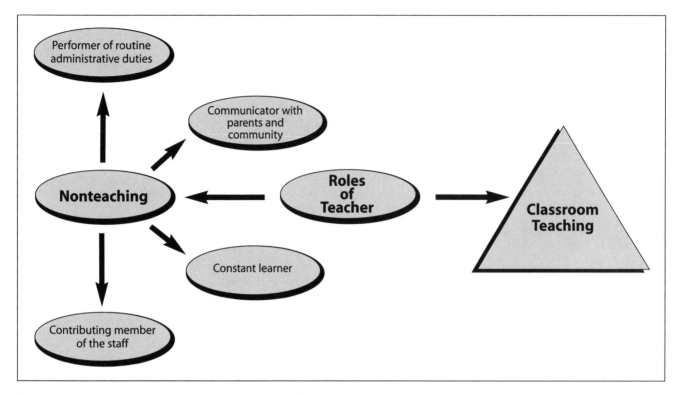

Figure 5-3   A teacher's performance roles. (Adapted from Saphier 1993)

individual such as John Whiner Collabnot (Chapter 3), we would want to focus on the nonteaching role as a contributing member of the staff since his classroom performance is quite competent. In this case we would want to collect information from observation outside the classroom.

The framework described below may resemble others defined by states or districts. To represent the framework as a working tool rather than a final document, we have used the question format. Leaders wanting to see a more standard format for contract use should refer to Appendix G "Performance Roles of Teacher and Related Competencies." District leaders can use this framework as a model to develop or examine their local district evaluation instruments to determine whether they need to add or refine certain areas of their performance evaluation.

Central office leaders may organize a discussion with their leadership team about evaluation priorities by rank ordering areas of performance using the framing questions. Participants could identify hard to assess areas (mostly on the high end of the triangle) and discuss how best to collect data on these areas, using Figure 4-2, the data sources checklist.

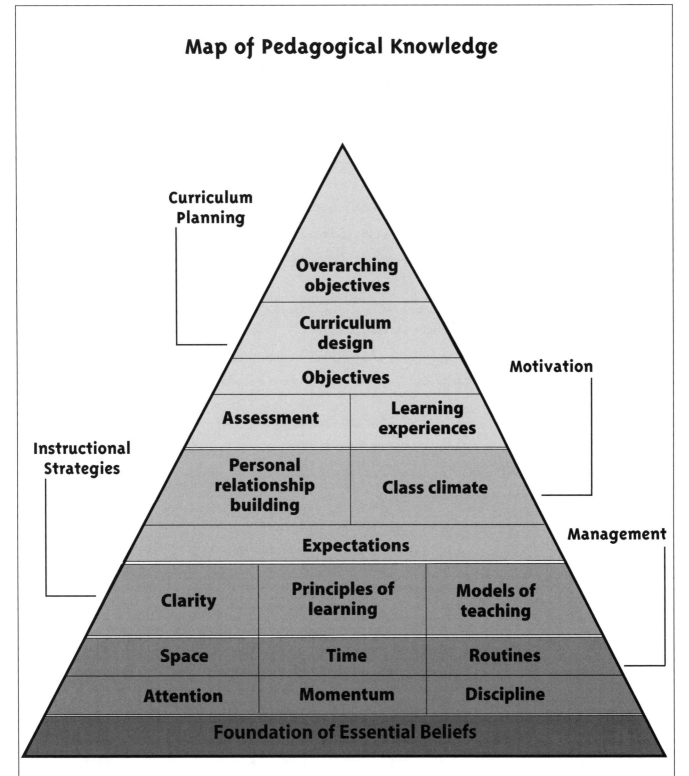

Figure 5-4 Essential elements of classroom teaching. (*The Skillful Teacher*, Saphier and Gower, ©1997 Research for Better Teaching, One Acton Place, Acton, MA 01720-3951)

Framing Questions for Evaluating Five Areas of Teacher Performance

CLASSROOM AREAS OF PERFORMANCE

Foundation of Essential Beliefs
Framing Question: Does the teacher believe that children's learning is primarily determined by their effort and use of effective strategies and that intelligence is not a fixed inborn limit on learning capacity? (Howard 1993)

Management
Framing Question: How does the teacher perform basic classroom management?

1. Attention: Does the teacher have the attention of the students?

❏ by using a variety of techniques to gain, maintain, and regain student attention to task?

❏ by displaying a pattern of attention getters that range when needed from desisting based on authority of the teacher to enlisting techniques that engage students in their work?

2. Momentum: Is the teacher well organized to minimize loss of learning time?

❏ by having materials prepared and ready to go and the space set up? (provisioning)

❏ by giving advanced warning of transitions?

❏ by subdividing students when it is necessary for them to move in order to minimize bottlenecks?

❏ by handling intrusions in a way that minimizes their effect?

❏ by providing fillers to occupy students productively when all students are able to begin or end an activity at the same time?

❏ by anticipating blocks to momentum and taking action to prevent or minimize them?

❏ by varying the format or changing the objective when the lesson "isn't working"? (lesson flexibility)

❏ by monitoring more than one activity at the same time?

3. Discipline: Does the teacher have a solid system of discipline?

❏ by diagnosing the cause of the disruptive or inattentive behavior so that the solution can be matched to the problem?

❏ by establishing a reasonable structure of rewards and consequences?

❏ by working on building cooperation and self-discipline among students as well as by enlarging his/her repertoire of ways to eliminate disruptions or inattentive behavior?

4. Routines: Does the teacher have work procedures and housekeeping routines that are taught, trained, and tested for?

❏ Start of class?   ❏ Getting materials?

❏ Seating?   ❏ Working with peers?

❏ Work noise level?   ❏ Raising hands?

❑ Distribution of materials?

❑ Making up work?

❑ Getting help?

❑ Leaving seats?

❑ Turning in work?

❑ Leaving the room?

❑ Sharpening pencils and getting materials?

❑ Transitions?

5. Time: How much time is allocated for student learning and how efficient is the teacher in ensuring that during this time students are actually working or attending?

❑ by matching his/her pacing and scheduling to the needs of different classes and individuals?

❑ by building in physical movement every 40 minutes or so?

6. Space: Is the physical space conducive to good discipline as well as instructional objectives?

❑ by allowing easily changed space to match different objectives and activities?

❑ by putting the least distance and fewest barriers between the teacher and any student in the class to help prevent or stop discipline problems?

Instructional Strategies

Framing Question: How does the teacher match the instructional clarity, including, for example, setting the context and selecting explanatory devices, to the content and to the students?

Clarity—the Context: How does the teacher set the stage for learning by putting learning into a context?

1. Does the teacher specifically communicate the objectives?

❑ by communicating orally and/or in writing what students will know or be able to do at the end of the class, unit, semester?

❑ by communicating the reason the objective is important and how it links to their lives?

❑ by checking to see if the students understand the higher level objectives?

2. Does the teacher specifically communicate the sequence of events?

❑ by letting the students know what the order or flow of events during the unit, week, or class period will be?

❑ by posting the schedule of the day or period?

3. Does the teacher specifically make connections for students?

❑ by showing resemblance of current learning to past knowledge?

❑ by making cognitive transitions between ideas being taught during a lesson?

❑ by making connections of current learning to future learning through foreshadowing?

4. Does the teacher specifically activate current knowledge?

❑ by finding out what students know or don't know about the topic in advance of new instruction?

❏ by modifying instruction based upon what students know?

❏ by motivating students to be interested in the new topic?

❏ by surfacing or anticipating previous misconceptions?

5. Does the teacher have students specifically summarize and process information?

❏ by adhering to the 10-2 principle by having students process new information approximately every 10 minutes? If so, how?

❏ by highlighting key points or having students process key information?

Clarity—Cognitive Empathy: How do teachers match their instruction to the conceptual understanding of their students?

1. Does the teacher anticipate student confusion?

❏ by anticipating "difficult to learn" concepts?

❏ by intercepting confusion "on the spot" before it actually occurs?

❏ by anticipating student's misconceptions?

2. Does the teacher have/use a variety of explanatory devices?

❏ by selecting strategies to reach the auditory, visual, and kinesthetic learner (mental imagery, analogies, modeling thinking aloud, graphic organizers, physical models)?

3. Does the teacher check for understanding?

❏ by monitoring broadly and frequently for understanding?

❏ by using a variety of questioning strategies that include open-ended, how and why questions as well as recall questions?

❏ by using appropriate signaling techniques to assess understanding?

4. Does the teacher unscramble confusion once it has been identified?

❏ by taking steps to find out where a student is confused and providing strategies to help the student unscramble the misunderstanding?

❏ by returning to the student to see if the confusion has been resolved?

5. Does the teacher communicate explicitly?

❏ by leaving few gaps and making no assumptions regarding a student's past knowledge or skill?

❏ by giving the necessary steps in directions?

❏ by giving the reason for the particular activity, explaining how it relates to the objectives?

6. What principles of learning does the teacher employ?

❏ by consciously integrating one or more principles of learning into every lesson?

❏ by consistently using those principles of learning designed to motivate and energize students to learn?

❏ by employing the principle of learning sequence that emphasizes the enhanced learning possible at the beginning and end of lessons?

❏ by using the "say-do" principle where the teacher uses a variety of modes of input and practice opportunities: seeing, hearing, moving, and touching?

7. What models of teaching are being used? Does the lesson plan have specified steps and sequence as well as content and thinking objectives?

Motivation

Framing Question: How does the teacher communicate high expectations and standards, build relationships with students, and establish a healthy classroom climate?

1. Personal Relationship Building: How does the teacher build mutual feelings of regard and respect?

2. Expectations: Does the teacher send messages of confidence and belief to students?

❏ by demonstrating that almost all children come to school with enough innate ability to achieve at a high level and by helping them to have confidence in themselves as learners so they can apply effective effort?

❏ by having clear, high standards and the conviction that s/he has the right to expect that students will reach them?

❏ by communicating the standards verbally and/or in writing to students and parents?

❏ by using a repertoire of strategies to enable all students to reach the standards?

❏ by communicating "what we're doing is important, you can do it, and I won't give up on you" messages in the following arenas:
—in responding to students' answers?
—in grading and grouping?
—in dealing with students who don't get it—yet?
—in praising and dealing with students who don't respond?

3. Classroom Climate: How does the teacher create a healthy climate for learning where there is cooperation, self-discipline, and respect?

❏ by building a classroom where students have a sense of community and are willing to take risks and have ownership in the class?

Curriculum Planning

Framing Question: What is the quality of the teacher's planning?

1. Objectives: Are several levels of thinking about objectives evident?

❏ by specifying what topic or content is being taught? (coverage level)

❏ by specifying what activities students are doing? Are activities congruent with mastery objectives? (activity level)

❏ by specifying how students get cognitively active and engaged through activities that complement and stretch various learning styles, personality styles, and need for physical movement? (involvement level)

❏ by specifying what students will know or be able to do and how students will know if they can do it, including content, physical skills, and social skills? (mastery level)

❏ by specifying what thinking skills will be explicitly taught and practiced? (thinking skill level)

2. Assessment: How will student learning be evaluated and assessed?

❑ by providing clear models of success and by developing a variety of assessment strategies that allow students to demonstrate their success?

3. Learning Experiences: What factors are being experienced by students in terms of: group interaction patterns, degree of abstraction, resources used, sensory input, and other planning variables ?

4. Curriculum Design: How is the curriculum designed so it has continuity, sequence, and integration?

5. Overarching Objectives: What are the embedded school or district core values and identified curriculum priorities, as determined by state or district guidelines?

NONTEACHING AREAS OF PERFORMANCE

Constant Learning
Framing Question: What evidence exists that the teacher is a constant learner?

1. Does the teacher demonstrate the characteristics of a reflective learner?

❑ by withholding judgment?

❑ by defining problems before attempting solutions?

❑ by analyzing from someone else's perspective?

2. Does the teacher practice change and experimentation?

❑ by considering new ideas?

❑ by experimenting and trying new things?

❑ by seeking change after five to seven years in a position?

3. How does the teacher keep current in the field?

❑ by maintaining membership/active participation in professional organizations?

❑ by reading about current research within field?

❑ by demonstrating awareness of state, county, or district standards?

Communication
Framing Question: What is the quality and quantity of the teacher's communication with parents and community?

1. Does the teacher communicate with parents?

❑ by following up on parent phone calls and notes?

❑ by delivering good news and bad news about student performance honestly and directly?

❑ by presenting high quality written communication?

❑ by seeking input from parents, not just reporting to them?

2. Does the teacher plan and carry out high quality open houses and back to school night presentations?[1]

❏ by communicating clearly about overall goals?

❏ by presenting high quality handouts?

❏ by handling questions with tact, respect, and clarity?

❏ by communicating criteria for good performance and expectations?

❏ by communicating belief in the importance of effort rather than innate ability as the vehicle to achieve success?

❏ by communicating how the teacher will be available for assistance for students and parents?

3. Does the teacher carry out high quality student reporting?

❏ by using specific feedback directly linked to individual student work?

❏ by addressing poor performance directly and fairly?

❏ by avoiding generalities and clichés such as "John is a wonderful boy, and I enjoy having him in class"?

Routine Administrative Duties

Framing Question: How does the teacher perform routine administrative duties?

1. Does the teacher carry out routine management duties?

❏ by arriving punctually?

❏ by reliably covering duties without reminders?

❏ by monitoring and anticipating problems during duty?

2. Does the teacher show high quality record keeping and paperwork?

❏ by being accurate, legible, and complete in paperwork requests?

❏ by punctually submitting grades?

❏ by completing educational plans thoroughly and accurately?

3. Does the teacher consistently carry out school policy?

❏ by enforcing policy, for example, if there has been an agreement relative to dress, does the teacher enforce this agreement?

4. How effective is the use of support personnel?

❏ by appropriately using aide and secretarial help?

Contributions as Member of the Faculty

Framing Question: What contributions does the teacher make as a member of the staff?

1. Does the teacher have high quality collegial relationships with peers and act as a team player ?

❏ by frequently sharing materials and ideas?

❏ by talking about teaching with colleagues?

❏ by participating in collegial activities, e.g., peer observation, study groups?

---

[1] As a resource to give teachers, see "Tips for Reaching Parents," William B. Ribas, *Educational Leadership* Vol. 56 (September 1998).

❑   by asking for assistance when necessary and providing assistance when asked?

❑   by assisting/mentoring new teachers?

❑   by participating in meetings?

❑   by volunteering to cover duties?

❑   by "pitching in" during emergencies?

❑   by taking responsibility for the behavior of students, even those who are not in his or her class?

2. How does the teacher practice honest, open communication?

❑   by communicating directly in addressing issues?

❑   by directly dealing with colleagues and parents, especially where difficult communication is involved?

3. How does the teacher fulfill responsibilities in meetings?

❑   by quality participation in:
    —grade level meetings?
    —special education plan meetings?
    —faculty meetings?
    —committees?

This comprehensive descriptive framework, which derives from *The Skillful Teacher* (Saphier and Gower 1997) and *How to Make Supervision and Evaluation Really Work* (Saphier 1993), is intended to give the supervisor a tool that will help focus attention and magnify strengths and problem areas. It is not intended to be used a checklist devoid of supporting evidence. These areas of performance provide the supervisors with categories that correspond well with most evaluation instruments. For a full development of these concepts, see *The Skillful Teacher* (Saphier and Gower 1997).

Observation Reports

Despite their limitations, observation reports are the most frequently required source of data in almost every evaluation system. Frequently they are written as chronological narratives describing a sequence of events in the classroom. They often lack specific detail and contain little analysis. Furthermore, they are not always connected to the categorical descriptions asked for in the evaluation. These reports may satisfy the legal requirements but are not always helpful in concretely identifying problems as well as the strengths—a major weakness in our quest to confront mediocre teaching.

Therefore, we include a model observation report based on this framework and a list of tips for supervisors to reference while writing an observation report on a mediocre lesson.[2] To provide continuity, we return to Sally Friendly, whom you met in Chapter 1 and got to know better in Chapter 3, "Profiles of Mediocrity." To put the case into a fuller context, you may want to refer back to these Sally Friendly profiles. The chapter will close with a final summary evaluation, also based on the Sally Friendly case.

[2] For more detail on the technical aspects of writing this type of report, see *How to Make Supervision and Evaluation Really Work* by Jon Saphier (1993).

Model Classroom Observation Report Based on the Case of Sally Friendly

Evaluation Cycle: Observation 3

Date: Monday 2/5/99

Time: 10:05-10:45

Grade/subject: 5th grade math

Twenty-two students present (three absent)

This is the third observation of the year. I conducted one on 10/22/98, and the curriculum coordinator conducted another one on 1/15/99. Three areas for attention that had been identified on these previous observations were the focus of this observation: (1) too much instruction focused on activities not connected to the curriculum, (2) no context set for learning, and (3) low expectations for student performance (see observation reports of 10/22/98 and 1/15/99).

Introduction

Mrs. Friendly was teaching a math lesson on multiplying fractions. Her objectives for students were listed in her lesson plan for the day:

To review addition and subtraction of fractions

To review math terms such as equivalence

To visually see the different amounts of 1/3 and 1/4

To play a math game, "Trivial Math"

These objectives focused on covering material and completing activities. There was no evidence of focused attention to what students should know or be able to do in the lesson plan or in the observed instruction.

Management

Mrs. Friendly has well oiled routines. Students, returning from physical education, entered the class and went right to their cubbies, sharpened pencils, and took out their math books. She played a name game to occupy the transition time. In pairs they began to work on the warm-up problem that was written on the board. As a result of these routines, the students lost little time and were on task in less than 2 minutes.

Mrs. Friendly was able to successfully bring the group back together with an attention signal of flipping the lights. She also was able to bring students back to task if their attention wandered. For example, when John and Bill were starting to get a little loud, she paused and looked at them and when Mary was out of her seat at the wrong time, Mrs. Friendly said, "Mary, you know the routine." As a result of these interventions, students settled back into their work.

Instruction

The teacher gave clear explanation for the directions to the activity she called "Trivial Pursuit Math." She said, "First you need to read the question and decide whether it requires addition, subtraction, or multiplication to solve. Write down the corresponding symbol in the blank. You should check your answer with your partner, then look it up on the answer page I will distribute. Mark it off as C for correct and X for incorrect." She asked for a thumbs up sign if everyone understood the directions. As a result, students knew the directions and went to work immediately.

As highlighted in my observation report of 10/22/98, I was looking for how Mrs. Friendly framed the lesson. In this observation, she still did not clarify the context for the lesson nor how it fit into the curriculum unit. She began the class by saying "we are covering some more fraction work today. Make sure you have your rulers. Okay, let's review adding fractions." This introduction did not set the learning into a context, nor did it communicate the student learning objective or the reason for learning. Later, when she made a transition to "Trivial Pursuit Math," she said " Okay, game time, get on your trivia hats." Again, it would have been helpful to tell why she had selected this activity and how it was connected to her objectives. I spoke with three students, Al (an excellent student), Bonnie (a good student), and Don (a below average student), and none of them could answer the question "why are you doing this activity? Don said " because Mrs. Friendly asked us to," and Al said "to get better in math." As a result, students did not know what they were supposed to be learning or why they were doing certain activities.

RECOMMENDATION: Mrs. Friendly should always frame the lesson for students by communicating the sequence of the class and by telling students what they will be able to do.

The teacher used few explanatory devices to explain difference in fractions and did not anticipate confusion regarding student use of rulers. Her objective stated that she wanted students to "visually" see the difference between one third and one half. She did have them look at their rulers, but it was confusing because the ruler was divided into eighths, so thirds were not clearly designated. One student said, "This does not make sense." It would have been a good place to use the overhead projector, but the overhead was unavailable as it was unplugged in the corner. When Mrs. Friendly saw that the rulers were confusing, she tried to unscramble the confusion "Okay, watch this. I am going to explain this with a pizza. What would you prefer, one third of a pizza or one fourth? She then drew two pizzas on the board. Mike started asking about mushroom and pepperoni, and in response she drew these on the pizza. This was a nice way of relating to students, but they lost the connection with fractions as several of them started talking about "Papa Ginos" and "Pizza Hut." There was no evidence at the time that students ever achieved the objective of seeing visually the difference between one third and one fourth. Mrs. Friendly shared copies of the tests administered the following week. Sixty percent of the students missed the example that asked students to represent visually the difference between one third and one fourth.

RECOMMENDATION: Mrs. Friendly should have passed out the cuisinaire rods for a more effective explanation. In the future, she should try to anticipate confusion and have several appropriate explanatory devices available.

Motivation

Class Climate and Personal Relationship Building

One of Mrs. Friendly's strengths is her warm, welcoming manner. On this day when students were returning from physical education class, she spoke to each one of them even though she had seen them when they arrived earlier in the day. " Did you have fun in the gym, Mary? Mike, I hear you are quite the soccer player! Bill did that cold hold you back today?" were some of the greetings. As a filler during the transition, she played a name game where she pointed to individuals and students called out first names or even middle names in unison. This helped to create a classroom spirit and a sense of community. Students feel that Mrs. Friendly does care about them. One student I spoke with said Mrs. Friendly is almost always nice.

Expectations

Both previous observations cited problems in the area of expectations and that these should be a focus for this last observation. In this observation there were also unclear expectations about the quality of work. After giving the directions she said "Do the best you can, don't worry about it, enjoy it. We can continue tomorrow. I don't expect all of you to be able to do this activity." As a result, students got two inappropriate messages: (1) their work wasn't important enough to merit their best effort and (2) the teacher did not believe all students were capable of doing it. There were no standards communicated for what constituted good work, and enjoyment was the explicitly stated objective.

In addition, Mrs. Friendly did not send positive expectancy messages to Brian and Judy. When Brian was having trouble understanding the fractional term "equivalence," Mrs. Friendly said (pleasantly), "That's okay, you can work on that in the resource room." When Judy said, "I don't get it," Mrs. Friendly said, "Judy, this is hard for you, maybe you will understand it after completing the worksheet." As a result, these students received no help and no encouragement from Mrs. Friendly that could improve their performance or bolster their self-confidence.

RECOMMENDATION: When students are seeking help or expressing confusion, Mrs. Friendly should assist them.

Conference Summary

At our conference, Mrs. Friendly said that she thought the lesson "went pretty well." I agreed that the class was well organized and established a friendly, supportive climate. I raised the three issues that had been highlighted in the two previous observations. These were: (1) Too much instruction focused on activities not connected to the curriculum, (2) no context set for learning, and (3) low expectations for student performance. I saw no improvement in any of these areas. In particular, when I raised concerns about the quality of the math instruction and questioned the purpose for the "Trivial Math" game, Mrs. Friendly agreed that involving the students was her main objective. I expressed the concern that despite areas of strengths detailed above, there was a lack of academic rigor in this class. We agreed that we would meet again after the Final Summary Evaluation in March to develop an improvement plan for next year and that Mrs. Friendly would act on the recommendations cited in this report.

Summary

Mrs. Friendly has some clear strengths. These include strong classroom management and the creation of a welcoming climate. She is clear about directions. However, she does not frame learning for students and does not communicate the levels of performance she expects. She fails to communicate strong belief systems to low-performing students. She failed to anticipate a mismatch between the rulers she was using to explain a concept. The lesson was focused on activity rather than being centered in the mastery of important learning. This lesson was unsatisfactory.

Tips: Writing an Observation Report on a Mediocre Lesson[3]

Annotated for Sally Friendly Observation Report

1. Connect Current Observation to Previous Reports
It is important to establish a pattern over time and not to view each observation as a discrete, isolated event.

SALLY: This observation from the outset is connected to issues highlighted in previous observations.

2. Write with Balance
These four elements should be used consistently throughout an observation report. They add specificity and meaning to the writing.

CLAIMS: Generalizations that serve as controlling organizers describing patterns and salient events.

SALLY: Each paragraph begins with a generalization about a pattern of behavior. Example: There are unclear expectations about the quality of work.

EVIDENCE: Specific examples are cited, including literal quotes when necessary. These quotes are extracted from literal notes taken at the time of the observation.

SALLY: Evidence accompanies each generalization. For example, in support of the claim listed above: "After giving the directions she said, 'Do the best you can, don't worry about it, enjoy it. We can continue tomorrow. I don't expect all of you to be able to do this activity.'"

INTERPRETATION: Writing should emphasize the effect of certain teacher behavior on students and highlight what was accomplished or not accomplished.

SALLY: As a result, students did not know what they were supposed to be learning or why they were doing certain activities. As a result, these students received no help and no encouragement from Mrs. Friendly that could improve their performance or their self-confidence. (A judgment is included as well.)

JUDGMENTS—PHRASES AND WORDS THAT PUT A VALUE ON THE BEHAVIOR: There should be few editorial digs and general judgments. Judgments should be concise and related to data, and strengths or problems should not be inflated or diminished. The summary should give a fair representation of the strengths and problems cited in the body of the report and not send mixed messages.

[3] Adapted from the work of Saphier 1993.

SALLY: There are no broad general judgments or editorial digs such as "It was too bad that . . ." or "Unfortunately." Judgments are limited to the observation. "One of Mrs. Friendly's strengths is her warm welcoming manner." "It was confusing because the ruler was divided into eighths, so thirds were not clearly designated." The summary judgment is fair and representative of the body of the report.

3. Be fair. Catch the teacher doing things right, but don't inflate or diminish their importance.

It is important to find and include strengths but to keep them in perspective. Although more evidence may be necessary to support negative claims, the evaluator should not underreport examples of strength in order to skew the report. In exceptionally sensitive cases, the number of examples of strength and problem areas should be in approximate balance in order to counteract accusations of unfairness during arbitration or legal proceedings.

SALLY: Several positive areas are mentioned, including management and class climate, in the body of the report and in the summary. There is a sense of proportion in that the strengths are acknowledged but do not average out the problems.

4. Be comprehensive. Include several areas, from management to curriculum planning.

SALLY: Management, instruction, climate, and expectations are all addressed. Curriculum planning is difficult to assess by observation alone and perhaps additional data need to be collected.

5. Stress missed opportunities and absence of skill or strategy.

Mediocre performance is often characterized by a narrow repertoire and by what is missing from the lesson.

SALLY: "The teacher did not, however, clarify the context for the lesson nor how it fit in the unit."

6. Include data from post-observation conference. Conduct the post conference before the write-up.

SALLY: Post-observation conference reference included that clearly gave teacher a chance to respond before the write-up.

7. Include focus on student data if possible.

SALLY: Reference to informal surveying of several students is included. Tests were collected and interpreted for student achievement related to the lesson objective.

8. Use categories rather than chronological narrative to concentrate evidence in areas of strength and weakness.

SALLY: Organized in categories according to the different areas of performance not chronological narrative.

9. Integrate directly practical recommendations in the body of the report rather than isolating them at the end.

SALLY: All recommendations are integrated into the text in the context of the observations.

10. Establish a serious tone.

SALLY: The report is written in the third person, which gives it a more formal tone. (Using second person "you" tends to over-personalize the judgments.) Using "Mrs. Friendly" rather than "Sally" sounds more serious and creates a professional distance.

11. Avoid weak language like "seems," "appears," or "possibly." Avoid hyperbole and unsubstantiated "edubabble" (see Figure 5-1).

SALLY: Weak and ambiguous language is absent.

12. Avoid inflated language to "soften the blow," especially apologetic language and positive endings such as "All in all, Mrs. Friendly is doing a creditable job."

SALLY: The ending accurately captures strengths and weaknesses.

13. Make a final judgment at the end of the report that describes the lesson as satisfactory or unsatisfactory.

SALLY: The language is unambiguous: "This lesson was unsatisfactory."

The Final Summary Evaluation Report

Most districts call for an end-of-the-year synthesis of multiple observations and the collection of other data to assess nonteaching areas of performance. What follows is a model final summary evaluation report based on the preceding observation, two additional observations, and other data sources including nonteaching areas of performance. Most summary forms are organized in categories corresponding to state or district principles of effective teaching. Increasingly, evaluators are asked to rate the performance in each category according to standards. If an individual's rating for a standard is less than satisfactory, there are two critical issues: first, the rating must be clearly connected to evidence in the evaluation; second, there must be an explicit problem statement that is linked to the deficient area of performance. This problem statement must cite the teacher's shortcoming and, when appropriate, the deleterious effect it has on students. Note that we do not advise including recommendations in a final summary evaluation report. Recommendations should await the design of an improvement plan, which will be fully discussed in Chapter 6.

Sally Friendly: Model Final Evaluation Summary
Springfield Public School
Final Summary Evaluation 1998–1999

Name: Mrs. Sally H. Friendly:

Assignment: Grade 5

School: Center

Primary Evaluator: Norman R. Smith, Principal

Supervisors/ Secondary Evaluators: Muriel Mclaughlin, Math Coordinator

This report covers from September 1, 1998 to May 30, 1999

Cycle: check as many as appropriate:

____Nontenured   ✓ Tenured   ✓ Formal evaluation cycle

____Professional development cycle   ____Improvement plan

Data Gathering Sources and Procedures

This report is based on three observations, two by me 10/22/9 and 2/5/99 and one by the curriculum coordinator 1/15/98. Other data sources used in this report include: student work, short queries of students, professional development survey, lesson plans, and gradebooks.

List of Attachments: Observation reports: 10/22/98, 2/5/99, and 1/15/98 (not actually attached)

Standards of Performance: As described in the framework agreed to by the Springfield Teachers Association.

Background and overall recommendation: Sally is in her 12th year as a 5th grade teacher. This year she had 25 students, two of whom were on educational plans.

Overall Performance Rating

☒ Below minimum standard

❑ Competent

❑ Distinquished

Overall Recommendations

On the basis of this report, Mrs. Friendly has been judged less than satisfactory and is being recommended to remain on evaluation and to have an improvement plan for next year. The plan for improvement will be developed separately.

Performance Summary

Standard: Management

Mrs. Friendly is well organized. She has a cubby for each student's work and has materials and supplies readily available. She has routines for getting attention, such as the triple clap and the light signal, which work well. She is good at anticipating downtime. For example she has "folder activities" available anytime a bus is late or a student returns late from the resource room and has 5 minutes before the changeover. She spends little time on attendance, and students know to get right to work.

☐ Below minimum standard

☒ Competent

☐ Distinguished

Management is a real strength for Mrs. Friendly.

Standard: Effective Instruction

In my three observations this past year, I have noticed several patterns. First, Mrs. Friendly is very clear in giving directions. On 2/15/99 she was explaining the directions to "Trivial Pursuit Math"æa complicated game with several steps. She used the blackboard and checked students' understanding before they started. As a result, they knew exactly what to do. The curriculum director also observed clear directions 1/15/99 when Mrs. Friendly's students do worksheets. She ended with "Now, wiggle your pinkie finger if you understand." Students went right to work.

A second pattern is that in three classroom observations neither I nor the curriculum coordinator had observed any context setting. Mrs. Friendly never told the students why what they were doing was important or what the sequence of the class was going to be. Students did tasks but were uncertain how they fit with the overall learning objectives. Groups of students were informally interviewed after each class to see if they understood the objectives of the activity. (See observation reports 10/22/98, 1/15/99, and 2/15/99.) None of the total of 12 students was able to give the learning objective.

A third pattern is that the three lessons consisted of a series of activities punctuated by giving directions and telling students what they should do but not communicating the importance of what they were learning and why they were learning it. Although the students were occupied and attentive, they were not engaged in important learning (see objectives below). During the three observations, the focus was on completing short-term work, which Mrs. Friendly would "check off." Mrs. Friendly did tell me at our post-conference after the 10/22/98 observation about the diorama project in social studies, but I was uncertain about its connection to the social studies curriculum. The curriculum coordinator's observation of 1/15/98 noted that the diorama project had been dropped from the curriculum because of the need to spend more time on state framework objectives. See Problem 5.

☒ Below minimum standard

☐ Competent

☐ Distinguished

Problem 1: Mrs. Friendly fails to frame learning (both the objectives and the sequence of activities) for students and does not regularly communicate the reasons for activities. Thus students have difficulty in determining what is important to know or to be able to do in transferring competencies from one subject to another and in making connections among concepts.

Standard: Class Climate

Sally's students feel welcome. On 11/5/98 during an informal walk by I observed her standing at the door greeting the students, "How are you Mike? Wow! I love your plaid shirt, Mary." On 2/5/99 she welcomed them warmly back from Physical Education (see Report 2/15/99). She cares about the students and treats them with respect. Most of the students like her and enjoy the class. She tries to create a sense of community and makes sure all students learn each others' names through several games, some of which she uses to fill time when students are coming in at different times.

❏ Below minimum standard

☒ Competent

❏ Distinguished

Establishing a welcoming, warm climate is a strength for Sally.

Standard: Expectations and Standards

Mrs. Friendly does not identify and communicate her standards and expectations. Mrs. Friendly is clear and forceful about her expectations for interpersonal behavior. She does not, however, identify and communicate consistent standards and expectations for quality and quantity of work or for study habits and work procedures to all of her students. Quoting from my 10/22/98 observation: "students asked over a dozen questions about an assignment, which ranged from 'How long does it have to be? What are we supposed to say about our countries? Do we need to label the maps?' to 'You did not tell us that we had to put this in our notebooks. What should I do if I didn't put it in?'" Mrs. Friendly's responses on that day included "Don't worry about that part, I know it is too hard for you. But those of you in Lavina and Stephen's group should be able to label the maps." "Well, some of you may be able to find more than three sources. Just do what you can." "I'd like you to try to keep your notebooks a bit neater. I know you like to be messy, but there's such a thing as too messy" (see observation report 10/22/98). The result of this is that students are clear on what it means to be to be a member of a group in terms of their response to one another but do not know what it means to be a successful academic member. Some students receive clear messages that Mrs. Friendly does not really believe they can perform.

On the 10/22/98 and 2/15/99 reports, I noted that no criteria for success were communicated. There was also evidence of low expectations for some of her students, as cited in the report of 2/15/99. This is a serious concern.

☒ Below minimum standard

❏ Competent

❏ Distinguished

Problem 2: Mrs. Friendly does not communicate expectations for high performance for all students. Thus students have difficulty determining what rigorous academic work should be.

Standard: Curriculum Planning

Assessment

During their evaluation year, all teachers submit samples of student work, homework, worksheets, and lesson plans over a six-week period of choice. Sally's selection, made during the period from Columbus Day to winter break, consisted of many holiday worksheets and seasonal projects (see attached). None of these projects had clearly specified criteria. The annotated student work had few comments except for a smiley face and some "good job!" and "well done!" comments. In discussing the selection of activities, Mrs. Friendly stressed the importance of keeping students engaged. However, Mrs. Friendly was unable to make clear connections to our district curriculum goals, which is critical at a time when students are required to pass area examinations at grade 6.

☒ Below minimum standard

❑ Competent

❑ Distinguished

Problem 3: Mrs. Friendly fails to plan a challenging, integrated curriculum that focuses on significant student learning. As a result, students spend considerable time on work that is not directly connected to district curriculum frameworks.

Problem 4: Mrs. Friendly fails to clearly state criteria for success, provide exemplars for different levels of performance, and give specific task-referenced feedback. Thus students are not always clear about the steps needed to achieve a high level of performance.

NONTEACHING AREAS

Standard: Routine Duties

Mrs. Friendly is very reliable in covering her duties. In her two, four-week stints with morning bus duty, she was punctual. On one occasion, she intervened with two students who were arguing and helped them settle their dispute before they entered the school. This was a nice example of anticipation. She also helps to build a welcoming school climate as she cheerily greets students. Her report cards are punctually submitted, and she completes all paperwork on time.

❑ Below minimum standard

☒ Competent

❑ Distinguished

Mrs. Friendly's performance of routine duties is a real strength.

Standard: Contributing Member of the Faculty

This is not an area for concern. Several past evaluation reports have lauded her for her contributions to the school community. As a member of the staff, Mrs. Friendly eagerly participates in all school events. This year, in addition to her hosting of the Annual Pitch and Putt Barbecue, she volunteered to serve on the Raising Expectations Committee. She attended every meeting and brought the refreshments. Mrs. Friendly always seeks out the new members of the staff and invites them to tea at her house the first week of school. She contributes to the congeniality of the school.

❏ Below minimum standard

❏ Competent

☒ Distinguished

Mrs. Friendly is a strong contributor to the faculty.

Standard: Professional Development and Constant Learning

Sally attends courses regularly. This year she enrolled in a Collaborative Associates workshop. On her Self-evaluation Questionnaire (SEQ), in answer to the question, What will be the main impact of this course on your teaching? she responded, "I will not hold my low-ability students as accountable. They are doing the best they can." The stated purpose of the course was to raise teacher expectations for all students.

❏ Below minimum standard

☒ Competent

❏ Distinguished

Although Mrs. Friendly does attend and participate, she should work to be more reflective as she translates the content of the sessions into her own classroom.

Standard: Communication with Parents

Mrs. Friendly maintains regular contact with parents through a newsletter. Two parents mentioned to me this past year that they are very pleased by the weekly contact, but they were concerned by the frequent misspellings and grammatical errors. Attached are two newsletters with the misspelled words circled. I sat in on the Back to School Night presentation, and I applaud the welcoming climate that she set when she asked parents to introduce themselves. However, this left only 4 of the 15 minutes for presentation of her program. She neither communicated the criteria for success and what her standards were going to be nor did she indicate how she would assist students to reach those standards.

☒ Below minimum standard

❏ Competent

❏ Distinguished

Problem 5: Mrs. Friendly's communication with parents does not meet pro-fessional standards for content or presentation.

Standard: Student Reporting

Student reporting is not thorough and may be inflated. For the first three marking periods, there were only four to five grading notations, and all of them were marked as quizzes. There was no designation of homework completion although Mrs. Friendly said she does check on homework. For example, three students, Jen Martin, Mary Payes, and Mike Deason, had very poor grades in grade 4 with Mrs. Jones (see enclosed). All of them have B's and A's the first half of the year. I would like to discuss the performance improvement of each of these students. In a scan of her grade sheets, no student received below a B, except for Brian and Abby, the special education students, who both had C's. Mrs. Friendly explained that she did not "want to discourage them."

☒ Below minimum standard

☐ Competent

☐ Distinguished

Problem 6: Mrs. Friendly does not establish clear grade reporting criteria.

Summary: Mrs. Friendly has been recognized for clear strengths, as cited above. However there are six key problem areas in which improvement must be made to reach the district's minimum level of performance. We will meet within a month to establish an assistance team to help Mrs. Friendly develop an improvement plan to address these problems. I have full confidence that Mrs. Friendly will continue her good classroom organization and welcoming climate and that she will forcefully address the problems cited. Because she is a competent, caring professional, I fully expect her to be able to address and improve these problems.

Date of Summary Evaluation Conference: June 5 , 1999

Date Evaluation Report Given to Teacher: May 15, 1999

Evaluator's Signature: *Norman R. Smith*   Date:_____

Teacher's Signature: *Sally H. Friendly*

My signature acknowledges receipt of this report on the date indicated and knowledge that it will be inserted into my personnel file. It does not indicate agreement or disagreement with its content. I understand that I have 10 days in which to submit a rebuttal statement, which will be attached to this report.

Teacher: _____ **Date:**_____

Tips: Writing a Final Summary Evaluation

Annotated for the Sally Friendly Case

1. Limit rating categories for performance standards to three and include documentation and references. The passing default is "competent," not "distinguished."

SALLY: Received only one "distinguished"

There is debate about the number of performance rating standards that should be used. Historically, evaluators have been asked to make four to seven distinctions on checklist ratings. There is little validity for this level of discrimination. Jon Saphier (1993) recommends a "pass" and "fail" two-category rating system to remove the necessity of making fine distinctions that end up being difficult to substantiate and a source for contention with teachers. Charlotte Danielson, in *Enhancing Professional Practice: A Framework for Teaching*, recommends four categories "unsatisfactory," "basic," "proficient," and "distinguished." She has organized these categories in a rubric making four categories reasonable. Here we illustrate the use of three ratings with the intent to recognize performance that exceeds standards as well as that which does not yet meet the standard. Leaders must ensure that the highest rating does not become the default rating and that "competent" is the commonly used category, saving "distinguished" for truly outstanding performance.

2. Use multiple data sources. Summary evaluations should contain multiple sources of data with multiple observers.

SALLY: Three observations are referenced from two different observers. Other sources of data include: observation of Back to School Night, the gradebook, lesson plans, newsletters, self-evaluation survey, student work, teacher handouts, and brief interviews with students.

3. Strengths and problems are stated clearly. Impact on students is cited when necessary.

SALLY: Six problems in five different areas of performance are listed. Strengths are clearly cited without "howevers" or "buts" to reduce the credit given.

4. Avoid recommendations. Many final evaluation summaries call for recommendations. We believe recommendations should be part of a plan developed separately and that Step 2 should be a process of describing strengths and problems.

5. Write a concise summary. The summary should avoid mixed messages. It should tie improvement to district standards, express confidence in the ability of the teacher to improve, and set a timetable for the next step: assembling an assistance team.

SALLY: All these characteristics are present.

Summary

Confronting mediocre performance requires: (1) a clear framework that addresses what is important in teaching, (2) supervisory competence in capturing what happens and in using the framework to analyze the effects of the teaching on students, and (3) a commitment to write about and conference about teaching performance with balance and detail. To be credible and convincing, evaluators should organize reports by areas or categories of performance and provide supporting evidence drawn from detailed notetaking. Observation reports and final summary evaluation reports reveal which parts of the classroom performance are substandard. Well written reports and clearly worded problem statements form the basis for the design of an improvement plan by clearly identifying problem areas.

6 Designing an Improvement Plan

The starting point of any effective plan of remediation is also an element likely to be missing from many typical performance improvement plans: the specific, clearly enunciated, straightforward statement of a problem. . . . Rarely if ever do they specifically address something so negative, yet so real, as the existence of a problem. (Brooks et al. 1997, pp. 3–7)

The process of designing an improvement plan should begin with clear statements of problems, not concerns, issues, or recommendations, but gaps that exist between a desired standard of performance and actual performance.

Improvement interventions can range from the formal processes stipulated in a contract to informal, unwritten teacher and supervisor—or even colleague to colleague—agreements to make changes. The most effective of these improvement efforts are driven by a straightforward acknowledgment that things are

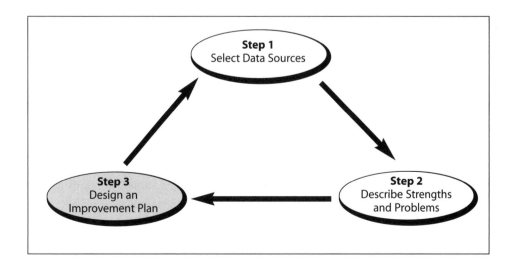

not what they should be. There is a problem to be solved, and there is an institutional commitment to do so. The planning concepts in this chapter apply to any improvement effort from an informal, teacher-driven goal-setting procedure to the more formal, contractually driven process of remediation or assistance. Once problems are identified, a well designed improvement plan becomes the primary tool in confronting mediocrity.

Avoiding the Rush to Recommend

Premature recommendations, however, often get improvement planning off on the wrong foot. Almost all districts have procedures that require the deadline-driven supervisor to hastily conceive recommendations and tack them onto the final summary evaluation. Here is a sample of typical recommendations:

1. Attend a conference on cooperative learning.
2. Observe Mrs. Smith, the math coordinator, teaching a lesson on pattern blocks.
3. Take a course on assessment.
4. Use more wait time.
5. Engage all your students.
6. Check more frequently.
7. Maximize students' time on task.
8. Continue to develop more rapport with your students.
9. Consult with the Reading Specialist.
10. Help students develop self-discipline through a variety of activities.
11. Increase the level of constructive communication with parents.
12. A more comprehensive approach to planning your lessons would be helpful to you and your students.

Unless they are tied to a problem-focused plan, these recommendations are likely to have little impact on teacher improvement. A closer look at these typical recommendations reveals why they do not work. The first three, for example, can be satisfied by the teacher "attending or doing." There is no direct impact on the teaching nor any meaningful way to assess the impact on students. Four through eight are very general. How would the teacher implement "using more wait time"? What does the phrase "continue to develop rapport" really mean? Is it a softener to avoid being directive, or is it a reinforcement of an existing strength? How would engagement be measured? What does "checking more frequently" mean? How is "time on task" defined? Number 9 is a special case because it implies the need to utilize an available resource, but the nature of the consultation is not spelled out. Recommendations 10 and 11 sound like general goals. Number 12 might be the basis for an entire plan rather than one in a series of recommendations. None of these recommendations is easily evaluated.

Another shortcoming of recommendations such as those listed above is that they can easily become isolated activities detached from district standards. Step 3 of the 3-D cycle, the design phase, should begin only after the supervisor has clearly laid out the evidence of shortcomings, as measured by district standards, and has defined the problems to be solved.

The "Reluctant Recipient"

While hastily conceived recommendations torpedo improvement plans, it is also true that plans often do not succeed because their designers pay little attention to the characteristics of those teachers who must implement the plan. "Succeed" in this context means the teacher has improved. It is, of course, true that a plan can be said to have succeeded if it serves as later documentation for dismissal, should this become necessary.

Hungerford et al. (1997) found that of 101 formal plans of assistance studied, very few were successful in changing and improving teacher performance. Focusing less on the plans and more on the plan recipients, whom they characterized as "reluctant teachers," they concluded that the receiving audience was a difficult group. Citing a 1988 interview conducted by Michele Howser (1989), Hungerford noted that many of the identified teachers were "heavily into denial or turning the issue into a battlefield. . . . [They are people] who spend a lot of time and energy denying, finding alternative explanations, attacking or just refusing to see the problem and are the teachers who tend not to get better." Howser describes these "reluctant teachers" as follows:

> They are typically middle aged (thirty-five to fifty-five) experienced (fifteen to twenty-five years of teaching). They are stagnant in their professional growth and resistant to change. Others view them as "frozen in their routines." Reluctant teachers have hundreds of reasons for not changing and are comfortable with the way things are "right now." Often much of their energy is invested in activities other than teaching (Howser 1997, p. 4).

For the resistant or "reluctant" participants particularly, there must be a formal follow-up plan with some design characteristics that maximize the likelihood of success. It is also important to remind ourselves that some resistance can be expected from individuals who have been given inflated ratings in the past. Unfortunately, most mediocre performers have had an evaluation history that has labeled them as good performers. In addition, poor performers often have less insight and are less capable of self-monitoring. An effective plan must be designed to respond to these characteristics.

A Place to Start

To succeed, a plan cannot be one-size-fits-all. It must be tailored to the complex personalities and histories of teachers such the Sally Friendlys and Donna D. Limits whom we met in Chapter 3. But every successful plan should be designed to anticipate and confront two of the most common characteristics of mediocre performance.

1. **Mediocre performers fail to take ownership for their problems** or for the initiative needed to improve. Lack of ownership can surface as subtle resistance or overt denial, but the fact is few individuals readily accept their low-performing status.

2. **Mediocre performers plan low levels of instruction** by failing to select and teach to objectives that promote significant student learning. Instead they plan with a focus of covering a certain amount of material and completing a designated list of activities. The plan needs to be designed to address both these problems:

Fostering Ownership

The supervisor owns the responsibility for defining the problems, but the teacher must share ownership for the development and implementation of the plan. Howser (1997) believes that the attitude of the teacher is the single most important variable in predicting improvement. We have found that a major contributor to a positive outcome is the teacher's willingness to accept responsibility for problems and to be an active participant in the follow-up. In Step 2 of the 3-D cycle, describing strengths and problems, the supervisor takes the first step toward creating ownership when he or she clearly defines the performance problems, supported by credible data sources. The teacher is likely to increase his or her ownership if the serious problems and their impact on the students and the school are clearly documented. If they are built on a credible base of multiple sources of data, these problem statements are nonnegotiable. The goal of the summary evaluation conference is simply to reach a common understanding of the problems and to enlist the teacher in designing a plan for his or her own improvement. To succeed, that is, to move beyond superficial compliance, the teacher **must make some choices**. Obviously, if the teacher refuses to cooperate, the supervisor builds the plan, but this defiance becomes another problem to be documented and tackled.

Fostering Better Planning

A good improvement plan not only structures opportunity for ownership but serves as good model of classroom planning—one that is goal focused rather than activity focused. Supervisors must ensure that mediocre performers improve their ability to plan and carry out instruction that focuses on significant student learning objectives. An improvement plan that itself is a poor model, e.g., consisting of isolated recommendations and activities, only reinforces the planning pattern where mediocre performers hitch up a series of unrelated activities. Thus the process of developing and carrying out the plan becomes an exemplar for the kind of planning we want teachers to carry out for their students.

A Model of Planning: Design Components

The following model represents a comprehensive approach to developing an improvement plan (see Figure 6-1). Not all intervention plans dealing with mediocre performance need to include all the steps listed below. Supervisors have to consider the circumstances and the appropriate allocation of time and resources. Implementing this level of intervention for all mediocre performers would drain the energies of even the most skillful leader. For example, with a teacher who readily accepts his or her deficiencies and pledges to improve, it is likely that the supervisor

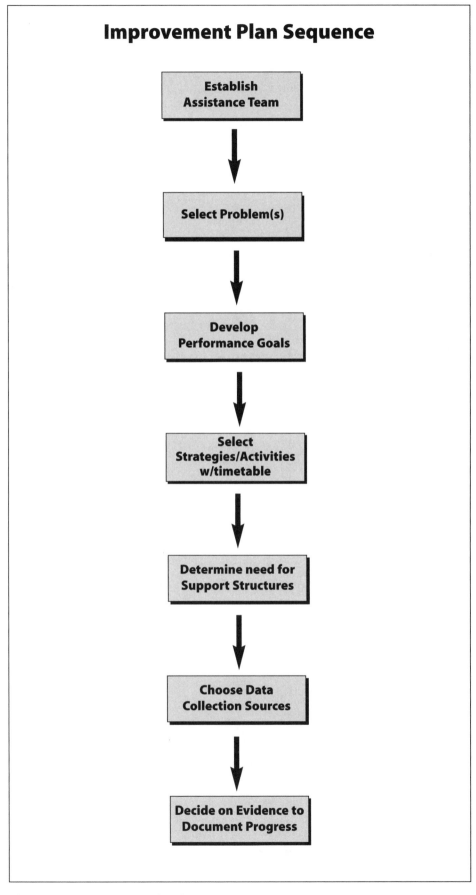

Figure 6-1 Improvement plan design.

> **LEGAL NOTE**
>
> An improvement plan should maximize the conditions that will lead to improvement. But supervisors should always keep in mind that the plan also becomes documentation of the assistance provided should it become necessary to seek termination or other disciplinary action. Specifying deficiencies with reasonable opportunities for remediation and periodic reevaluation fulfills the ethical and legal requirements of fairness and due process.

could develop a plan without a full team. What follows is the "Mercedes" plan—one that could certainly serve as documentation should the teacher fail to improve and dismissal become a consideration. The reader will see that there are many legal issues related to designing a plan. Even though the focus is on improvement, skillful leaders always prepare themselves for the possible move to dismissal. These legal safeguards only offer more incentive for the identified teacher to participate in his or her own improvement and do not prevent the supervisor from using a less formal plan when that is sufficient.

Establish Assistance Team

Establishing the Assistance Planning Team and Planning Process

Both individual and institutional participation in the improvement plan can be increased by having several people share in setting goals and developing the plan. For a formal improvement plan dealing with multiple complex problems, a support team helps provide the institutional capability to respond to less than satisfactory performance. A team can consist of five or six members, including the identified teacher and supervising administrator, and might include any of the following:

Identified teacher

Primary supervisor

Curriculum specialist with expertise in an identified problem area

Teacher association representative

Trusted teacher colleague

Teacher mentor or colleague trained in peer coaching

A supervisor unfamiliar with the teacher

Outside consultant

Central office representative

> **LEGAL NOTE**
>
> Most negotiated evaluation procedures are likely to include the so-called "just cause standard" and the requirement that the teacher be given a reasonable opportunity to improve before any personnel action can be taken. More often than not, this takes the form of a written remediation or improvement plan that must be developed by the principal in cooperation with the teacher and with the possible requirement that the teachers' union be involved.

Team members should be chosen for their ability to support the teacher's improvement efforts and for their competence in assessing data drawn from multiple sources. Team members should have strong communication skills and share the conviction that all children deserve competent instruction. Although outside consultants do not routinely serve on formal improvement teams, they can be valuable assets when districts lack internal expertise or when internal resource staff are not perceived to be credible by the teacher being supported. Outside consultants can be assigned to work with teachers or administrators as confidential helpers to the teacher, as advisors or facilitators for the planning process, or as supporters and monitors of the implementation of various strategies incorporated in the plan.

Example: Sally Friendly's Assistance Team

Sally Friendly, Teacher

Norman R. Smith, Principal and Primary Evaluator

Muriel Mclaughlin, Math Coordinator and Secondary Evaluator (Observed Sally Friendly as a secondary evaluator and identified several gaps in her math instruction.)

Nancy Kerr, Mentor Teacher (Selected by Sally Friendly, Nancy has been trained as a mentor teacher and has 20% released time to work with identified teachers.)

Doug Bates, Association Representative (Doug was nominated by the teachers' association.)

Emily Henderson, Principal from another school (Emily has had no contact with Sally Friendly and could be an objective voice in the planning.)

Creating a team accomplishes several things. First, it clearly communicates that the institution has commitment to improvement that goes beyond the individual supervisor-supervisee relationship. Second, if there is resentment or resistance from the summary evaluation process or if the identified teacher is "reluctant," it increases the pool of personalities to include some supportive colleagues for both the supervisor and the teacher. Third, it clearly separates the development of a plan from the descriptive step that focuses on collecting data and stating problems. It makes the team responsible for developing goals and appropriate recommendations and removes this task from the busy, deadline-driven administrator.

LEGAL NOTE

Unions are likely to seek to have a role in drafting an improvement or remediation plan. While it may be helpful to involve the union in consultation with the teacher in preparing a plan, the principal and superintendent should always preserve the final decision as to the need for and content of an improvement plan to the employer. The need for and content of a plan should not be grievable.

LEGAL NOTE

Except where there would be potential serious harm to students, which is not the situation we are dealing with in confronting mediocrity, any adverse employment decisions such as dismissal proceedings must await sufficient time to complete the plan. Sufficient time is usually a year or two.

The team should have an organizational meeting and agree upon its charge and operating ground rules:

1. The primary charge should be to develop and support the implementation of an improvement plan and to provide formative feedback during the plan. (Figure 6-1 page 123 lays out all of the steps.)

2. Unless the district has adopted a formal peer assistance process that gives evaluation authority to the team, the main purpose of the team is to assist the teacher. (See Chapter 9 for a discussion of peer assistance.) The primary evaluator is still responsible for the ultimate evaluation of the success of the teacher in improving performance. Formative evaluation can be built into the plan.

3. The team should establish agreements about frequency of meetings and set a schedule. For example, during the improvement period, the Sally Friendly team will meet every six weeks.

4. Roles and responsibilities of each member of the assistance team should be made clear. It is important that supporting roles are separated from evaluation roles. In order to have an objective neutral leader, we recommend that a supervisor other than the primary supervisor be chair. In our example Emily Henderson will chair the Sally Friendly team.

5. There should be an agreement about the number and sequence of problem interventions and which tasks will be carried out by the full team and which by individual team members.

6. Decide on the duration of the plan. Plan duration should be matched to the number of deficiencies and years of employment of the identified teacher.

7. Make certain that everyone who is involved in implementing and monitoring the plan has received a copy of it and signed it.

LEGAL NOTE

The duration of a plan must in the first instance comply with the requirements of any collective bargaining agreements and promulgated policies regarding such plans. Some agreement and/or policies will stipulate a minimum period of time during which the plan must be in effect. Ideally, the employer should retain the discretion to determine how much time the teacher should be given to improve.

Selecting Problems and Establishing a Sequence for Problem Intervention

> **Select Problem(s)**

We have already stressed the importance of the supervisor's stating problems in a way that clearly communicates the message of underperformance to the teacher. We suggest that all problems be identified in order to counter potential charges of "He is always coming up with new criticism; this is harassment." As institutional guardians of high performance standards, the team selects a few of the problem statements to be the starting point for improvement planning.

Improvement plans should initially address only a few problem areas and only one at a time. Otherwise the plan is very difficult to implement, monitor, and assess. Madeline Hunter used to say it took poor teachers many years of practice to get bad. Confronting mediocrity means building new practice patterns. It will not happen overnight. The team's goal is to provide the conditions for success, not just to document the intervention for dismissal. Problems should be ranked and addressed in order of the likelihood of successful intervention. As progress is made, the plan evolves and other problems may be selected for focus. Here is the menu of problem statements developed for Sally Friendly (see Chapter 5).

STANDARD: EFFECTIVE INSTRUCTION

Problem 1 Mrs. Friendly fails to frame learning (both the objectives and the sequence of activities) for students and does not regularly communicate the reasons for activities. Thus students have difficulty determining what is important to know or to be able to do in transferring competencies from one subject to another and in making connections among concepts.

STANDARD: EXPECTATIONS AND STANDARDS

Problem 2 Mrs. Friendly does not communicate expectations for high performance for all students. Thus students have difficulty determining what rigorous academic work should be.

STANDARD: CURRICULUM PLANNING—ASSESSMENT

Problem 3 Mrs. Friendly fails to plan a challenging, integrated curriculum that focuses on significant student learning. As a result, students spend considerable time on work that is not directly connected to district curriculum frameworks.

Problem 4 Mrs. Friendly fails to clearly state criteria for success, provide exemplars for different levels of performance, and give specific task-referenced feedback. Thus students are not always clear about the steps needed to achieve a high level of performance.

Nonteaching Areas

STANDARD: COMMUNICATION WITH PARENTS

Problem 5 Mrs. Friendly's communication with parents does not meet professional standards for content or presentation.

STANDARD: STUDENT GRADING

Problem 6 Mrs. Friendly does not establish clear grade reporting criteria.

Where should the teacher start? All of these are important problems that relate to district standards, and all should be addressed at some point. As we have stressed, however, it is important to confront mediocrity through stages. Work one step at a time and work for depth rather than coverage. The team should select a reasonable menu of problems where improvement is likely to better conditions for students. The team should not predispose the plan to failure by asking a struggling teacher to tackle all problems simultaneously. The following criteria will help determine which problems should be addressed first.

Criteria for Selecting Problems

- Clear ownership, e.g., the teacher's choice of a place to start
- Significant impact on improving instruction
- Likelihood of near-term success (in three to four months)
- Teacher's willingness to make reasonable short-term effort
- Low cost in supervisory time to assess (easily assessed)
- Direct impact on student learning

LEGAL NOTE

Great care should be taken in drafting an improvement plan. Avoid making too many commitments with respect to what the employer will be responsible for doing to make employees efficient in the performance of their duties. Make certain that you will be able to follow through on all of the commitments that you make in the plan.

The Problem: Mrs. Friendly fails to frame learning (both the objectives and the sequence of activities) for students and does not regularly communicate the reasons for activities. Thus students have difficulty in determining what is important to know or be able to do in tranferring competencies from one subject to another and in making connections among concepts.

If there are problems with management, which is not the case with Sally Friendly, we might counsel beginning with management because of the adage "management comes before instruction." In this book we do not focus extensively on management problems because there is a wide knowledge base on this topic. If management is the primary presenting problem, our advice would be to remember that when the teacher improves his/her management skills we should not assume this leads automatically to good instruction. "Management sets the table. Instruction provides the meal." Therefore, in most cases, the team should focus its primary energy in raising the level of instruction and remember that mediocre performers might achieve a "satisfactory" in management but still be "less than satisfactory" in instruction.

In the Sally Friendly example, let us assume that the team applied the criteria and selected the problem above. They further agreed that if sufficient improvement is made with lesson planning they would move to Problem 3, "Mrs. Friendly fails to plan a challenging, integrated curriculum that focuses on significant student learning" as a more specific focus for the spring semester.

We will use this selected problem to illustrate the steps needed to develop a plan with components that maximize success. Developing goals to address this problem is the next task of the planning team.

Developing Performance Improvement Goals

Whether the teacher and the supervisor or the team jointly set the goals, they should be directly linked to the identified problem. Performance improvement goals are statements of what needs to happen to eliminate the problem and improve learning for students. While ownership is more likely when the teacher sets goals, it is important to remember that mediocre performers may not know how to do this stage well. Failure to set effective goals may itself be one of the underlying symptons of their mediocre classroom performance. Coaching, modeling, and patience may be required.

| Develop Performance Goals |

Criteria for Good Goals [1]

There may be more than one goal per problem, but there should not be more than one problem per goal.

Each goal should be related to solving the stated problem.

Each goal should be specific enough so that it can be determined when the goal has been met.

A goal should be capable of being implemented and practiced in a specific context but should have application across a wide range of teaching applications.

[1] Adapted from Brooks et al. 1997, pp. 3–9.

This stage is difficult and can be time consuming but is well worth the effort for the long-term learning it fosters. If teachers can improve in goal setting, this skill can be transferred to their own classroom. One or more goals should be established for each identified problem.

Applying these criteria to illustrate the steps, we once again pick up with Sally Friendly. Our hypothetical team selected the following goals.

Performance Goals Mrs. Friendly should regularly communicate to students the lesson and unit objectives and the sequence of lesson and unit events.

Mrs. Friendly should provide frequent opportunities for students to process and integrate information.

Selecting Activities and Strategies

Select Strategies/Activities w/timetable

Once final performance goals are settled, the teacher, with the help of the team and/or evaluator or other resource person, selects implementation strategies and activities matched to the goal. They should be sequentially listed with time frames for completion.

Sources for Strategies and Activities

The following are all good resources to find appropriate implementation strategies and activities.

- **Curriculum support documents** ranging from national (e.g., NCTM), state, and local frameworks to teacher's manuals for formal programs adopted by the district.
- **Colleagues with expertise** in particular areas of curriculum design, instruction, and assessment required by the district's performance standards. These individuals could model techniques for the identified teacher.
- **Professional journals, books, and articles** on specific models of teaching, e.g., *Teaching for Understanding* or *Cooperative Learning*, or key research on generic pedagogy or content-specific pedagogy.
- **College courses, workshops, and local inservice offerings** targeted to the problem being addressed, e.g., teaching students to write, reading in the content area, advanced placement laboratories, discrete mathematics.
- **Technology:** resource tapes and audio, quick take cameras, videotaping as a source for ideas or as follow-up.

Criteria for High Quality Strategies and Activities

Excellent strategies and activities have the following characteristics:

- They are targeted directly to the goals.
- They are specific enough to be implemented effectively.
- They can be assessed.
- They assign the teacher responsiblility for doing much of the work.
- They specify a timetable.

See the attachment at the end of this chapter, "Idea Bank of Activities for Improvement Plans." We have selected strategies and activities from this bank of ideas and modified them for Sally Friendly.

Strategies, Activities, and Timetable
1. Agenda will be posted and reviewed. (daily)
2. Curriculm-relevant mastery and thinking objectives will be listed in the plan book and be written on all assignments given to students. (daily)
3. Lesson plans will designate time and type of processing activity and annotations of their success. (weekly)
4. At the start of a fraction unit, Mrs. Friendly will give an overview of the entire unit including the objectives, components of the unit, and the connection to district goals or standards.
5. Mrs. Friendly will create a survey to collect information from students about how well she is succeeding in communicating the context for the fraction unit and about the experience that students are having with the expanded repertoire of processing strategies.

Establishing Support Structures: Personnel and Material Resources

Determine need for Support Structures

In this stage, the necessary support structures are identified. They may range from a resource book, to assistance from an identified team member, to financial support or released time for coursework. Support structures should be linked to underlying causes of the mediocrity. Teacher problems can be attributed to lack of expertise (Sally Friendly), inappropriate belief systems (Peter Passable), or external problems such as alcoholism (Louise Biere, see Chapter 3). The teacher may lack expertise in a particular goal/activity area and need support to acquire that expertise. In order to succeed in the classroom, the teacher may even need counseling or therapy as part of the support provided by the district. Some strategies may be easily implemented without much training or support; others require training or learning before implementation.

Strategies, Activities, and Timetable	Support Structures
1. Agenda will be posted and reviewed. (daily)	1. None.
2. Curriculm-relevant mastery and thinking objectives will be listed in the plan book and be written on all assignments given to students. (daily)	2. Mentor provides plan book models and sample assignments. Curriculum coordinator provides curriculum guides and frameworks.
3. Lesson plans will designate time and type of processing activity and annotations of their success. (weekly)	3. Mentor provides plan book models and sample assignments. Principal provides book resource: *Summarizers: Activity Structures to Support Integration and Retention of New Learning.*
4. At the start of a fraction unit, Mrs. Friendly will give an overview of the entire unit including the objectives, components of the unit, and the connection to district goals or standards.	4. Provide Sally with released time to observe another grade level teacher who is skilled at framing the context of a new unit.
5. Mrs. Friendly will create a survey to collect information from students about how well she is succeeding in communicating the context for the fraction unit and about the experience that students are having with the expanded repertoire of processing strategies.	5. District will pay for attending a workshop session "Interviewing Students: Getting Important Feedback." (9/30)

Choose Data Collection Sources

Choosing Data Collection Sources and Assigning Responsibility

For every activity or strategy, there should be a matched method of collecting data. The team should agree on what sources of data will be used and who will collect it. For the plan to foster ownership, the teacher should be responsible for collecting much of the data. As we discussed in Chapter 4, multiple sources of data should be incorporated to ensure depth of information. The menu of data sources in Figure 4-2 can be a useful tool to help assess progress and build accountability in the implementation and assessment of each goal. This kind of depth can only be achieved by focusing on a few goals at a time. Moreover, because teachers and evaluators determine the data sources together, there are no secrets about what is expected or how the teacher can meet expectations. Notice in the "Data Collection Method and Sources" list below that for each activity there is a corresponding identification of how information will be collected.

Strategies, Activities, and Timetable	Data Collection Method and Sources
1. Agenda will be posted and reviewed. (daily)	1. Observation: Four random drop-by visits by principal. (by 10/5) Artifact: Six Polaroid photographs taken by teacher. (by 10/5)
2. Curriculm-relevant mastery and thinking objectives will be listed in the plan book and be written on all assignments given to students. (daily)	2. Artifact: Plan book examined by curriculum coordinator. (by 10/15) Artifact: Ten sample assignments given by teacher to curriculum coordinator. (by 10/15)
3. Lesson plans will designate time and type of processing activity and annotations of their success. (weekly)	3. Observation: Unannounced visit by curriculum coordinator. (by 10/15)
4. At the start of a fraction unit, Mrs. Friendly will give an overview of the entire unit including the objectives, components of the unit, and the connection to district goals or standards.	4. Observation: Principal observes 20-minute introduction to a unit on multiplying fractions. (10/20) Artifact: Principal examines introduction of materials given to students on 10/20.
5. Mrs. Friendly will create a survey to collect information from students about how well she is succeeding in communicating the context for the fraction unit and about the experience that students are having with the expanded repertoire of processing strategies.	5. Survey: Teacher interviews three students of different performance levels and reports to the team. (by 11/3))

Establishing Evidence of Progress

Decide on Evidence to Document Progress

There must be evaluation of progress toward the identified goal. To help make this assessment more concrete, it is often necessary to further specify the evidence that could be used to document progress.

The complete plan for the defined problem, including the second performance goal, would look like Figure 6-2 (page 137).

LEGAL NOTE

The timing of follow-up evaluation can be very important in fulfilling the requirement for reasonableness. If a teacher is assessed as unsatisfactory and recommendations for improvement are made, there must be an adequate opportunity for a follow-up evaluation. What is adequate can vary from case to case, depending upon the specific circumstances involved.

Strategies, Activities, and Timetable	Evidence for Progress
1. Agenda will be posted and reviewed. (daily)	1. Clear, legible agendas present during all four visits and represented by the Polaroid pictures.
2. Curriculm-relevant mastery and thinking objectives will be listed in the plan book and be written on all assignments given to students. (daily)	2. Mastery and thinking objectives are listed in the plan. There is evidence of direct connection to the district frameworks. Collected assignments show evidence of explicitly stated objectives.
3. Lesson plans will designate time and type of processing activity and annotations of their success. (weekly)	3. Plans show frequent notations with the name of the processing activity, estimated amount of time to be spent, and follow-up notations commenting on the impact on student learning.
4. At the start of a fraction unit, Mrs. Friendly will give an overview of the entire unit including the objectives, components of the unit, and the connection to district goals or standards.	4. There is evidence of all three components: objectives, components, and connection to district goals.
5. Mrs. Friendly will create a survey to collect information from students about how well she is succeeding in communicating the context for the fraction unit and about the experience that students are having with the expanded repertoire of processing strategies.	5. There is evidence that the teacher can create and administer a short survey interview by developing meaningful questions, analyzing the data in terms of student learning, and communicating these findings to the team.

Referral of Disagreements

In cultures where there are hostile union-administration relationships and/or in the case of an uncooperative teacher, it is possible that the plan contents could be grieved even if the district procedures are adhered to.

Progress, Backsliding, and Dismissal

In our example we have chosen one problem to illustrate the design features of a good improvement plan. These features can be replicated for other problem areas. As in the Sally Friendly example, there was another problem the team identified that could be addressed during the second half of the year. Readers may be overwhelmed by the prospect that there are several other problems that need attention, considering the amount of investment needed to address each problem. We should remember, however, that initially we are seeking to develop conditions to ensure success in one or two areas. If progress is demon-

LEGAL NOTE

"Backsliding" refers to a situation, following an unsatisfactory appraisal and remediation period during which an employee is deemed to be satisfactory, where manifestations of prior deficiencies reappear. A second unsatisfactory rating does not necessarily entitle a teacher to another remediation period.

"Given D.'s long history of occasionally remediating but then falling back to her unacceptable teaching performance over a period of three years, and given the inordinate time extended by the system in an effort to assist her in remediation but to no avail, I find the District did not act unfairly in not extending the Tier 2 status for another year.... The evidence shows that her deficiencies are too pervasive and without lasting remediation. It would be patently unfair to the students of Lexington, who have a right to expect the best possible teaching, to subject them to an "experiment" with (D.), with every expectation that it would fail." Lexington Public Schools, AAA Case # 11-390-00571-94 (Arbitrator Bruce Fraser, July 14, 1995).

strated, "success breeds success" and often spills into other areas. Teachers often will begin to take more personal growth initiatives with fewer formal intervention structures. We might call this scaled-down intervention a monitoring status.

If success is not evident in spite of the maximum conditions, then perhaps this is no longer a case of mediocrity and we are moving toward confronting and documenting incompetence.

Success can occur only to be followed by backsliding. In this situation, improvement has been demonstrated, the teacher has been removed from a formal assistance plan, but there is a subsequent lapse to previous poor performance levels. The case of Brenda in Chapter 8 illustrates how, despite sucessful intervention, a teacher can easily fall back into old patterns. If backsliding occurs, the skillful supervisor assesses what needs to be put in place to maintain a satisfactory level of performance. It is made clear in the legal notes that a district is under no commitment to continue to provide support in the face of constant backsliding.

Should the supervisor conclude that the performance cannot be remediated, there may need to be a new round of performance evaluations after the period of assistance to document the continued low performance.

LEGAL NOTE

You need not put up with unsatisfactory performance indefinitely. Usually, the longer an employee has been with you the longer the remediation period you will be required to provide them. Someone who has been evaluated as satisfactory for 20 years will be entitled to more time to improve than someone who has only been with you for one, three, or five years.

Designing a Plan: A Summary Checklist

The following checklist summarizes all of the steps involved in designing an improvement plan.

1. The supervisor clearly identifies all of the problem areas in the final summary evaluation report. The plan should based on problems and performance goals, not on recommendations, concerns, or issues.

2. Keep plan development separate from the summary evaluation meeting. If possible and appropriate, include a team with participants selected by the teacher and the supervisor.

3. Address the two supervisory challenges of lack of ownership and low level instructional planning.

4. Select only a few problems areas on which to begin work. Keep the focus on testing capability for improvement, not on transforming the teacher in two months. Think instruction and instructional goals. Think intensive, not extensive.

5. To increase ownership of the plan, require the teacher to participate fully in setting goals and selecting activities and data to be collected.

6. Continually monitor congruency among problems, goals, strategies, and data collection and evidence for progress. Internal consistency ensures that what is implemented is connected to the problem identified and that assessment of success is built in from the beginning.

7. Make the teacher responsible for most of the data to be collected as evidence of progress. Have some of the data collected from students.

8. Focus the plan on measurable change in behavior rather than fulfilling an activity carried out. Agreeing on evidence that documents progress helps to keep all parties focused on observable changes.

9. Include multiple data sources and collection procedures.

10. Spell out roles and responsibilities and distinguish evaluation roles and events from development roles and events. Clarify resource and support team roles.

11. Specify the timetable for completion, which anchors the plan in specific context over a limited period of time.

LEGAL NOTE

Decision Following an Opportunity for Remediation
[W]e believe it was incumbent on the Board in this case to ground its dismissal decisions on observations and evaluations made after, and not during, the remediation period. Observations during the remediation period could be properly used to evaluate improvement, but the absence of any evaluation at the conclusion of the period made it impossible for the Board to make a reasoned decision. *Board of Education of School District No. 131 v. Illinois State Board of Education,* 403 N.E. 2d 277 (1980).

Figure 6-2 Model Improvement Plan

Team Members	Teacher	Teacher Representative	Supervising Principal	Curriculum Coordinator	Mentor Teacher	Nonsupervising Principal
	Sally Friendly	Doug Bates	Norman R. Smith	Muriel Mclaughlin	Nancy Kerr	Emily Handerson
Signature:	*Sally Friendly*	*Doug Bates*	*Norman R. Smith*	*Muriel Mclaughlin*	*Nancy Kerr*	*Emily Handerson*
Date:	6/10/99					
Standard Area:	Instruction					

The Problem: Mrs. Friendly fails to frame learning (both the objectives and the sequence of activities) for students and does not regularly communicate the reasons for activities. Thus students have difficulty in determining what is important to know or be able to do in tranferring competencies from one subject to another and in making connections among concepts.

Performance Goals	Strategies, Activities, and Timetable	Support Structures	Data Collection Method and Sources	Evidence for Progress
Mrs. Friendly should regularly communicate to students the lesson and unit objectives and the sequence of lesson and unit events. Mrs. Friendly should provide frequent opportunities for students to process and integrate information.	1. Agenda will be posted and reviewed (daily).	1. None.	1. Observation: Four random drop-by visits by principal. (by 10/5) Artifact: Six Polaroid photographs taken by teacher. (by 10/5)	1. Clear, legible agendas present during all four visits and represented by the Polaroid pictures.
	2. Curriculm-relevant mastery and thinking objectives will be listed in the plan book and be written on all assignments given to students. (daily)	2. Mentor provides plan book models and sample assignments. Curriculum coordinator provides curriculum guides and frameworks.	2. Artifact: Plan book examined by curriculum coordinator. (by 10/15) Artifact: Ten sample assignments given by teacher to curriculum coordinator. (by 10/15)	2. Mastery and thinking objectives are listed in the plan. There is evidence of direct connection to the district frameworks. Collected assignments show evidence of explicitly stated objectives.
	3. Lesson plans will designate time and type of processing activity and annotations of their success. (weekly)	3. Mentor provides plan book models and sample assignments. Principal provides book resource: *Summarizers: Activity Structures to Support Integration and Retention of New Learning.*	3. Observation: Unannounced visit by curriculum coordinator. (by 10/15)	3. Plans show frequent notations with the name of the processing activity, estimated amount of time to be spent, and follow-up notations commenting on the impact on student learning.
	4. At the start of a fraction unit, Mrs. Friendly will give an overview of the entire unit including the objectives, components of the unit, and the connection to district goals or standards.	4. Provide Sally with released time to observe another grade level teacher who is skilled at framing the context of a new unit.	4. Observation: Principal observes 20-minute introduction to a unit on multiplying fractions. (10/20) Artifact: Principal examines introduction of materials given to students on 10/20.	4. There is evidence of all three components: objectives, components, and connection to district goals.
	5. Mrs. Friendly will create a survey to collect information from students about how well she is succeeding in communicating the context for the fraction unit and about the experience that students are having with the expanded repertoire of processing strategies.	5. District will pay for attending a workshop session "Interviewing Students: Getting Important Feedback." (9/30)	5. Survey: Teacher interviews three students of different performance levels and reports to the team. (by 11/3)	5. There is evidence that the teacher can create and administer a short survey interview by developing meaningful questions, analyzing the data in terms of student learning, and communicating these findings to the team.

Idea Bank of Activities for Improvement Plans

1. **Problem Area: Management—Lost Instructional Time** Students are not paying attention.

Sample Activities and Strategies

- Identify three additional techniques to keep and get attention. Try them out and record the response in a log.
- Observe a teacher who is known to have good class attention. Be prepared to share what you learned from your visit and how you will apply it in your classroom.
- Have all materials organized in advance of class. Keep track of your progress and note results in a journal.
- Record estimated time for each activity segment and then compare with the actual time spent.
- Identify a routine that is not working. Plan a lesson to teach, practice, and test students' acquisition of the modified routine. (Example: making a transition from language arts into recess.)

Resource: *The First Days of School (1991)*

2. **Problem Area: Instruction—Communicating the Context for Learning** Students have little sense of what they are learning, how, and why.

Sample Activities and Strategies

- Post/communicate the itinerary each day.
- Communicate objectives regularly.
- At the end of each week, ask students what they have learned.
- After every 10 minutes of instruction, have students summarize and process new information for 2 minutes. Use an hourglass to cue yourself.
- Use an audiotape of your teaching to listen for transitions then report on your findings.
- List rationale or the "why" for objectives in lesson plans.
- Communicate the importance of each instructional objective in terms of student lives.
- At the start of a unit, give an overview of the entire unit, including the purpose of major activities.
- Create questions and interview students of different performance levels about their understanding of purpose and context of a unit.

3. **Problem Area: Instruction—Checking and Explaining** Students are regularly "lost," and retention of concepts is poor because the teacher has little or no repertoire for checking for understanding.

Sample Activities and Strategies

- Teach students how to use a particular graphic organizer.
- For each lesson objective, list the explanatory device to be employed.
- Use at least three explanatory devices for each instructional segment:

one keyed to the auditory learner, one keyed to the visual learner, and one keyed to the kinesthetic learner. Examples include: modeling thinking aloud and mental imagery.

- In lesson plans, note what strategy will be used to check all students' understanding at critical junctures during instruction. After class, note how particular strategies worked and the impact of the data on the next stage of instruction.

- Ask students to write about the impact of different kinds of explanatory devices on their learning and to identify which were most effective in helping them to understand and retain a concept. Bring learning log entries to the supervisory conference and report on the decisions made about subsequent instruction as a result of information gained from students' responses.

- Invent ways to incorporate technology to both explain concepts and check understanding.

- Invent and test a concrete model or graphic organizer that helps students better understand a concept or series of concepts they need to master.

4. **Problem Area: Motivation—Engaging Students** Students are bored, perhaps quiet or not disruptive, but academically disengaged.

Sample Activities and Strategies

- Implement the 10-2 principle (see above)

- Use strategies to activate students' knowledge in advance of instruction.

- Implement signal-checking strategies.

- Vary instruction: use pair-based cooperative learning strategies such as: think-pair-share, teammates consult, paired verbal fluency, and a three-step interview. (See *Summarizers*, Saphier and Haley 1993.)

5. **Problem Area: Planning** Students experience disconnected activities. There is little continuity of instruction.

Sample Activities and Strategies

- List curriculum-relevant mastery and thinking objectives in the plan book and on all assignments.

- On lesson plans, designate time and type of processing activity and annotations on its success.

- Create unit plans that detail key questions and key organizing themes, the thinking level objectives, how they are taught, and what methods of assessment are used.

- Create opportunities for students to reflect about learning in a journal.

- In a unit identify the thinking skills and how student work will be used to assess whether students are transferring that skill to their work.

- Establish criteria for getting A's, B's, C's, etc. and communicate these to students.

6. Problem Area: Motivation—Expectations

Sample Activities and Strategies

- Work to use effective praise that states specifically what students did to earn that praise.
- Increase methods of having students self-assess progress.
- Create strategies to reward progress and effort.
- Choose one or two students to carry out a focused case study to get them to achieve at a higher level.
- Get a peer to observe three high-performing students and three low-performing students and your responses and interaction with them.

7. Problem Area: Personal Relationship Building

Sample Activities and Strategies

- Administer an anonymous student survey.
- Get a colleague to observe and take notes on responding to student answers.
- Videotape interaction patterns and sit down with a colleague and watch the video together.
- Develop a routine of greeting students each day by first names as they enter the class.

7 Model Contract Language

Supervision, Evaluation, and Employee Discipline

In earlier chapters we discussed institutional deficiencies and supervisory problems that contribute to mediocre teaching. We looked at specific patterns of excellence and mediocrity in teaching. In the "3-D" chapters, we considered better ways to collect data for evaluation, to describe teaching strengths and problems, and to design an effective plan to improve substandard performance. In this chapter we will look at the wording of teachers' contracts and policy handbooks concerning procedures for supervision, data collection, evaluation, improvement plans, and discipline and dismissal. Strong contract language enables district leaders to add control to the competence and conviction needed to confront mediocrity.

In any collective bargaining agreement or school board policy manual, the language that describes the supervision, evaluation, and discipline of teachers is critical. This language defines the employment relationship. It also empowers third parties, especially labor arbitrators, to substitute their judgment for that of the employer whenever an employee or the union challenges decisions that affect the employment relationship. Such challenges do not have to involve suspension or dismissal. Increasingly, teachers have challenged evaluation reports that characterized their work as unsatisfactory or below the district's performance standards.

Collective Bargaining May Be Required   It is important to realize that some states, such as Massachusetts, mandate that before a public employer can do anything to change either evaluation standards or evaluation procedures, it must first notify the union. If the union so requests, the employer must engage in collective bargaining at least to the point of impasse before the employer can implement any change from the status quo, i.e., from the conditions existing before the proposed change.

This chapter gives a detailed analysis of contract language and provides a model to follow. This model contract language could also be used in a policy manual if your state does not require negotiation over any or all of the topics discussed in this chapter. The contract language given in the following sample is grounded in Massachusetts law. Be sure that you have your local school counsel review this language for conformity with your state's laws and regulations before adopting any policies or making any new contract proposals based on this material.

See Chapter 5 for a complete framework describing a teacher's roles and competencies. We have included in Appendix G a second source document organized in a contractual format. This document, "Performance Roles of Teachers and Related Competencies," was developed in 1964 by the California Teacher's Association; it has stood the test of time as a good working model.

Forms play a very important role in the process of supervision and evaluation. They focus the evaluators on the information that must be documented. They can also ensure that the evaluator is given the procedural safeguards set forth in the contract or policy statements relative to evaluation. A simplified "Model Final Summary Evaluation Report Form" is included in Appendix F.

SAMPLE CONTRACT LANGUAGE

Introduction

This Article is divided into the following parts: Supervision Procedures, Evaluation Procedures, Personnel Files, Employee Discipline and Just Cause,[1] Grievances, and Dismissal Procedures.

Definitions

Certification—Massachusetts teachers' certification issued pursuant to Massachusetts General Laws, Chapter 71, Section 38G and the regulations[2] pertaining thereto as promulgated by the Department of Education.

Committee or Board—The School Committee of the Town of (insert the name of the school district). In all cases referring to the Committee or the employer, except for those specifically reserved by law exclusively to the Committee, the Superintendent or a designee shall be the Committee's agent(s) for purposes of this ARTICLE.

Evaluation—means the process of defining goals and identifying, gathering, and using evidence as part of a process to improve professional performance and to assess job effectiveness by determining whether the facts substantiated by the evidence that has been documented satisfy the school district's performance standards.

Evaluation Report—a narrative report that is prepared by an evaluator (i.e., principal, assistant principal, or other designated administrator) and set forth on the Evaluation Report Form.

Evaluator—any person designated by the Superintendent with responsibility for conducting evaluations. All evaluators must be certified for the positions they hold and be trained in the process of evaluation.

Observation—a classroom visitation or conference conducted by a supervisor or evaluator specifically for the purpose of gathering data to be used in preparing an Observation and/or Evaluation Report.

Supervisor—any employee of the school district whose job description assigns responsibility for the supervision and/or evaluation of personnel.

Observation Report—a report that is provided to the teacher following an observation/conference or series of observations/conferences.

Teacher—all personnel serving in those positions that are included in the bargaining unit represented by the (insert the name of the bargaining agent).

---

[1] "Just cause" is a term of art in the context of labor law and collective bargaining agreements. It is the standard that labor arbitrators generally apply in reviewing disciplinary action taken by employers. In some states, such as Massachusetts, it is actually mandated by state law.
[2] See 603 CMR 44.00.

General Principles

The purpose of this article is to set forth the process that will be followed to supervise, support, evaluate, and, if necessary, discipline employees when there is "just cause" for doing so.

In all aspects of their work, teachers are subject to supervision and evaluation. Therefore, any interaction that a teacher has with supervisors, evaluators and/or administrators, students, their parents, or other persons are potential sources of evidence that may be used in the process of supervision and evaluation.[3]

Except as otherwise qualified by this article, all observation of the work performance of a teacher will be conducted openly and with the full knowledge of the teacher. The employer specifically reserves the right to use video surveillance to the extent permitted by law in the investigation of suspected illegal activity or misconduct in office.[4]

Teachers will be informed, by no later than October 1st of each school year, of the identity of their supervisor(s) and evaluator(s) for that school year; provided, however, that the superintendent shall have the right to change said supervisor(s) and/or evaluator(s) with prior written notice to the teacher involved and the (insert the name of the bargaining agent). Normally, teachers will be evaluated by their building principal, assistant principal, or other designated administrator, with supervision conducted by building-level and systemwide supervisors who possess subject matter expertise and/or have administrative responsibility for the programs involved (e.g., special education, physical education, music, etc.). Personnel assigned to more than one building or department will be supervised by the principal and/or supervisor in the place where they spend the most time. The Superintendent and assistant superintendents may participate in the supervision and/or evaluation of any member of the bargaining unit.

Whenever a supervisor or evaluator has any concerns about a teacher's performance, it is the supervisor's and/or the evaluator's responsibility to so inform the teacher in writing by describing the specific concerns involved to the teacher and using the term "less than satisfactory."[5]

---

[3] The concepts in this section are very important to include in any contract or policy language that establishes the procedures to be followed in the evaluation of all employees. Teacher unions try to limit the potential sources of the data that evaluators may use in the evaluation process to evidence that has been observed on a first-hand basis by the evaluator. This paragraph puts teachers on notice about the fact that any interactions that they have with anyone within the scope of their employment may be used in assessing the performance of their duties.

[4] The use of video surveillance is a crucial tool that employers should be prepared to use in all appropriate circumstances. Unfortunately, many evaluation procedures already contain language that restricts the use of any kind of electronic monitoring in the evaluation of personnel. Some decisions from administrative agencies and arbitrators have distinguished between the use of information gathered through electronic surveillance for purposes of evaluation as opposed to disciplinary action taken when employees violate laws (e.g., prohibition of corporal punishment or sexual harassment).

[5] Many times in their efforts to deal with colleagues whose performance is less than satisfactory, supervisors and evaluators fail to communicate the degree of their concern. Requiring the use of specific terminology such as "less than satisfactory" leaves little doubt that the supervisor has concerns regarding the quality of the teacher's performance.

The evaluation instrument and procedure will be distributed to each teacher prior to any evaluation of that teacher. There will be a pre-conference,[6] observation(s), observation report(s), summary evaluation, and evaluation conference. A consistent uniform procedure will be followed for all members of the Bargaining Unit who serve in similar positions. An Evaluation Committee[7] will review and make recommendations to the Superintendent, who will have the final decision on the evaluation instrument and procedures to be used.

Supervision Procedures

The primary goal of the supervision process is to facilitate professional growth.

Tenured Employees   Every tenured employee will participate in a minimum of two Supervision Cycles every other school year. Supervision Cycles will normally occur between October 1st and May 1st.

Nontenured Employees   Nontenured employees will participate in a minimum of two Supervision Cycles each school year. The Supervision Cycles will normally occur between October 1st and June 1st.[8] During the first school year, the supervisor will perform a general assessment of the teacher in relation to all of the criteria set forth in the Evaluation Criteria and, when available, the Job Description. The first Observation Report must be completed by December 15th. The second Observation Report must be completed by May 15th. The second report must contain a recommendation with regard to the reappointment of the nontenured teacher using one of the following options:

Reappointment recommended

Reappointment with tenure recommended

Reappointment not recommended

---

[6] Pre-conferencing should be part of any evaluation procedure, however, contract language should not require that each observation be proceeded by a pre-observation conference. Such a requirement would mean that every observation would have to be a pre-announced observation.

[7] There should be an ongoing committee with participation involving members of the bargaining unit and individuals whose duties involve responsibility for supervision and evaluation. The function of such a committee would be to advise the superintendent regarding any proposed changes in the procedures to be used in evaluating personnel. Unions will often resist such committees and insist upon collective bargaining unless they can designate a majority of the membership of such committees and require that any proposed changes be subject to ratification by the union.

[8] The date for the conclusion of the second supervision cycle and the completion of evaluation reports should coincide with the contractual and statutory deadlines for notifying nontenured personnel about reappointment for the following school year. Many states have statutory deadlines that must be adhered to. The failure to meet such deadlines will usually result in automatic reappointment for the forthcoming school year. See, for example, Mass. Gen. Laws c. 71, s. 41, which specifies that teachers who are serving without professional status who do not receive written notice by June 15th that they will not be reappointed for the forthcoming school year are deemed to have been reappointed. If your district has a collective bargaining agreement or a policy statement that specifies an earlier date than that specified by law, the earlier date is controlling because an employer can always agree to give employees earlier notice than the statute otherwise requires.

Cycles of supervision shall be conducted in accordance with the instruments and procedures set forth in or made a part of this ARTICLE or otherwise agreed to in writing by the supervisor/evaluator and the teacher involved.

All Observation Reports must be signed by the supervisor(s)/evaluator(s) and, at the time of supervisory conference, by the teacher. Said signature in no way indicates anything other than the fact that the teacher has been given a copy of the report. The teacher shall have the right to attach a rebuttal to the Observation Report.

All Observation Reports will be forwarded to the Central Office with the Evaluation Reports completed at the end of the school year.[9] All Observation Reports must indicate whether the performance observed was satisfactory or less than satisfactory.

In the event of a change in assignment (i.e., teaching in a different certification area, courses not taught within the previous three school years, grade level changes of two grades or more at the elementary level, or assignment to a different school building), a tenured teacher may be designated for supervision during that school year.

In the event that the second Supervisory Cycle is rated as "less than satisfactory," then a third Supervisory Cycle of at least thirty (30) school days will be added in that school year or the following school year.

Each supervision cycle will consist of three phases: a pre-conference, data gathering, and preparation of the supervisory report.

Pre-Conference

The supervisor/evaluator and teacher will meet to discuss the cycle including goals, evaluation criteria, and procedures for supervising the teacher's work. Within five (5) school days of the conference in which all or part of a teacher's performance has been rated as "less than satisfactory," the supervisor/evaluator will produce a written improvement plan. The plan will include specific goals and objectives for the cycle, the method(s) for gathering data, and a date for completion of the cycle. At least one cycle will include a classroom visit (sufficient in duration to observe a complete teaching sequence) for classroom teachers and, in the case of non-classroom teachers, a direct observation by the supervisor. If a Supervision Cycle results in a "less than satisfactory" rating, the following cycle must focus on the identified problem(s) and must include direct observation by the supervisor. If the teacher disagrees with any aspect of the plan, the teacher must notify the supervisor in writing within five school days. If the disagreement is not resolved between the teacher and the supervisor within three school days thereafter, the plan and the teacher's objection will be referred to the Superintendent, who will make the final decision as to the content of the plan.[10]

---

[9] The purpose of this language is to ensure that all documentary evidence that supports the judgments made in evaluation reports is available to the employer in the event that a personnel action is challenged.

[10] Whenever an improvement plan is used, there should be an opportunity for the employee involved to participate in its development and acceptance prior to implementation, however, in the event of disagreement, there should be an expeditious resolution procedure. Some contracts call for participation by the union and include expedited mediation and arbitration. In any event, neither the employee nor the union should be able to delay the implementation of an improvement plan.

Data Gathering

The exclusive means of gathering data for observation and evaluation reports are classroom observations, direct observations by the supervisor/evaluator, and other data that have been documented and made a part of the teacher's personnel file.[11] Teachers are encouraged to provide their supervisors/evaluators with any information they would like them to consider in preparing observation/evaluation reports. Observations may be announced or unannounced.

Preparation of the Observation Report

The supervisor/evaluator will prepare a draft Observation Report that has the following parts:

1. Goals, if any, set for the cycle
2. Description of data gathering procedures
3. Report of the data collected
4. Perceptions and judgments, including commendations and recommendations
5. An overall rating of "satisfactory" or "less than satisfactory"
6. Suggestions for growth. Suggestions for professional growth or development should be made for all teachers.
7. All relevant documentation

Teachers will be given a complete copy of any Observation/Evaluation Report(s) normally within seven (7) calendar days following a supervision/evaluation cycle and at least one day before the conference. If the report is not available within seven (7) calendar days, the teacher and the Superintendent will be notified in writing as to the reason(s) why. The teacher and his/her supervisor/evaluator will review the report, and the teacher will sign the report solely for the purpose of acknowledging receipt of a copy. The teacher may submit a rebuttal statement, in which case it will be attached to and become a part of the observation/evaluation report.

The official written reports of each cycle will be kept at the Office of the Superintendent. The teacher will be given a signed copy of the Observation Report.

---

[11] This language enables supervisors and evaluators to use information from sources other than their own first-hand observations. This is essential` if the employer wants to be able to utilize information from sources such as students, parents, or employees who are not supervisory personnel. Because of the limited opportunities that a supervisor has to observe teachers performing their duties, it is important for the evaluator to be able to utilize information from other sources. Fairness also dictates that the teacher should have an opportunity to know what this information is and to comment upon it before it is incorporated into an evaluation report. It is important to note that nonsupervisory personnel are not being relied upon to make judgments about the quality of the teacher's performance. They are, however, being given an opportunity to provide evidence that the supervisor may or may not choose to use in the evaluation process. This is a controversial and sensitive area. Nonetheless, consumers of educational services should have some meaningful way to provide feedback both to teachers and the administrators who are charged with assessing their performance.

Evaluation Procedures

The purpose of evaluation is to improve and assess a teacher's professional competency and to provide a record of facts and assessments for personnel decisions.[12]

Tenured teachers will be placed in an Evaluation Cycle if, following two Supervision Cycles that have been rated "less than satisfactory," the Superintendent determines that the teacher requires evaluation. In such cases, an "Improvement Plan" must be developed.

All Evaluation Reports must be signed by the evaluator(s) and, at the time of the evaluation conference, by the teacher, to acknowledge receipt. A copy of the Evaluation Report will be furnished to the teacher. All Evaluation Reports will be forwarded to the Superintendent's Office no sooner than six (6) school days following the evaluation conference. Each Evaluation Report must include the following parts:

1. Goals set in the "Improvement Plan"
2. Description of the data gathering procedures
3. Report of the data collected
4. Comments and judgments
5. An overall rating of "satisfactory" or "less than satisfactory"
6. A recommendation either to return the teacher to the normal supervisory cycle or to take personnel action
7. Attachments to include any relevant documentation

A teacher may submit a written reply to any evaluation report. Said reply will be attached to the Evaluation Report placed in the teacher's personnel file.

While classroom observation is the primary source of information regarding the performance of a teacher, evaluators are expected to gather information in as many different ways as possible to produce the most complete and accurate record of the teacher's overall performance. These may include conferences with the teacher, the review of materials produced by the teacher and/or students, communications from other teachers, parents, and other persons who provide first-hand information that has a bearing on the teacher's performance and is appropriate to consider in the evaluation process. In all cases, written communications must be shared with the teacher.

Improvement Plan

When a teacher's performance has been rated as "less than satisfactory," by a supervisor in two consecutive Observation Reports, the Superintendent may require that the teacher be placed on an Improvement Plan. Said Improvement Plan shall set forth the specific criteria that must be met, the evaluator's specific expectations, the indicators of satisfactory performance, how the evaluator will assist the teacher, when appropriate, in meeting these expectations,

---

[12] It is important to emphasize that there are two equally important reasons for evaluating personnel. The first is to improve the quality of instruction, and the second is to provide the information necessary to make personnel decisions. Unions will often try to emphasize only the improvement component of the evaluation process while downplaying the personnel decision-making aspect as being punitive in nature.

the time that will be allowed for improvement, and the date by which another Evaluation Report will be completed. Before any Improvement Plan goes into effect, it must be reviewed by the teacher, the Principal, the Superintendent, or the Superintendent's designee, and, at the teacher's election, a union representative. Upon satisfactory completion of an Improvement Plan, the teacher will be returned to the normal cycle of supervision during the next school year.

Following two Observation Reports in which a teacher's overall performance is rated as "unsatisfactory," the Superintendent may withhold a step increase or freeze the salary of a teacher who is on maximum.[13]

The following documents attached to this Article are hereby incorporated and made a part of this Agreement:

Areas of performance: teaching and nonteaching

Evaluation criteria

Profile sheet

Observation report form

Evaluation report form

Improvement plan form

Personnel Files

No derogatory material, including any document specifically addressed to the teacher, shall be placed in a teacher's personnel file without his or her knowledge and unless the "Complaint Procedure" has been followed. This knowledge will be indicated by the teacher's signature affixed to the material being placed in the file. Teachers will have the right to submit a written answer to such material, and this answer shall be reviewed by the Superintendent and attached to the file copy.

The official personnel file for each teacher shall be kept at the Office of the Superintendent of Schools. Other files may be maintained by supervisors and evaluators, however, their contents may not be used for personnel decisions unless the documents have been forwarded to the Office of the Superintendent by October 15th of the school year following the school year in which they were developed or received. The teacher shall have the right to review and to copy the contents of any files that pertain to their work. A teacher may, if he/she wishes, have a representative of the union accompany him/her during such a review. No documents or materials specifically concerning the teacher found or kept in any other place can be used to the detriment of any teacher. The right to review and duplicate files does not extend to confidential recommendations received by the school system prior to a teacher's employment.

With every personnel file there shall be a log sheet. Access to a personnel file by anyone other than Central Office personnel or legal counsel will be recorded on the log sheet by setting forth the date, name of the person reviewing the file, and the reason for access.

---

[13] While clauses such as this often meet with substantial resistance from the union, they are important to consider. They serve two useful purposes. First, they put the teacher on notice regarding the seriousness of the evaluator's concern about the quality of the teacher's performance. Second, it represents the type of progressive discipline that arbitrators look for when asked to review more serious disciplinary action such as suspension or dismissal.

Employee Discipline and Just Cause

The evaluation and supervision procedures do not preclude an administrator from using employee discipline[14] to deal with a situation in which the Superintendent determines that a teacher's actions or behaviors are unacceptable. Progressive discipline will be followed (i.e., oral reprimand, written reprimand, suspension without pay, dismissal), unless the Superintendent determines that the seriousness of the teacher's actions warrants initiating discipline beyond an oral reprimand.

No teacher will be disciplined, reprimanded, dismissed, or reduced in rank or compensation without just cause.[15]

If the supervisor or evaluator intends a conference to be the first step in the process of employee discipline, the supervisor or evaluator must so inform the teacher in advance of the conference and advise the teacher of the right to be accompanied by a representative of the union.[16] The supervisor or evaluator may have other persons present at any meetings and shall notify the teacher as to who the supervisor will have at the meeting.

Evaluation Reports shall be subject to "just cause," but the opinions/judgments of the evaluator are not subject to just cause review. The facts, procedures, the appropriateness of personnel actions taken as a result of the evaluation and the Improvement Plan are subject to review by the arbitrator.

The criteria for determining whether there was "just cause" for employee discipline are as follows:[17]

1. Did the employer give the teacher forewarning or foreknowledge of the possible or probable disciplinary consequences of the teacher's conduct? In cases of dismissal for inefficiency and/or incompetence, did the employer comply with all requirements of the Evaluation Procedure, including the criteria, instrument, and Improvement Plan?

---

[14] Employee discipline applies to circumstances in which a teacher has engaged in inappropriate behavior that rises to the level of insubordination, conduct unbecoming, or criminal activity.

[15] Before agreeing to include a "just cause" standard in your collective bargaining agreement or personnel policy, be certain that you understand its ramifications. Briefly put, the concept of "just cause" allows an arbitrator to substitute his/her judgment for the judgment of the employer in those circumstances in which the employee challenges any personnel action that they grieve. Some states such as Massachusetts have incorporated a just cause standard into those statutes that deal with employee discipline and dismissal. See Mass. Gen. Laws, c. 71, s. 42.

[16] As a result of decisions by the National Labor Relations Board and various state labor relations agencies, employees have been accorded what is often referred to as "Weingarten Rights," i.e., the right to have a union representative present at any meeting which the employee subjectively believes will result in disciplinary action. While the supervisor who is conducting the meeting is not generally required to advise the employee of their Weingarten Rights prior to the meeting, the supervisor must recess the meeting until the employee is given a reasonable period of time to obtain union representation. Said representation need not necessarily involve an attorney. Again, some states, such as Massachusetts, have created an affirmative obligation on the part of a public employer to advise employees of their right to have an attorney present. See Mass. Gen. Laws c. 71, s. 42D.

[17] The following description of the "just cause" standards is but one example based upon the decision of arbitrator Daugherty in Enterprise Wire Company 46 LA 359 (1966). Another example adapted especially to teaching situations is that articulated by arbitrator Archibald Cox in the Needham Case. Cox stated that "just cause" is absent unless three requirements are satisfied: (1) The teacher committed the offense or was guilty of the shortcoming ascribed to him. (2) The misconduct or shortcoming justified the disciplinary measure. (3) The procedure was consistent with fundamental fairness.

2. Was the rule or managerial order reasonably related to (a) the orderly, efficient, and safe operation of the schools and (b) performance that might reasonably be expected of the teacher?

3. Did the employer, before administering discipline to a teacher, make an effort to discover whether the teacher did in fact violate or disobey a rule or order?

4. Was the employer's investigation conducted fairly and objectively?

5. Through the investigation did the employer's representatives obtain substantial evidence or proof that the teacher was guilty as charged?

6. Has the employer applied its rules, orders, and penalties even-handedly and without discrimination to all similarly situated teachers?

7. Was the degree of discipline imposed by the employer in a particular case reasonably related to (a) the seriousness of the teacher's proven offense and (b) the record of the teacher's service with the school system?

It is understood that some conduct does not require forewarning or a detailing of the possible or probable consequences in advance of imposing discipline (e.g., conduct unbecoming a teacher or criminal conduct).

Grievances Involving Supervision, Evaluation, and Discipline

Suspensions pursuant to a criminal indictment shall not be subject to the grievance and arbitration procedure.

The dismissal of a nontenured teacher, prior to the completion of ninety (90) school days, is not subject to the grievance and arbitration procedure.

The failure to renew the contract of a nontenured teacher or failure to renew appointment to a stipended position is not subject to just cause and the grievance or arbitration procedures except as to an allegation that a specific procedure provided for in this Agreement, as opposed to the judgments of the supervisor, evaluator, or Superintendent, has not been followed. In such cases, the arbitrator's award shall be limited to the amount of the stipend or a financial award not to exceed the salary for one school year.

A grievance alleging deviation from the procedures established by this Agreement for the evaluation of a teacher who has not been dismissed may be processed only through Level Three of the grievance procedure and shall not be subject to the arbitration provisions of this Agreement, provided that any denial of said grievance shall be without prejudice to refiling of the grievance in the event that said teacher shall subsequently be dismissed, and provided further that said grievance, if so refiled, shall be subject to the arbitration provisions of this Agreement. The teacher may at his/her discretion file a written notice of an alleged procedural violation within five (5) school days of the event(s) that gives rise to the notice, in lieu of filing a grievance. Said notice will preserve the teacher's right to subsequently file a grievance based upon the same events, provided the teacher has given a copy of said notice to the teacher's principal and the Superintendent.

Evaluation reports shall be subject to just cause, but the opinions/judgments of the evaluator are not subject to just cause review. The facts, procedures, and/or the appropriateness of personnel actions, other than nonrenewal, taken as a result of the evaluation and the Improvement Plan are subject to review by the arbitrator.

Dismissal Procedures

In order to dismiss a tenured teacher for inefficiency and/or incompetency, as opposed to incapacity, conduct unbecoming, insubordination, or other just cause, the following procedures must be followed:

1. The teacher's supervisors and evaluators must follow the requirements of this Article and shall, if they agree, reasonably aid the teacher in removing any substantial constraints that the teacher identifies during supervision or evaluation as obstacles to satisfying the evaluation criteria.

2. The Superintendent must place the teacher in an initial Evaluation Cycle of at least sixty (60) school days from the date of delivery to the teacher of an Improvement Plan following two (2) consecutive Supervision Cycles in which the teacher's performance was rated "less than satisfactory" by the supervisor. In no case shall fewer than sixty (60) school days elapse between the start of the first Supervision Cycle and the end of the second Supervision Cycle. The Improvement Plan must be provided to the teacher within thirty (30) calendar days of the teacher's receipt of an Observation Report for the second Supervision Cycle.

3. An Evaluation Report must be prepared within thirty (30) calendar days of the close of the initial Evaluation Cycle.

4. If the teacher's performance is rated as "satisfactory" at the end of the Evaluation Cycle, the teacher shall be returned to the normal Supervision Cycle during the next school year. If the Evaluation Report rates the teacher's performance as "less than satisfactory," a meeting will be held with the Superintendent, at which time the Improvement Plan will be reviewed and the teacher will receive a written warning that if, following a second evaluation cycle of at least (60) school days, the teacher's performance is still "less than satisfactory" in the areas identified for improvement, the Superintendent will recommend to the Committee that the teacher be dismissed. Two such Evaluation Reports with an overall rating of "less than satisfactory," subject to the provisions of this Agreement, will constitute grounds for dismissal of a tenured teacher.

5. In no event may a tenured teacher be dismissed for inefficiency or incompetence any sooner than 180 school days following the receipt of an Improvement Plan.

8 A Principal Confronts Mediocre Teaching

Good supervision is hard work under the best of circumstances. Supervising a teacher who is performing at a mediocre level is a significant commitment of a supervisor's time and energy. It is some of the most difficult work any supervisor will do in a school setting. The work is intellectually difficult, and it will challenge a supervisor's most fundamental beliefs about teaching and learning. The following case study describes the process of evaluating a mediocre teacher, designing an improvement plan, and tracking the teacher's progress.

I met Brenda during my summer interviews of faculty at my new school. She was a self-described "teacher of literature and woman of ideas." I developed a mental image of Brenda sitting at an outdoor Harvard Square cafe wearing a wrinkled linen dress and a pair of well worn Birkenstocks. She held a collection of Chekov's short stories and sipped Bordeaux from a small glass. Brenda was involved with high school drama, and my image of her was a nice match with her theatrical manner.

Unfortunately, this image started to fade during my first observation of one of her English classes. Sixty minutes into the observation I realized that while Brenda may have been a "woman of literature," she also exhibited clear signs of being an absent-minded professor. There was an unacceptable amount of chaos in her classroom. Brenda's objectives were vague, students were confused and inattentive, there seemed to be no set routines for the operation of the class, and her expectations were not clearly communicated to students. I observed numerous other things in class that left me full of questions. After my first observation of Brenda, I tried to sort these questions into categories I could explore during our post-observation meeting. I was feeling very uneasy and a bit overwhelmed by the realization that this nice woman was exhibiting marginally competent teaching behavior.

I was a new principal in a new school in the first month of classes with a 25-year veteran teacher who appeared to be performing at a mediocre level. She was well liked and overly self-confident. To make matters just a bit more complicated, Brenda had a personnel file six inches thick, stuffed with evalua-

I knew that I could accentuate the positive and ignore the evidence of poor instruction

tions from administrators and department heads who graded her as outstanding and good in all categories of performance. Evaluator comments like "the whole faculty appreciates Brenda's work with the Sunshine Fund and the annual faculty socials she hosts at her home . . . she does so much to positively impact faculty morale . . . she has generously given her free time to assist new teachers" ran throughout her evaluations. Missing from the stacks of evaluations, however, were any comments about consistently good teaching behaviors. It was amazing that although a few "check mark" evaluations categorized Brenda's teaching over the years as acceptable, good, or excellent in several instructional categories, not one of the narrative sections said much about teaching performance.

I could not decide whether to pack my bags and return to northern New England or to bury my head in my other work and pretend that the teaching I had just observed was better than mediocre. I knew that I could accentuate the positive and ignore the evidence of poor instruction. I knew that Brenda was not incompetent and that I could easily let this one go. I was unlikely to get a great deal of grief from parents or the superintendent for letting this one slide. I knew because I had done it before and learned that high school kids did not complain too much about their teachers, at least not to their parents and the superintendent.

I cannot pinpoint when I decided to become a kids' principal. I always liked working with adolescents. Despite all the heartburn and heartache they caused, these thousands of young people brought me great pleasure as both a teacher and an administrator. But I had always tried to be a teachers' principal. I believed that if I worked to provide teachers all the support and resources necessary to teach adolescents, then they would do the right thing by their students. They would spend newly found free time developing new curriculum and new lessons for their students. Or teachers would design new assessment measures that might truly measure how much the kids understood about what was being taught, and they would scrap most of the quick and dirty test measures designed to take little effort and time to correct.

But four or five years into my first high school principalship, it became clear that this was not necessarily true. While many teachers knocked themselves out for kids, some were just doing the minimum and putting in their time. I witnessed situations where administrators and teachers had lobbied successfully to have teaching loads reduced from five to four classes, but the newly won time didn't translate into an obvious benefit for kids. When block schedules were adopted at the secondary level and contractual guarantees of longer prep periods were made at the elementary level, teachers benefited more than students. I entertained serious arguments as to why high school teachers' schedules should allow the freedom to come and go from campus the way their university counterparts did. While such schedule changes were usually initiated with the best of intentions toward students by faculty and administrators, the bulk of this time was eventually spent on reducing teachers' after-school workload instead of increasing the time spent conferencing with students or collaborating with colleagues on interdisciplinary curriculum or improved assessment practices. In the end, teachers applied the additional time to easing the pressures of their everyday workload. Any uses of time that would more directly and specially benefit students were given short shrift.

In the same manner, budget increases implemented to benefit students also became teacher centered. Book money increases were often spent on workbooks and activity books that focused more on task completion than learning.

I cannot pinpoint when I decided to become a kids' principal

An entire decade of technology purchases focused on making the lives of teachers and administrators more efficient rather than orienting the purchases toward improving student performance.

Two small personal experiences may provide a small window into my eventual shift to becoming a kids' principal. The first experience is the story of a 4th grader in rural Vermont, John Harris. John and my son, Zach, were good buddies in 4th grade. John helped Zach figure out mechanical devices like bicycles and lawn mowers and how things in Vermont were a bit different from those in Zach's native Massachusetts. Zach helped John with spelling and math. It was a good match.

John and Zach shared a wonderful teacher for that year. He was a person parents asked to have teach their children. Kids learned a lot in his class, and they had some fun doing it. But even with this skilled teacher, the focus sometimes drifted away from what made sense for students. He and I had been discussing his use of pre-tests with short spelling units. I praised his desire to know where each kid stood prior to teaching the unit. But I was curious about the ending assessment. In the pre-test, John demonstrated mastery of 10 percent of the words he would be learning and Zach knew 90 percent. At the end of the unit, John mastered 55 percent of the words and Zach, 100 percent. John received an F for the unit test and Zach an A, despite the fact that John learned almost five times as many words as Zach over the same period of instruction. When I questioned the teacher about this apparent inequity, he lamented that time and state curriculum frameworks forced him to move on without John (and others like him) having the time to master enough words.

I also experienced something similar in another town in another state where the issue was grading. The discussion boiled down to something quite simple. Should we abandon our traditional grading practice of A through F in favor of a system of A, B, or incomplete (do over)? Teachers overwhelmingly wanted to keep the traditional system despite the apparent benefits of a new practice that would not allow kids to hand in substandard work and be rewarded with a passing grade of C or D through the process of averaging. "The new system would be too darned time consuming, and it would be an organizational nightmare to keep track of all those redos," teachers said in opposition.

In this same time period, I was hearing bits of teacher room conversations about what was "good for teachers." The great national education debate that began with the publication of *A Nation at Risk* and intensified as the national economy went sour in the late 1980s seemed to cause many teachers to go into a self-protective mode and focus solely on what was good for them.

Sometime during the criticism of public schools and competition for diminishing resources in the later 1980s, I came to the conclusion that teachers had the National Education Association and the American Federation of Teachers to lobby and advocate for them, parents had the National Parent Teacher Organization, and my assistants and I had the National Association of Secondary School Principals. I realized my students had no such advocates.

It was at this time that I promised myself that I would be a kids' principal. I committed myself to making sure that certain difficult questions always got asked. How does this benefit students? Would I put my son or daughter in this situation? Is this designed to improve student performance? I decided that it was the principal's job to ensure that these questions got asked and answered. It was the job of the principal to advocate for kids!

The conviction to be a kids' principal seems obvious. After all, isn't public school education for kids, and shouldn't kids be at the center of every decision

How does this benefit students? Would I put my son or daughter in this situation? Is this designed to improve student performance?

made about teaching and learning in the school environment? Well, of course, the welfare of kids should come first in schooling, but in practice that policy is too difficult and too risky. Principals always need the support of faculty, parents, superintendents, and the school board to retain their jobs. Student support is nice but rarely pivotal in the longevity of a principal. The choice of being a kids' principal is not as simple or practical as it may appear. However, keeping a sharp focus on kids is absolutely essential for the improvement of student performance. "The reality is," says Robert Fraser, attorney and coauthor of this book, "that the only thing that stands between a kid and an incompetent or mediocre teacher is the evaluator."

In Chapter 2 we talk about the importance of the three C's when confronting mediocre teaching (competence, conviction, and control). It is essential that a principal has the supervisory competence to manage the complicated task of remediating mediocre instruction.

The principal must also have the administrative control necessary to take on this challenge. Micromanaging school boards and superintendents can easily derail such an effort. The most important component of the three C's model is that of conviction. A principal who does not believe that students are the focus of what he or she does or who does not hold the conviction that student learning is the single most important thing a school does will not be able to take on the challenge of mediocre teaching. Confronting mediocre teaching is so time consuming, so intellectually challenging, and so threatening to many established and accepted school practices that only principals who are truly convinced that student learning should be their primary goal will take on the challenge.

My apologies for the digression on conviction, but it was within this context that I decided several years ago to take on the challenge of Brenda's mediocre teaching. It was a much greater challenge than I expected. Ultimately, the experience has been rewarding for both Brenda and for me; mostly because time and effort has paid off for both of us. Many others, too numerous to name, have contributed to this success.

LEGAL NOTE

All personnel who supervise and/or evaluate teachers should be certified and qualified for that work. This involves appropriate academic preparation in educational administration and subject matter pedagogy, as well as subject matter expertise. Ideally, the supervisor should have certification or a substantial amount of academic preparation in the subject matter that the supervisee is teaching. If a supervisor does not have expertise in a teacher's subject area, then he or she should have substantial academic work in that subject, e.g., English, calculus, physics, history, etc. Alternatively, the supervisor should consult with someone who has relevant subject matter expertise. Supervisory training should be ongoing, with constant updating in legal and contractual requirements for the school district's evaluation procedures. Some states and/or contract language specify that the employers must conduct training for all supervisors before the employees can be evaluated. This may also be required by state law and/or regulations.

The Improvement Process

Toward the conclusion of one of the education reform movement's first books published after *Nation at Risk*, Ted Sizer concludes, "The visitor to schools repeatedly looks for signs of good quality and patterns that promise success. Inescapably, they point to the teachers . . . an imaginative, appropriate curriculum placed in an attractive setting can be unwittingly smothered by journeymen instructors. It will be eviscerated by incompetents. On the other hand, good teachers can inspire powerful learning in adolescents even in the most difficult circumstances" (Sizer 1984, p. 180).

In Brenda I knew I had a teacher stuck somewhere between incompetent and skillful. The authors call this the land of mediocrity. My job as principal and evaluator was to follow up my "gut reaction" from my first observation of Brenda with a much more detailed assessment of her teaching. If, in fact, I needed to confront a 25-year veteran teacher, I needed data to support my conclusion. Data collection began at our first post-observation conference.

Our first meeting was awkward. We did not really know each other or what to expect from each other. I did not want to come off as too critical, and Brenda was nervous in anticipation of my critique of her teaching. I began our meeting by asking Brenda what she had wanted to accomplish in the class I observed and how she thought it went. She responded by saying that she wanted the kids to work in groups, do a collage on personality types, and start *Catcher in the Rye*. She thought it went pretty well with the exception that several students were whining about grades. Brenda's response to my questions gave me considerable insight into the scope of the problem. Her response also started to give me data about the quality of her teaching and of her thinking about her teaching.

Our conversation about this class indicated that Brenda's thinking ended with the expectation that her students would complete the activity of doing a collage representing certain personality types. The focus on activity superseded serious consideration of other expectations for student learning. For example, what were the roles that individuals in the small groups were supposed to perform, what things would the students know or be able to do as a result of the collage activity, and how would Brenda know (assess) how well the students learned those things she wanted them to learn?

Although Brenda identified that student whining detracted from the class, she failed to identify what teaching behaviors might have contributed to some of the whining. Consider the following exchange between Brenda and some of her students, "People who want some extra credit can do poetry tomorrow." "How much is it worth, Mrs. Smith?" "I'm not sure, Amy." "Well, what else are we doing tomorrow?" "I have not decided yet." "Mrs. Smith, it would help me decide about the poetry if I knew how much it would count! When are we getting our last extra credit assignment back, the one we handed in two weeks ago?" "Can we still hand in the last extra credit thing?" "Yes, Courtney, but I'm not sure how much it will be worth."

This brief exchange indicated some possible reasons for the whining from students: the lack of explicitness about what "doing poetry" meant, what value this assignment might contribute to a student's average, and what were the

The focus on activity superseded serious consideration of other expectations for student learning

expectations about the timelines of assigned work. In addition, it raised questions about the promptness of Mrs. Smith's feedback to students on their written work and other questions about planning and organization.

When I asked Brenda specific questions about her objectives in the collage lesson, she could describe a goal for students to learn about a commonly accepted variety of personality types and to understand that writers frequently drew upon these types when developing characters in a book. I asked Brenda if she thought the students were aware of these objectives. She was reasonably sure that they were aware. I was more sure that they were not because I had asked five different students during class, "What is the purpose of the collage?" Their responses uniformly identified "doing collages of famous people" or "I'm not sure."

Our first post-observation conference ended with Brenda's lament that I obviously did not see anything good in her teaching. I responded defensively by reminding her of several positives I had mentioned. In fact, I was relieved that the bell had rung and Brenda was off to a class.

The remainder of our first year together consisted of my alternating between collecting data (evidence) about Brenda's performance and wondering if I really wanted to take on what was beginning to look like a huge challenge. Brenda was beginning to complain within earshot of her colleagues in the teacher's lounge. Although presumably some teachers knew of her shortcomings, they were not going to confront her. It was easier for them to circle the wagons to support her, focusing more on her kindness and generosity toward them than the effectiveness of her teaching.

My assistant principals were helpful in gathering some of the data I needed to support my view that Brenda needed some serious improvement in her teaching. Brainstorming ideas and data sources about Brenda's teaching became a regular part of our weekly meetings. From these meetings I got great ideas about information sources outside Brenda's classroom that might speak to her effectiveness (progress reports, discipline referrals, grade distributions, attendance patterns, parent requests for changes out of her classes, and teacher/student loads within her department).[1] In addition, my assistants, all of whom had evaluative responsibilities, could provide the moral support and understanding to help me stick with it. And while our regular conversations about teaching and learning were helpful to all of us, it was their ongoing moral support and observational expertise that would prove invaluable in analyzing Brenda's teaching and prescribing some approaches to improvement.

As spring arrived, it was time for me to stop collecting data about Brenda and to put together an overall summary of Brenda's teaching. I needed to write a final evaluation that would describe the situation, diagnose the problems, and finally design a plan for the next year. Because I had already decided to recycle Brenda back into another evaluation year and because the end-of-the-

---

LEGAL NOTE

Whenever a supervisor is dealing with a situation in which a teacher's performance is unsatisfactory, it is always desirable to involve other supervisory personnel in the process. "The school district's evaluation procedures are a model of how a professional employee should be rated. The evaluations occur at two levels. At the first level is the principal; if he rates a professional employee unsatisfactorily, the matter is referred to the second level, the superintendent, for further evaluation. While a teacher might object to being rated so often in a short period of time by different persons, such a procedure is clearly in the employee's best interest since it brings into the evaluation different viewpoints thereby lessening the influence personal bias can have … with respect to teaching methods." *Rosso v. Bd. of School Directors*, 380 A.2d 1328 (Penn. 1977).

---

year administrative tasks were consuming large chunks of my time, I postponed designing the improvement plan until the fall (in Chapter 5 we recommend separating the development of the improvement plan from the final evaluation). This turned out to be a wise decision because communication between Brenda and me was about to come to a standstill.

I wrote a final evaluation that I thought was carefully crafted to provide a balanced description of Brenda's teaching for the year. I was very conscious of walking between the errors of leniency and severity (see Chapter 4). I did find positive occurrences to mention in the beginning of the evaluation. My assistants thought my description overemphasized the positive. Brenda's department chairperson, with whom I shared a draft, thought it was devastatingly negative. I guessed that I had just the right balance given these two contradictory reactions. I tried to focus my criticisms on several key areas so that neither the evaluation nor next year's plan for improvement would be overwhelming. I concentrated on planning and organization, expectations for student performance, and objectives for thinking and learning. I decided that addressing these three critical areas of concern would be necessary and sufficient for the following year's improvement plan. I was not prepared for Brenda's response to what I had written.

Brenda broke the awkward silence at the beginning of our final evaluation conference by saying, "I have thought long and hard about all the negative things that you have said about my teaching. Since my previous principals have always concluded that I was either good or excellent over the years and you have found nothing good to say about me, I have concluded that you simply do not understand me. You have no idea of who I am philosophically, psychologically, or intellectually. So, I would like to use this time today to talk about who I am so that you will finally understand why the things I do in my classroom are good and when things went wrong, you'll understand that was because kids just are not what they used to be."

I sat in stunned silence for about 30 minutes while Brenda rambled through everything from the beliefs of Thomas Dewey to the personality and leadership theories of Myers and Briggs and Hersey and Blanchard. She concluded her comments by claiming that we were such total opposites that I might never appreciate what a truly good teacher she was and that she, therefore, felt it necessary to write a rebuttal to my evaluation. Unable to recover in

---

[1]Chapter 4, which introduces the 3-D framework, gives a detailed list of data sources to assist a supervisor who is trying to complete a comprehensive assessment of a teacher's performance.

time from Brenda's unexpected monologue, I mumbled a few questions like, "Was there anything in the evaluation that you did not understand?" The passing bell sounded, and Brenda excused herself to go teach a class. I was simultaneously relieved that the meeting was over and sick that I had failed to communicate the central message about her mediocre teaching and the critical need for improvement.

I grew increasingly annoyed with myself as the day went on. I had lost my courage by the middle of Brenda's rebuttal. I got sucked into responding emotionally to the situation rather than responding with all of the data I had collected throughout the year that suggested this entire situation was about mediocre teaching (and some pretty mediocre conferencing on my part) and not about misunderstanding.

I held another meeting with Brenda the following day. I decided that the simple and direct approach was best given the emotional nature of the previous meeting. I informed Brenda that I thought that we had an almost insurmountable problem between us. She thought the problem was that I did not understand or appreciate her. I thought that the problem was that her teaching was mediocre. And to make matters worse, if she did not think that she was part of the problem then she could not very well respond with any changes that would improve the situation. Consequently, I ended the meeting by concluding that if she were not able or willing to see the problems with her teaching and therefore would not change some of her instructional practices, that I would remain dissatisfied and would have to fire her. I promised to work with her if she were willing to make the effort to improve and to do whatever I had to do to dismiss her if she did not want to make the effort.

Our meetings had come around the end of the school year (as late as I could put them off, I think). The consequences of these two meetings would now occupy me for a significant part of the next two years.

 ## Designing the Plan

The summer provided a welcome relief from the tension of my supervision of Brenda. It also gave me some time to reflect upon what had happened and to plan for the upcoming year's improvement plan. Summer also provided a generous opportunity to discuss and plan strategies with my assistants.

A request that summer from Brenda to have her evaluator changed was promptly refused by the superintendent. However, the request gave me an idea that I thought might help Brenda buy into my supervision plan. I decided to begin the new school year by offering Brenda the opportunity to invite any trained evaluator in the district (approximately 20 had similar training in "Observing and Analyzing Teaching" courses by Research for Better Teaching) to observe several of her classes in September and early October. Brenda could pick the person. I proposed that if the guest evaluator identified in the observations any of the problem areas that I diagnosed previously, Brenda would fully cooperate with an improvement plan. If the guest evaluator did not identify problems or concerns in the areas of planning/organization, expectations, and objectives about the level of thinking skills, then I would back off from the improvement plan.

This strategy worked beautifully. Brenda picked a long-time administrator whom she trusted and respected. My faith in our administrative team's training and skills paid off when the guest evaluator's observations revealed problems not only in the same three areas that I had diagnosed, but in several of the areas I had been chastised by my assistants for downplaying. Brenda now accepted the idea that she was part of the problem and worked to participate in an improvement plan that would lead to better instruction for kids! The key element of this strategy was that it forced Brenda to take ownership of the problem. (See Chapter 6 for more about ownership issues.)

In their study, *Bringing About the Best in Teachers* (Blase and Kirby 1992, pp. 77–88) the authors discuss the effectiveness of suggestion versus direction when working with most teachers in most situations. In a section on "Knowing When to Push and When to Nudge," they note, "Effective principals do not hesitate to give specific, direct instructions during crises." I felt that the situation with Brenda was critical enough that I needed to be very directive and not very collaborative in the development of her improvement plan. I did, however, leave some room for Brenda's input to help foster her ownership of the plan. I designed a plan that required Brenda to do the following:

- Achieve professional development in identified problem areas
- Prepare written, detailed lesson plans for each meeting of each class with specific objectives for what students would know and be able to do
- Focus on higher objectives for thinking skills
- Focus on establishing and communicating clear and appropriate expectations for student performance

While I was more directive in developing this plan than I normally prefer to be, I did allow Brenda to shape enough of the requirements of the improvement plan to feel that she was a part of it. For example, she was able to choose her professional development opportunities. Brenda asked if she could write broad, weekly lesson plans for her classes and then do individual, detailed plans for the day of the class meeting that she would share with students via an overhead or handout. I agreed to these suggestions. Brenda's input resulted in improved plan requirements and her feeling that she contributed to the development of her improvement plan.

The improvement process took two years. In the beginning, it consumed significant amounts of my time (and Brenda's). I gave detailed, written or verbal feedback on the first detailed lesson plans. In some cases, we spent hours reworking Brenda's objectives about student thinking from statements like: "students will note the theme of prejudice in *The Merchant of Venice*, consider a few lines of the play, examine several works of art from the period, and recall two different styles of writing." Eventually, it became easier for her to push her thinking objectives to higher levels. This same lesson transformed might have evolved to: "students will define prejudice and describe how prejudice affects Shylock in *The Merchant of Venice*," or "students will identify two paintings from the time and setting of *The Merchant of Venice*, describe how the paintings depict Venetian society, and compare or contrast that portrayal to Shakespeare's descriptions in *The Merchant of Venice*."

Brenda's input resulted in improved plan requirements and her feeling that she contributed to the development of her improvement plan

"Collaboration can be a powerful force for improvement."

Many good teaching behaviors are generic and therefore applicable across department lines, and no supervisor can be expected to know the content details of every discipline. When instructional problems are evident in a teacher whose subject area is one of particular weakness for the supervisor, however, high-quality supervision can be difficult. If Brenda had been teaching German, my ignorance of the language would have presented just such a problem. In situations where content expertise is perceived, either by the teacher or supervisor, to be a problem, I suggest collaborating with another supervisor (department chair or assistant principal) who is more knowledgeable in the subject. The collaboration among three individuals can be a powerful force for improvement.

Another strategy I used was to have Brenda provide examples from her lessons of how she incorporated newly learned instructional strategies from professional development opportunities into her day-to-day teaching. My constant expectation in this area reinforced the notion that professional development was not a spectator sport. Brenda's experimentation with instructional strategies was something she and I routinely discussed in each pre- and post-observation conference. She learned that it was okay to try and then discard strategies if they did not fit a learning situation. Brenda began to see positive results from her new efforts to improve. The tone of her classes changed from somewhat chaotic and whiny to more focused and cooperative. Kids seemed to know at all times what they were doing and why. Expectations about when things were due and how much they were worth were more clearly communicated and understood. Brenda's classes were better, and Brenda was much more satisfied with herself. Brenda's effort was paying dividends.

Outside of the obvious benefits to Brenda and her students, the school grapevine was beginning to pick up some interesting opinion shifts. While some faculty crabbiness persisted about, "They're out to get the senior faculty," and, "After 25 years, why aren't they happy with Brenda's teaching?" The conversation was beginning to come around to, "Well, it really is about time someone got Brenda on the stick; she was kind of an embarrassment to the department" and "I guess it is time to take the evaluation process seriously." High-performing teachers were quietly taking pride in the fact that not everyone was graded excellent on their evaluations in every category all the time. Good feedback from evaluators and good conversation and reflection about teaching and learning between teachers and evaluators was beginning to permeate the atmosphere of the school.

An Afterthought

After three years of working with Brenda to help her improve her teaching from mediocre to effective, I was feeling cautiously smug about having "fixed" the problem. Within a year, however, some symptoms of mediocrity in Brenda's teaching were beginning to reappear. After almost a two-year absence, "cranky" behavior referrals from Brenda were showing up on my assistants' desks. Parent and student complaints about a variety of teaching issues went from nonexistant to occasional. It appeared that once outside the direct supervision of our improvement plan cycle, Brenda relaxed and started to slide back into a pattern of pedagogical laziness that would eventually bring her right back down to where we began four years earlier. Consequently, I increased the number of formal and informal visits to Brenda's classroom and reinstituted the practices of regular pre- and post-observation conferences.

Good teaching and good supervision are hard, time-consuming work. Self-satisfied after three, long years of supervision and improvement, both Brenda and I got lazy. Our reduced effort resulted in Brenda's students being short-changed once again. We are both back on track now. We now know that there needs to be constant attention to "staying in shape" intellectually for teaching and learning just as an athlete must stay in shape. We realized we could not simply get in shape and then stop working out.

Organizational Support for Brenda's Improvement

Cases such as Brenda's challenge the organization's capacity to confront mediocrity as much as that of the individual supervisor. Principal lore is full of cautionary tales about the fate of those who seek to take on entrenched veterans. Here, the district's leaders had established several essential institutional conditions to support the principal's efforts.

Control

- Contract provisions allowed multiple observers and observations, multiple sources of data, the opportunity for pre-and post-conferences, and the supervisor's requirement that the teacher set and report on her goals.

- When "end runs" were attempted, the superintendent supported and reinforced the principal's authority and protected his work from outside interference.

Competence

- Evaluators within the school had sufficient background and training to be able to analyze the import of what was happening in the classroom and help the teacher determine what strategies and actions helped or hindered student learning.

- Evaluators in the district had received the same training, were working with a common language and concept system, and had reasonably consistent standards for performance. Thus the principal trusted that his colleagues could provide a fair and credible second opinion.

Conviction

- Key members of the organization, ranging from the superintendent to the assistant principals, shared a belief system that said (1) the work of getting Brenda to change was important; (2) given adequate support, clear goals, and focused feedback Brenda could reasonably be expected to improve; and (3) when the situation became tense, it was not okay to give up.

- Regular communication about difficult cases among supervisors, primary evaluators, and the central office built common purpose and allowed evaluators to take advantage of one another's expertise. It also enabled evaluators and supervisors to practice writing, conferencing, and coaching skills. Regular practice and communication helped administrators to deal effectively with challenges such as Brenda's request for a different evaluator and to support one another during difficult stretches. In this case, the supervisor was part of a culture that demanded and supported raising teacher performance. The message was clear: children deserve competent teachers, and "just okay" is not good enough.

9 Preventing and Detecting Mediocrity in New Teachers

Won't all the thousands of new teachers cure the problem of mediocre teaching? After all, those teachers will bring to the profession enthusiasm and, in many cases, current knowledge in areas such as computer technology and brain theory learning. (New England district administrator)

There is no doubt that new teachers will give our schools renewed vitality, but we cannot assume an influx of youth will mean excellent teaching for all students. As the "kids" replace the veterans, confronting mediocrity brings special challenges. First, along with mediocre performers, many talented teachers will be retiring, taking with them a storehouse of rich experiential knowledge. Most schools have not yet set up structures to transfer that knowledge to the new teachers. Second, there are already teacher shortages that will cause limited applicant pools. Finally, will we be successful in retaining good new teachers in light of the sometimes discouraging conditions and competition from better paying professions? Urban districts and lower paying regions will have to settle for second or third choice candidates and are already being forced to implement the unpromising practice of hiring uncertified teachers. As a result, districts will have to grow teachers, not just select them. Will leaders have the additional time and energy to develop their teachers in light of their often heavy workloads?

Even as we worry about these challenges, however, we celebrate an opportunity to create new high performance learning cultures with these enthusiastic new teachers. We may have more influence on these new recruits. While most of this book has focused on confronting mediocrity among veteran teachers, we now shift our attention to new teachers and the special challenges and opportunities that they bring to our schools. Leaders need to do three things to prepare for the influx of new teachers:

1. Select the best possible candidates.
2. Prepare the institution to nourish, grow, and retain new teachers.

3. Look for early signs of mediocrity and release teachers if certain competence and convictions are not in place after two years.

Selecting the Best Candidates

There are only two ways to improve your school. One is to improve the teachers you have. The other is to hire better ones. . . It is much easier to hire a good teacher than to fire a bad one. (Whitaker 1999, p. 117)

We can increase our hiring accuracy by screening candidates for certain skills and beliefs that are good predictors of success. Because of the increasing teacher shortage in certain regions and disciplines and the growing prevalence of alternative licensing programs, the hiring process becomes critical in predicting candidates who have growth potential. Here are a dozen ideas to help guide the selection process.

Candidates should have a solid knowledge of their subject matter and should be constant learners in their field.

If we are going to expect teachers to teach to high standards, they should have a rigorous academic background. Many teachers have not experienced a rigorous academic curriculum with a strong academic major or graduate program. They should also demonstrate that they are constant learners within their specialty areas. To assess ongoing learning, interviewers should probe for evidence of independent learning beyond the formal classroom.

Suggested Interview Questions: "Tell me about a rigorous and demanding course you have taken and what you learned about yourself as a learner. How do you keep current in your area of specialty? Describe how you intend to become a lifelong learning role model for your students."

Candidates should have a good overall academic record but may have experienced some low grades.

An experienced Vermont principal has a formula that has resulted in an enviable recruiting record. She hires teachers with good academic records, but she seeks out those with one or two low grades. She claims these people make better teachers because they have had to struggle and can better empathize with students. She will never hire a teacher with a poor overall record. We want to leave room for some candidates with a mixed record but would discourage anyone being hired with a GPA of less than 2.75.

Another source of information is test scores. While success is not defined nor predicted by a high score on a single test such as a state teacher test, tests add to the pool of information about a candidate. Discipline-based tests such as in mathematics can be very helpful. We would be concerned about hiring a candidate who barely passes a subject matter test. (Georgia and Tennessee, for example, allow 50% to be the passing score in mathematics. Source: *USA Today*, June 8, 1999). Some studies have shown "the verbal ability of teachers as measured in their standardized test scores is positively related to their students' test scores" (Latham p. 24).

Sample Interview Question: "Describe your most frustrating academic experience and what you discovered about yourself as a learner."

Candidates should like students and care deeply about children as learners.

Teachers often "love kids," but are they equally passionate about what or how the students are learning? Can they motivate students to achieve at high standards of performance? Loving kids is important but not enough.

Sample Interview Questions: "Describe how you will convert your love of children into helping them achieve at high levels of performance. What does it take to get an A in your classroom? How would your students describe you? How would you like your students to describe you?"

Candidates should be able to write concisely and quickly.

Writing is linked to thinking and planning. Every candidate should be asked to provide a timed writing sample on site. Provide a computer if requested. Do not judge handwriting. Several of the authors would not have received their first teaching jobs if handwriting had been a major selection criterion.

Sample Interview Questions: Invite candidates 30 minutes early to the interview. Give them a question to respond to in writing such as: "Identify a situation from your most recent experience (job or university) that you thought needed to be improved. How did you go about it? Were you successful? What did you learn?"

Candidates should be able to be able to describe management routines that they would implement.

No one expects new teachers to have a complete repertoire of discipline strategies. However, especially in certain settings, having management skill becomes crucial to survival. New teachers will need on the job training in dealing with difficult discipline cases, but they should have thought through some basic organizational issues.

Sample Interview Questions: "Describe your routine for passing in papers. For students entering class? For making up missed work? How would you handle a difficult student who continually interrupts the class?" (See one principal's method for assessing this skill in the next section.)

Candidates should have a variety of interests.

Studies have shown that excellent teachers usually have many areas of interest outside the school. For example, they are very active in church, or in scouts, pursue hobbies, or enjoy travel. These out of school interests provide outlets and growth opportunities as well as breeding grounds for new ideas. Having a variety of interests is also a predictor of the ability to manage multiple demands on time.

Sample Interview Question: "Tell me about a hobby or interest outside education and how that hobby or interest plays a role in your personal growth."

Candidates should be flexible.

There will be many demands for change during a teacher's career. Interviewers should probe to see whether change causes undue stress and how the candidates have adapted to changes in their lives. Look for substantive anecdotal data rather than platitudes. Probe what adds stress to their lives and how they handle stress.

Sample Interview Question: "Tell about your most difficult personal or professional situation and how you coped with the situation. What did you learn about your strengths and weaknesses and how you cope with stress?"

Candidates should be responsive to feedback.

Candidates may tell an interviewer they are open to feedback, but can they give a recent example of when they received and acted on feedback? The presence of this quality is a good predictor of growth potential; the absence of this quality is a strong predictor of mediocrity.

Sample Interview Question: "Give an example of seeking and/or receiving critical feedback and your response to this feedback."

Candidates should be able to think and respond quickly but also reflectively.

Interviews are often conversations that may reveal aspects of personality and on the spot articulation. We suggest that two or three thought questions perhaps on flexibility, risk taking, or response to stress be posed in writing, with the candidate being given 5 minutes of preparation time followed by a presentation of answers. This could be a break time for the interviewer.

Sample Interview question: "Take 5 minutes to jot down some thoughts about the three most important qualities you will bring to this job and areas of support you will need from the district. Be prepared to present a 2 to 3 minute verbal response."

Candidates should be able to participate on a team.

This does not mean they should have been a council president or a team captain, although these are promising indicators. Rather it means they bring some collaboration skills to their job. We need people who are willing to assume and share leadership and to be followers. However, there are occasional noncollaborating individuals who are magnificent in the classroom. Collaboration is still secondary to classroom instruction.

Sample Interview Questions: "Do you consider yourself a team player? Describe yourself as a leader and/or team member. Be specific about times you have assumed leadership or played a role on a team of any kind."

Candidates should be able to articulate how they will communicate with parents and how they would deal with difficult parents.

It is important for novice teachers to be able to handle situations but also to know when to ask for assistance from the administrator.

Sample Interview Questions: "What three things would you tell parents at back to school night? Assume a parent is very upset and criticizing you for the workload, which is too difficult for her Molly. How would you handle this situation? How would you decide when to use an administrator as a resource for dealing with a difficult student? A difficult parent?"

Candidates should be able to make modifications for special education students and for students with learning challenges.

Inclusion and integration skills are crucial to assess during the hiring process.

Sample Interview Questions: "Ask candidates to bring three artifacts that give insight into how they think about their teaching. Suggestions include unit plans, project expectations, and tests or student products. Using any material, please describe a unit when you modified curriculum to adjust to auditory, visual, and kinesthetic learners. How might you modify a test for a student on an Individualized Educational Plan with severe writing difficulty?"

Candidates should be asked either to teach a class or provide a video of their teaching.

We believe that a video may provide better data because it captures work with students in their own setting. Studies of expert teachers reveal that knowledge of the students is crucial to skillful teaching (Berliner 1986).

Sample Interview Question: (After showing a video or teaching a demonstration lesson) "What are your reflections and insights about the class?"

LEGAL NOTE

Be skeptical about references. In the current legal climate, references should be interpreted cautiously. We know of many teachers who are passed on with glowing recommendations. They often result from implicit deals "I'll give you a recommendation if you give me your resignation."

A teacher who was not renewed after two years rewrote a cool reference from his principal by cutting and pasting new language into the body of the letter.

Give credence only to superlative references, but even then be careful.

Selecting the Best High School Teachers

Michael Fung, Headmaster of Charlestown High School, Boston, Massachusetts, has compiled an enviable record of hiring talented new teachers over the past few years.

He has developed interview questions that cover five areas:

1. Teacher's fundamental belief system
2. Teacher as lifelong learner
3. Content knowledge
4. Instructional skills
5. Classroom management skills

He uses five stem interview questions to get at these five areas and then asks follow-up questions.

Teacher's Fundamental Belief System

Interview Question: "Using the *American Heritage Dictionary*, please look up the definitions of the word "teach." The dictionary gives six different definitions. Take a few minutes to look them over and comment on each of them. There are no right answers or wrong answers, but please tell us which of the definitions is most consistent with your belief system."

Fung's Observations: "This past year I have interviewed more than 40 teachers. The large majority chose the fourth definition: to cause to learn by example or experience. Only one chose the first definition: to impart knowledge. I use this question (and sometimes some follow-up questions) to find out two things: first in terms of teaching, what does the teacher believe in? Second how articulate is the teacher? How well can she or he organize his or her thoughts without preparation time?"

Teacher as Lifelong Learner

Interview Question: "Can you describe a book in your field (for example, in mathematics) that you read in the past two years? Tell me what you think of it."

Fung's Observations: "I use this question to discover whether the teacher is a lifelong learner and keeps up with the latest developments in the field. One would think that this is a simple, easy-to-answer question. In reality, a large majority of the candidates cannot name a book in their chosen field. One math teacher said that he had not read any math book in the last six years. Nevertheless, his resume contained a full page of staff development workshops he has attended during those years. I did not hire him, but someone else did."

Content Knowledge

The candidate is given three to five questions in writing. They are asked to respond either orally or in writing, except that English candidates must answer the question in writing. Here is one sample with an interesting twist.

Written Question: Please comment about the prose style of this passage. If this were a Massachusetts Comprehensive Assessment System (MCAS) 10th grade writing sample, how would you grade it? Justify your judgment.

Interview Question: The following passage is taken from a recent report on high school restructuring.

The preceding reframing of pedagogical practice forced teachers to shift the ways in which they viewed and assessed their students. The implementation of common planning time engendered a more holistic view of individuals and gave rise to a reformed rubric, rendering "one teacher/one grade" obsolete. Team teaching quickly expanded to include team grading. Student work was scrutinized daily through a myriad of lenses. Cross-unit objectives maintained a thread of cohesion despite disparate disciplines, emphasizing critical thinking skills along with improvement in writing and communication. The increased contact teachers had with one another enabled them to develop deeper insight into each student's strengths and weaknesses. Trouble spots, such as difficulties in reading and math, were noted more efficiently.

Fung's Observations: "This passage was included in a report on high school restructuring. In my view, it could only be interpreted as a parody of the 'high institutional' style of writing that appears frequently in educational journals— what might be referred to as 'edubabble.'"

NOTE In the future Mr. Fung is considering including some actual samples from students to evaluate teachers' assessment skills in the content area of writing. He believes that knowledge of assessment is integrally connected to content knowledge.

Instructional Skills

"One of the most difficult tasks a teacher has to face is to anticipate conceptual confusion or conceptual difficulties on the part of students. I then give a few examples of confusion: the Underground Railroad is not the subway, oxymoron is not an insult, and so on. Sometimes the term "targets of difficulties" is mentioned. An example of conceptual difficulties in history would be the concept of B.C. and A.D. (now common era). In physics, an example would be the concept of a heavier object dropping to the ground at the same speed as a lighter one, and not any faster."

Interview Question: "Let me give you an example of anticipating misconceptions in math. For example, $1/2$ plus $1/3$ cannot be equal to $2/5$, a very common error, (demonstrate by using block diagrams to show students that $1/2$ is larger than $2/5$). Now, in your lessons can you give me an example of conceptual difficulties that your students might encounter? How do you help your students overcome these conceptual difficulties?"

Fung's Observations: "Most candidates have a problem with this question. Apparently very few have been taught to anticipate conceptual difficulties in their lesson planning. A few were able to give an example, usually with a reasonably good solution. Those individuals inevitably turned out to be good teachers. All the candidates thought that this was a good question to ask. Several said that they had learned a lot from this line of questioning."

Classroom Management Skills

I call this the "toughness question," although on the surface it seems nothing more than a question on classroom management. Basically, I present a situation to the candidate and ask a question. Before the candidate can complete the answer, I interrupt and present an escalating situation.

The interview often goes like this:

Interviewer: "Suppose you were teaching a class, and a student just stood up and walked around, what would you do?"

Candidate: "I would ask him to go back to his assigned seat."

Interviewer: "But the student not only refused to sit down, but he said 'Make me!' right in front of the class."

Candidate gives an answer, but before she finishes her sentence . . .

Interviewer: "But instead of saying 'Make me!' he said 'Make me you f__ing bitch!' Now the whole class was watching, what would you do?"

Candidate tried to give another answer. Again, before she could complete her all her statements . . .

Interviewer: "But the intercom was not working, and the student you wanted to send for help was just standing there. Now the whole class was laughing. What would you do?" And so on, and so on.

Fung's Observations: "With over a hundred interviews, I have discovered that the teachers who cannot give more than one or two answers inevitably had serious classroom management problems. (Typically, after one answer: 'I'd send the kid to the headmaster's office.' Slightly better, but not much: 'Oh, this never happened to me!') Those who could give five or six answers usually turned out to be exceptionally good teachers. The best were the ones who first presented their 'guiding principles,' and then provided answers based on those principles. A couple of exceptional candidates were even able to slow me down so that they were not interrupted as much."

"It is not difficult to understand how and why this approach works. Teachers who can provide four or five answers have spent time thinking how they should manage their classes. Moreover, they are committed to dealing with their own problems. As a consequence of this commitment, they become better teachers along the way through observation of their colleagues, studying the literature on the subject, or through their own reflection and self-examination. On the other hand, those who give up after one or two answers are usually the ones who habitually pass their problems to others, so they never quite learn how to handle the learning issues of their students, whether they be disciplinary or instructional."

CAUTION   Mr. Fung reports several embarrassing moments with long periods of silence. He has made it a rule to explain to the candidates after the interview why the interview questions are presented in that manner, and that the interruptions are deliberate. This technique might be disconcerting to teachers during an interview, especially for a complete novice who might not yet have had a chance to develop the experience-based repertoire.

After the tough interview and selection process, Michael Fung immediately begins a development program. He believes that new teachers learn from taking risks with support. Let's examine how leaders can prepare the institution to nurture new teachers.

Institutional Practices

Preparing the Institution

Leaders must adopt institutional practices that nourish new teachers. The good news is that the enthusiastic newcomers may themselves be both the beneficiaries and the resources for building growth-sustaining schools. They are likely to be receptive to new collegial practices that should start the day that they are hired. Creating favorable conditions will not only help retain good teachers but will serve to attract better candidates.

Hold a multi-day new teacher orientation.

Every college in this country provides new students with a multi-day orientation that consists of survival training and introduction to the values of the institution. Association and district administrators should take note and negotiate language that would permit a substantial orientation program in place of the "Hello, here are the keys, welcome."

Establish formal mentoring and induction programs.

Some states have mandated some form of induction programs; even if they are not mandated, organizations need to develop strong novice support programs. Districts could hire recent retirees to serve as mentors on a consultant basis. But some new teachers might benefit more from interactions with younger staff. Perhaps teachers in their 30s who are competent and who remember what it is like to be a new teacher could be paid a coaching stipend. Money should be allocated from the rollover surplus resulting from replacing veteran teachers with low salaried teachers. A good first reference is ASCD's network on mentoring (www.mentors.net) or the May 1999 edition of *Educational Leadership* with the theme "Supporting New Teachers."

Establish a regular support network for new teachers.

Novice teachers should meet biweekly, preferably with two experienced mentors or facilitators. There are two purposes for these meetings. New teachers can receive specific assistance through joint problem solving, and they can learn and practice collegial interaction patterns. The group can utilize a problem-solving model such as the following:

1. Teacher presents a problem.
2. The group helps the teacher to define the problem in terms of a question, How might I . . . ?
3. The group brainstorms solutions.
4. The teacher evaluates options.
5. The teacher plans for implementation.
6. The teacher implements the solution, evaluates it, and reports back at the next meeting. A variation of this is cited in *Breaking Through Isolation with New Teacher Groups* (Rogers and Babinski 1999).

Secondary teachers need within-department curriculum support that goes beyond being handed the curriculum guide. Experienced staff should help the novice to troubleshoot problems with particular units or lessons.

Anticipate the "nickel and dime" management problems.

Before the school year begins, hold a "novice's pitfalls" meeting. Most schools orient new teachers to the discipline code but fail to help them anticipate and handle the "nickel and dime routines" such as how to handle the 3 P's: pee, paper (and books), and pencils. These rather minor management issues often become testing grounds for new teachers and, especially at the secondary level, can escalate into subsequent discipline problems.

New teachers need to anticipate responses to these "nickel and dime" violations. One new teacher received conflicting advice about pencils. One veter-

LEGAL NOTE

While we want to support novice teachers, leaders need to be aware that many states have a 90-day period when teachers can be removed without legal restrictions. In some cases there is confusion whether this is 90 school days or 90 calendar days. To be on the safe side, unless clearly stated in the statute, evaluators should assume this refers to calendar days and move on cases of extraordinary problems during this time.

an told her, "They will take advantage if you pass out pencils." Another said "Nah, not worth it; keep a supply on hand, that way you won't have to deal with the intrusion." Whatever the decision, all new teachers should clarify their expectations for minor work procedures before the first day of class.

Lighten the task difficulty.

How is it that leaders permit senior teachers to have easier conditions and often inflict "boot camp" on new teachers? To prevent an early sense of helplessness and discouragement, consider the following list and work to lighten the task conditions, especially in the first semester. Providing optimal circumstances in all areas will be difficult, but leaders should consider maximizing the conditions for early success.

- Number of daily preparations—One or two.
- Traveling—Give own room.
- Prep Period and scheduling—First period prep and/or prep midmorning.
- Level of Class—Avoid low-level class assignment for first semester.
- Textbooks—Provide textbooks and sample lesson plans. New teachers should not have to invent the curriculum.
- Block schedule—Difficult for new teachers to manage 90 minutes.
- Extra duties—None for first semester.
- Professional development—Focused on support for first semester.
- Class Size—18 to 20 is a good start.
- Students—Reduce to a minimum students with intensive needs for first year.

Forgive first year mistakes.

Novice teachers in their first year will make many mistakes. The question is what they are learning from these mistakes.

Forgiveness Sticks

Michael Fung invented forgiveness sticks. "Usually I went into a class, took notes, and then discussed them with the teacher. I found it worked better if I videotaped the class. The teacher then reviewed the tape either alone or with me. Any criticism, no matter how well intended can lead to problems. A year ago one young new teacher I had worked with for four months resigned even though she was making significant progress. I found out that she thought I was too demanding with my constant suggestions. That came as a shock to me, as I thought we got along well. As a result of this experience, I invented 'Forgiveness Sticks.'

I give each new teacher three forgiveness sticks with the name and date of employment. If the teacher becomes unhappy about his or her relationship with me, he or she can ask for one of the sticks. It is *my responsibility* to find out why the teacher is unhappy and to do something about it. Another way this works is that if a teacher makes a mistake she or he can give me a forgiveness stick. One teacher, for example, made a sarcastic comment to a student. She did apologize, but she felt she needed additional forgiveness from the headmaster. By asking for a stick, the teachers are alerting me that something is not quite right. Since I, as the one in authority, must discover the reasons, it makes it easier for the new teacher to air his or her grievance or mistake. It gives them more control."

Give Control and Provide Support and Incentives

When the National Center for Education Statistics asked dissatisfied teachers what specifically prompted them to leave, the factors in order were student discipline problems, poor student motivation to learn, inadequate support from administration, poor salary, and lack of influence over school policies and practices. (Hardy 1999, p.14)

To be effective in a high accountability environment, teachers, like administrators, need to develop competence, conviction, and control. Leaders must seriously consider how they can provide the institutional support to provide the control that will help to retain new teachers. These include:

- A consistent discipline policy with effective backup consequences
- Instructional coaching on how to motivate students

Once teachers have mastered basic survival skills, perhaps after a semester or a year, leaders need to invite new teachers to participate in curriculum decision making and to provide opportunities for ongoing professional growth.

Negotiate for performance-based evaluation.

Mediocrity is institutionalized when reduction in force decisions on staffing are exclusively based on seniority. Either budget constraints or enrollment declines can cause a district to reduce staff. The newer teachers are almost always the first to lose their positions. Two of the authors were part of a school district that implemented a performance-based reduction in force agreement in which seniority became the determining criterion only if there was equal performance. This concept was sustained in an arbitration decision upholding the school committee (Layoff/Reduction in Force Grievance of F. Shulowitz (Wayland Public Schools, Massachusetts 1980 Case #1139-0682-79).

LEGAL NOTE

"Measurable standards for meeting the incentives shall be established and agreed upon by the administration and the Association. These standards shall be listed clearly and made available to all teachers. The administration shall decide whether a teacher has qualified for the Locally Assessed Incentive payment, based on the quantifiable assessment of the standards." (Contract between Carlisle Teachers' Association and the School Committee of the Town of Carlisle, Massachusetts, July 1, 1998 to July 30, 2001.

LEGAL NOTE

The contract language is very important in sustaining a performance-based reduction in force agreement. Here is the language upon which the arbitrator upheld the performance-based reduction in force:[1]

"Decline in student enrollments, changes in curricular offerings, economic restraints, or other pressing conditions may necessitate the reduction of a number of professional positions in the school system. When the school committee (board) determines that staff reductions are necessary, it shall, consistent with applicable laws, determine the order in which teachers shall be reduced in the following manner: unless within the difference there is a significant difference in the teacher's performance as evidenced by evaluations from up to the previous five years, length of service shall prevail. In determining whether a significant difference in the evaluation exist, the judgment of the COMMITTEE shall prevail unless it is determined that the COMMITTEE's decision was not made on a reasonable basis. The evaluations shall be considered to be an accurate reflection of teacher performance and shall not be subject to contrary testimony except as to statements based on facts, e.g., attendance records, as opposed to questions of judgment" (Agreement between the Wayland Public Schools and the Wayland Teachers Association 1980).

---

[1] Districts negotiating for this language should consult the local state statutes on dismissal or demotion of teachers as that language may render local performance-based language irrelevant.

The Carlisle Massachusetts Public Schools has organized a performance based professional development program which gives both competence and control to newer teachers and veterans alike. David Mayall, President of the Carlisle Teachers Association, describes an innovative professional development program in Carlisle which has grown out of a school board and teacher association alternative compensation committee.

We wanted to implement Peter Senge's ideas on becoming a learning organization devoted to continuous improvement. The timing was perfect to try some new ideas. First we negotiated for a change in the salary scale from M +30 to M+60. This gave senior staff another salary target. Then we developed the idea of Carlisle College with a goal of providing professional development by teachers and for teachers, keyed to locally defined priorities. A great by-product is that veteran teachers are given a new opportunity to offer courses to other staff in their areas of expertise. Teachers receive double credit for offering a course. Another incentive is that teachers can earn $500 when they demonstrate proficiency in an identified target area. In our first year we offered a technology incentive. We are adding a systems thinking target area and a 'repertoire incentive' where teachers will need to prove through a portfolio that they are using certain identified instructional techniques in the classroom. Again, veteran teacher will be offering courses to help their peers gain the needed proficiencies. This is a great way for new teachers to expand their repertoires. For example, if they take the cooperative learning course and submit a successful portfolio, they receive $500 plus salary credit. A commission, consisting of two association members and the superintendent, administer the program to ensure rigorous standards. An additional incentive has been offered of $1000 to $2000 for participation in the National Board for Professional Teaching Certification. A successful participant can receive a salary increase of $1000 per year for five years. These incentives have added little to the school budget as we use grants and a negotiated reallocation of 50% of the tuition reimbursement. It is win win."

The Carlisle example provides a model of shared leadership; the school board, the administration, and the association collaborate in encouraging continuous growth for both veterans and new teachers. The contract language in the legal note in the margin makes it clear that this is a standards-based professional development program. Carlisle is not holding just students to high standards.

Detecting Early Signs of Mediocrity

One of the major causes of mediocre teaching is giving a permanent contract to low-performing teachers. Even as leaders support new teachers for early mistakes, they need to be alert to early warning signs that distinguish expected beginner problems from predictions of more entrenched mediocrity. Certainly it is difficult to predict whether novice teachers will develop, later in their career, personal problems such as Hank Frail or Louise Biere (Chapter 4). Our favorite guideline is: help new teachers out for two years, then help them out of the district if they don't measure up. It is one thing if mediocre performance develops: it is another to hire mediocrity from the start. Let's examine some warning signs.

Warning Signs

1. **Failure to manage routines and discipline.** All teachers deserve a year of struggle. Learning to teach is difficult, and few teachers are fully prepared to assume the challenge of a classroom even with student teaching experience. Leaders need to expect some on the job training. Looking back at their own first year of teaching, leaders often say it would not have been a good predictor of their future career path. However, after a year of struggle *under reasonable conditions*, marked improvement (not perfection) should be expected. If a teacher's classroom is chaotic and disorganized by February of year 2, we believe it is time for them to look elsewhere. Do not add this teacher to your list of problems.

2. **Absence of desired skills and attitudes predicted during the hiring process.** Look back at the interview suggestions earlier in this chapter and assess how the teacher is doing. For example, if the teacher turns out not to be receptive to feedback or to lack passion about subject matter, do not believe that good supervision will improve the teacher. Cut the cord after two years.

3. **Failure to plan a coherent, thoughtful lesson.** We have emphasized that many mediocre performers have learned the skills of management in the sense of "setting the table for instruction" but have not yet learned to provide an "instructionally nutritious meal." We might give teachers who have improved in management in year 2 another year to assess their growth in instructional planning, especially if they are open to feedback and show signs that they are reflective about their teaching. But we would not award a permanent contract unless sufficient growth has been made in this area.

4. **Evidence of limiting beliefs.** We have written about the different profiles of mediocrity (see Chapter 4), and the competence, conviction, and control needed by leaders to confront mediocre teaching. There are some common corrosive beliefs that erode conviction and can lead to a Donna D. Limits type low expectations teacher (see Chapter 3). If supervisors detect any of these beliefs in beginning teachers, we recommend nonrenewal. Limiting beliefs are very difficult to change. If provisional teachers hold any of these beliefs, it is time to move them out.

The Permanent Teacher/Tenure Decision

Why do teachers tend to get tenure as a matter of routine? There are three major reasons why few teachers are denied tenure. Principals especially, become invested in their personnel. "I hired her. She is coming along "and the leniency effect kicks in (see Chapter 3). Second, there is the perception that it is easier to stick with "a known commodity than risk going outside." Third, there is an aversion to searching for new personnel because of the time involved in posting and interviewing. We often convince ourselves to stick with the known mediocrity.

Limiting beliefs

Mediocre performers do not believe in constant learning. As a result, courses and workshops are more for the purpose of acquiring recertification points, and there is little evidence of transfer of learning into the classroom.

Mediocre performers do not believe that learning is a risky business. As a result, they model that learning is linear, predigested, and rote.

Mediocre performers do not take responsibility for their students' learning. As a result, they blame the parents and the students for lack of progress.

Mediocre performers do not believe that students will have questions or are confused. As a result, they teach by "mentioning" and assume all the students "got it" or all the students "should get it."

Mediocre performers do not believe all students can learn. As a result, they accept low performance from certain groups or individuals as all that can be expected.

Leaders who advocate for students and for excellence do not give teachers a permanent contract without convincing evidence of promise.

This is a reversal of current practice, as typically tenure is a semi-automatic "default" decision. The principal makes the tenure decision, often with very little consultation and with few district accountability mechanisms.

The first thing a district should do is to announce to candidates that tenure must be earned, that it is not automatic, and it is reserved for proficient performers, not just average performers. John Mudry, principal of the Gaineville Elementary School Region 15 in Middletown, Connecticut, says, "In Connecticut we have four years before we have to make the tenure decision. During the new teacher orientation, we tell them we are not looking for average teachers here. To get tenure we are looking for above average performance. We do not give tenure to everyone."

We recommend that no teacher receive a permanent contract without the principal or primary evaluator justifying the recommendation to a tenure advisory committee or a group of peers. The burden of proof is shifted from an assumption that you really have to screw up not to get tenure to, you really have to perform at a high level to get tenure.

We encourage supervisors to create supportive conditions in the first year or two. Leaders beware, however, and do not try to create ideal conditions in a last year before making a permanent personnel decision. In a case we are aware of, a mediocre performer was shifted in his third year to a lower grade level with a very strong team. This might be a good thing to do with an underperforming veteran, but, in this case, the improvement that occurred resulted in a "false positive" reading. Tenure was granted. However, under less optimum conditions a few years later, the problems resurfaced and mediocrity "returned."

The message is clear. If in doubt give the benefit to the students and don't renew. It is always easier earlier in a teacher's career. Just as baseball teams occasionally trade away future stars, mistakes will be made, but the standards will be clearly communicated, and, in the long run, students will be better served.

Using This Book to Develop Novice Teachers

This book focuses primarily on confronting veteran mediocrity, but some of the resources can be helpful in assessing and especially in assisting new teachers. For example, to assist new teachers to develop images of excellence, leaders might discuss the case descriptions in Chapter 1 and focus on Nancy Kerr. Chapters 4, 5, and 6 are especially helpful with appropriate modifications to match the supervisory circumstances unique to new teachers.

Chapter 4 Selecting Data Sources

Expanding the data sources used to evaluate and coach new teachers can encourage the use of multiple assessment techniques with their students. Supervisors can support data collecting practices of a Nancy Kerr by jointly examining artifacts such as grade distributions, progress reports, discipline referrals, as well as student products (see Figure 4-2). Increasing reflective skills could be achieved through a portfolio (see Chapter 9).

Chapter 5 Describing Strengths and Problems

Leaders can use Chapter 5 to define for new teachers what an excellent teacher does. The chapter also can be used as a tool for self-assessment and goal setting (Figure 5-4).[2]

New teachers need encouragement and cheerleading, but they also need specific feedback to grow. This includes clearly stating problems, as discussed in Chapter 5. With novice teachers, we would frame problems incrementally, rather than comprehensively as we recommend when confronting mediocre "experienced" teaching. Our goal is to develop and support more than to document, although descriptions serve both purposes.

Chapter 6 Designing a Plan

The full comprehensive planning process, as described in this chapter, would not be appropriate for new teachers, but more informal applications of the stages of designing an improvement plan are very helpful in identifying areas for growth (see Figure 6-1).

The 3C's allow the supervisor to maximize the specificity of the feedback given to new teachers in evaluating performance. More important, the 3 C's provide a data-based decision making environment where reflection and learning for adults are not just valued but required.

The 3C's and New Teachers

This book has focused on confronting mediocrity at three levels—the teacher, the supervisor, and the institution (see Figure 1-1). The need to deal with the influx of large numbers of new teachers creates new stresses at all these levels. It focuses us again on our three essential conditions (Figure 1-2). Leaders need **competence** to select promising candidates, predict future mediocrity, and to support and develop new teachers. They need **conviction** that new teachers

---

[2] You may want to purchase *The Skillful Teacher*, available from Research for Better Teaching, for a fuller development of the concepts in this chapter.

can and should be expected to meet high standards and expectations. They also need **conviction** to act decisively when certain skills and beliefs are not evident after two years. Finally leaders need **control**; they need to design, assemble, and use institutional structures and resources to build lasting cultures of exellence. In the following chapter, we consider future trends and initiatives that may help us to build and sustain those essential conditions.

10 Evaluation in the Early 2000s

Teachers say that evaluation, as it is currently practiced in schools, does not help them to improve instruction. We might ask whether evaluation has even accomplished its primary job—that of judging performance against high minimum standards. Truthfully it can be said that evaluation and supervision have largely failed to ensure that each child has a competent teacher and to foster individual and institutional growth. Some readers, therefore, may dismiss our work as simply another prescription for improving traditional, hierarchical evaluation procedures. They may chide us for not overthrowing old thinking and advocating a major shift to a collaboratively based system. Ultimately, we are committed to a two-pronged approach to confronting mediocrity: first to making existing systems actually do what they were intended to do and second to building strong professional communities capable of upholding high standards for all members and of resisting second-rate work.

We have begun by focusing on leaders' courage, vision, and competence. Even if we substitute new evaluation systems and structures, these leadership conditions must be in place. Leaders are responsible when mediocrity is tolerated over time. At the same time, we do not want to ignore initiatives that have the potential for creating powerful professional partnerships and collective responsibility for student learning.

In this chapter we will look at four movements that together could have major impact in creating new cultures and in confronting mediocrity. These initiatives become especially important as we look ahead to bringing thousands of new teachers into the profession; they are:

1. Peer assistance
2. The standards movement
3. Use of teacher portfolios for assessment
4. Use of data about student achievement

Peer Assistance[1]

So far we have examined how supervisors can develop the conviction, competence, and control they need to recognize mediocre performance and to do something about it. Supervision and evaluation matter and school leaders need to put the improvement of teaching onto their busy schedules.

While we do not shrink from calling on school leaders to do the job right, some school systems have learned how to share the responsibility for maintaining standards of teaching performance with practicing teachers and their unions. Generally called peer assistance and review (PAR), this model assumes that teachers care about the performance of their colleagues and are uniquely qualified and positioned to offer the kind of assistance that can improve mediocre teaching.

While peer assistance programs differ slightly among the school districts that embrace them, most programs share some common characteristics. First, the programs are cooperative efforts between teachers and administration. Second, the programs almost always combine attention to the needs of novice teachers with intervention programs for experienced teachers whose performance has fallen below local standards. Most peer assistance programs employ teachers of recognized capability as consulting teachers who carry responsibility both to recognize mediocre performance and to help correct it. Finally, like the principal in Chapter 8 who chose to become a kid's principal, peer assistance focuses on the students and their learning as the ultimate goal of all school efforts.

Peer assistance and review programs are always collaborative efforts between teachers and administrators. In the school systems where this model thrives, teacher unions often lead the way in design, development, and implementation. Since 1981, the Toledo Public Schools and the Toledo Federation of Teachers have enacted the Toledo Plan, in which a Board of Review, made up of practicing teachers and administrators, reviews requests for intervention plans to help struggling teachers and decides if intervention is necessary. In Columbus, the peer assistance program is directed by the seven-member PAR Panel, made up of four members appointed by the Superintendent of Schools. In Cincinnati, the Peer Assistance and Evaluation Program is managed by the Peer Review Panel, a committee comprised of members appointed by the union and members appointed by the administration. In Rochester, intervention efforts on behalf of teachers experiencing serious difficulties in the performance of professional duties are the responsibility of the Joint Governing Panel, whose members include six representatives of the Superintendent of Schools and six representatives of the Rochester Teachers' Association.

Peer assistance programs usually attend to novice teachers as well as teachers with performance problems. While both are offered the assistance of able peers, the purpose of the program for novices is primarily to ease entry into the profession. Many of the problems of experienced teachers who are candi-

---

[1]Our thanks to our colleague Dr. Gregory Ciardi from Research for Better Teaching for contributing this section.

dates for peer assistance fall under our definition of mediocre teaching. Intervention programs for teachers in trouble follow a protocol similar to what we offer supervisors dealing with mediocre teaching. The essential components are referral, investigation, intervention, and assessment.

Referral of a teacher experiencing difficulty is the first step in peer assistance. While the specifics vary from district to district, in general, referrals may be made by supervisors, (union) building representatives, or the teachers themselves. The kinds of teaching performance that might lead to a referral are like those in our profiles of mediocre teaching in Chapter 3. Columbus offers the following symptoms of teaching that might generate a referral:

Serious discipline or classroom problems

Frequent conflicts with students

Noisy classroom atmosphere

Children frequently out of the classroom and in the halls

Total lack of student interest in classroom activities

High incidence of discipline referrals

Unduly harsh and unreasonable treatment of students

Frequent parent complaints and difficulty resolving problems with parents

Lack of planning and preparation for instruction

Disorganization about meeting professional responsibilities

Extremes in grading as reflected by grade inflation or excessive failure rates

Lack of student growth and achievement

Tardiness and high absentee rates

Sarcasm and demeaning comments in relation to students

General negativism toward all facets of the job

Difficulty with routine tasks

Failure to comply with district policies and administrative requests

Linda Lohr, who served as a consulting teacher in the Columbus Public Schools, has found that the problems of teachers experiencing difficulty fall into three general categories: (1) poor management of students, time, or tasks, (2) difficult personal relationships with students of colleagues, and (3) a general lack of interest in the responsibilities of the job.

After a referral, peer assistance programs require a formal investigation, which corresponds to the data collection activities we describe in Chapter 4 as the first step in developing an improvement plan for mediocre teaching. In an investigation, a trained consulting teacher visits the classroom of the referred teacher to talk with the teacher and to conduct a formal classroom observation. If that conversation and observation confirm the issues raised in the referral, the consulting teacher recommends further action in the form of an intervention plan.

Intervention plans are the heart of peer assistance and review. As Bob Chase, the president of the National Education Association, has said, peer assistance is not about getting rid of bad teachers, it is about helping colleagues who are experiencing difficulties in the performance of their duties.

The procedures described in Chapter 6 "Designing an Improvement Plan" are compatible with peer assistance programs, but the responsibilities for evaluating the success of plans in peer assistance programs rests with the assistance

In the development of goals, consulting teachers decide how directive or collaborative to be in the goal setting process.

team instead of the primary evaluator. Intervention involves the development of improvement goals, an action plan to meet those goals, and a series of classroom observations to support and document progress toward their accomplishment. In the development of goals, consulting teachers decide how directive or collaborative to be in the goal setting process. Adult learning theory holds that teachers need to be as involved as possible in the development of their improvement goals, but consulting teachers know that, in some circumstances, clear direction to the teacher is most likely to achieve a successful outcome.

During an intervention, the consulting teacher meets regularly with the teacher. Classroom observations are preceded by planning conferences and followed by reflecting conferences. Other members of the staff who might be helpful, such as resource teachers or curriculum specialists, might be consulted. Principals are kept informed of the goals, the intervention, and the progress of the teacher toward improvement.

One of the most compelling features of the peer assistance program in Toledo is that the decision about how and when to end an intervention is left to the consulting teacher. During an intervention, the consulting teacher monitors the teacher's progress toward meeting the accepted improvement goals. There is no predetermined time limit set for intervention. The consultant decides when the teacher has either made significant progress and no longer needs assistance or has shown so little progress that it appears that further assistance would not help. The report is forwarded directly to the personnel department of the school system. In Columbus, the consulting teacher submits the final evaluation report to the Peer Assistance and Review Panel, which considers the consulting teacher's recommendations. The panel then makes a formal report to the personnel department. Both of these models place the primary responsibility for determining if the progress of the teacher has been sufficient with the consulting teacher.

Peer evaluators need conviction, competence, and control to do the job, just as supervisors do. The difference in peer assistance and review programs is that those qualities are held to exist in peers as well as in supervisors. Consequently, school systems that use peer assistance and review make sure that those who would serve as consulting teachers have those qualities.

In Columbus, Peer Assistance and Review Consulting Teachers must have the following attributes:

Minimum of five years' experience teaching in Columbus

Demonstrated outstanding teaching ability

Proven abilities in oral and written communication

Proven ability to work cooperatively and effectively with colleagues

Extensive knowledge of a wide repertoire of classroom management and instructional strategies

In Cincinnati, consulting teachers work out of a shared office and serve for two years. By working together in the same place, second-year consultants are available to help first-year consultants gain the conviction, develop the competence, and learn the control to become effective supervisors and evaluators for the teachers they serve.

In a true profession of teaching, the responsibility for maintaining standards of practice would reside with practicing teachers. Peer assistance and review is a step in that direction. By placing the responsibility for identifying and remediating mediocre teaching with consulting teachers, peer assistance makes plain that teachers care about the quality of their teaching and about that of their colleagues.

Linda Lohr, a consulting teacher from Columbus, talked about this at the first national conference on the topic of peer assistance, held in Columbus in May of 1998. She explained that decisions to recommend that a colleague be asked to leave the profession are the most difficult a professional teacher could ever be asked to make, reached only after hours and hours of sitting in a classroom watching kids try to learn and not be able to. That is what we mean by conviction. That is what a kid's teacher sounds like.

Mediocre teaching is what is preventing some of our students from achieving at levels they need. Peer assistance and review expands the responsibility for addressing it to colleagues and in the process raises the standards of the profession. We support these initiatives in the job of confronting mediocre teaching.

The Standards Movement

At the national level, a very diverse group of alliances, projects, and organizations seeks to improve learning for America's public school students. Taken as a whole, these efforts are commonly referred to as the "standards movement." Although this movement is extremely diverse and the groups have different political, social, and religious agendas, there is a common theme tying the various groups together: that learning and success for all students should be tied to high performance standards and performance assessments that require a great deal from our young people and their teachers. These standards are generally thought to be associated with benchmarks established from within each of the academic disciplines. These so-called benchmarks establish the minimally acceptable levels of successful performance for every student. The essence of the standards movement is a desire to eliminate an educational system that allows for, and in many ways promotes, different expectations of academic performance for different students.

Forty states now have standards in all four core subjects (as of September 1999); an additional eight states have adopted standards in at least one subject. That leaves only Idaho and Iowa with no official standards in English, Math, Science, or Social Studies, according to *Education Week* (January 11, 1999).

In the majority of these states, the identified standards are tied to some type of test. The fundamental assumption throughout the states is that an individual student's performance on a particular test is an accurate measure of what the student has learned. Consequently, test results are now being analyzed relative to established minimum standards of performance. The stakes are high and getting higher in most states. In some states, a student's graduation will depend on passing these tests. In other states, teachers, schools, and school districts are being evaluated on the basis of their students' performance on the tests.

School-to-school and state-to-state experiences with standards-based testing vary widely across the nation. According to Sherman Tinkelman, "New York State has been administering curriculum-based Regents Examinations to high school students ever since June of 1878 . . . these instruments presuppose and define standards . . . they are effective in stimulating good teaching and good learning practices" (Bishop, Moriaty & Mane, 1997). This long-term practice of holding some students accountable for high standards in New York is now headed toward a goal of testing all students in 2003. In Massachusetts, educators are just embarking on the standards journey with the establishment of Curriculum Frameworks in all core disciplines. Yet, despite their short history with standards-based testing, all members of the Class of 2003 will be required to pass Massachusetts Comprehensive Assessment System tests in English, Mathematics, Science, and Social Studies in order to graduate from high school.

While anxiety grows among school people who worry about how they will make students ready for these high stakes tests, every conceivable national organization from the American Association for the Advancement of Science to the National Association for Sport and Physical Education adds to the stress by publishing its own version of new standards for its discipline. Unfortunately, the focus on what students should know and be able to do has obscured any serious discussion of how teachers are going to improve their instructional practices so that they can help students reach these new, high standards.

This book helps fulfill the goals of the standards movement by addressing the issues of what teachers and supervisors need to do to improve instruction in our schools. America's failure to have all of its teachers performing at the highest levels in the classroom will result in an unacceptably high number of students who will fail to achieve the high level of expectations inherent in the standards movement. High levels of student performance are unlikely to occur without consistently high levels of teaching performance.

Those who believe that high standards testing based on state frameworks will by itself improve the quality of teaching are deceiving themselves. However, the marriage of the standards movement with a systemic focus on the improvement of classroom teaching may provide the most powerful catalyst for substantive improvement. The standards movement and the accountability it brings will not go away. They offer us genuine tools to help all teachers perform at high levels.

Teacher Portfolios

Teachers have used portfolios for a number of years as a way to present information when they are job hunting. We need to focus on making portfolios more central to teacher development and evaluation. Portfolios are perhaps the most promising source of performance data because they present authentic views of contextual learning and teaching over time. They present a more valid picture of what the teacher knows and can do (Schuman 1998, Wolf 1997). Lee Schuman provides a nice working definition of this portfolio:

A teaching portfolio is the structured documentary history of a carefully chosen set of coached or mentored accomplishments substantiated by samples of student work and fully realized only through reflective writing, deliberation and serious conversation. (Schuman 1992)

Most of the work with teacher portfolios has been preservice and for development rather than evaluation purposes. However, the Teacher Assessment Project (TAP) directed by Lee Schuman laid the groundwork for the National Board for Professional Teaching Standards (Wolf 1991). This stimulated a national discussion on wider use of portfolios, and they have begun to serve as an alternate to traditional clinical-observation-based evaluation.

In Chapter 4 we listed teacher portfolios as one source of data to assess teacher quality (see Figure 4-1). Portfolios have special features worth highlighting further.[2] They can more accurately reflect the teaching-learning processes we want our teachers to use with their students. "I would be doing exactly what we ask our students to do: self-assess, self-evaluate, and self-regulate" (Wagenen et al., p.28) is the way one teacher put it from Middletown, Connecticut, Region 15. This district has been a national leader in developing a culture to unite evaluation and professional development by using portfolios. John Mudry, Principal of Gainesville School in Middletown, Connecticut, Region 15 says:

In collaborative portfolio evaluation we are not interested in having teachers update their resume but in getting teachers to focus on some type of instructional strategy—what is happening in their classroom. Good teachers reflect about their instruction. It gets rid of the observation-based dog and pony show. (Interview May 7,1999)

Thus teachers using portfolios are practicing the same kind of analytical thinking as their students. Evaluating how teachers carry out this thinking may give us a more accurate picture of their teaching than the more traditional observation-based evaluation observation.

Another feature of evaluation portfolios is the shift of the responsibility for data collection from the observer to the teacher, making evaluation a more collaborative enterprise. This works well with high performing teachers. However, the assembly of a portfolio is very teacher-labor intensive and requires teacher ownership. To use as a tool to improve substandard teaching, portfolios must become a part of the overall culture. Bruce Labs, principal of the Woodsville High School in New Hampshire requires portfolios for all teachers as a supplement to observation-based traditional evaluation. "The portfolio gives you additional data because you see the teacher from many different angles [not observed in the classroom]. Their portfolio is a reflection of their passion for their subject matter and how many things they are involved in." Bruce returns portfolios that do no show adequate support data or reflection about the standards. He said after a year when teachers put together portfolios with "all their good stuff," they chose the National Board Certification Standards as guidelines for selecting and evaluating material to be included.

---

[2]For an intelligent discussion of teacher portfolios, see *Evaluating Teaching: A Guide to Current Best Practice*, editor James H. Stronge 1997, especially the chapter "Portfolios in Teacher Evaluation" by Kenneth Wolf et al.

PORTFOLIO TIPS[3]

Following are several suggestions for developing quality portfolios.

- Focus on instruction, not assembling a job interview portfolio.
- Structure around specified performances standards and goals.
- Establish careful selection criteria to avoid a barrage of unfocused data.
- Focus on portfolio selection, choosing appropriate artifacts, and reflection, annotations by the teacher explaining why the artifact was selected and what it reveals about their teaching.
- Caption all items with concise comments indicating the connection between the item and the portfolio goals.
- Create a support team or a mentor-colleague rather that having a teacher develop a portfolio in isolation.
- Provide time and resources. Teachers need time during the year to sit and talk and time and money during the summer to write their reflections. (It is unrealistic to expect high quality work without district support.)
- Consider developing an administrative portfolio.

Content Checklist

Suggested teacher-produced artifacts

- Lesson plans
- Unit level plans developed complete with goals, activities, and assessment strategies
- Copies of project guidelines
- Copies of all quizzes and tests
- Sample homework assignments
- Record keeping
  - Number of days/time extra help after/before school/free time
  - Number of students sent from class
  - Arrival and departure times
- **Videotape** of teacher analyzing a lesson or peer discussion feedback
- **Audio tape** for specific focus

Student Products

- Sample student products and criteria for grading
- Corrected tests and projects sample A's, B's, F's, etc.

Client Surveys

- Student survey
- Parent survey

[3]Thanks to John Mudry and Bruce Labs for several of these suggestions.

Reflection Pieces

- Philosophy connected to specific classroom practices
- Post-unit analysis. What did I learn? How I would improve it?
- Grade distribution: analysis and insights
- Study group reflections
- Self-assessments and reflections based on student products or surveys
- Goal setting reports

We believe the best use of portfolios is as an alternative option to traditional evaluations or as a menu choice in a teacher's improvement plan. Mandating portfolios would in many cases undercut the desired goal of developing more collegiality and collaboration.

Data about Student Performance

Our fourth promising initiative involves incorporating concrete data about the success of instruction into the evaluation. This idea is controversial. There is much confusion about what form of student performance data is appropriate to use for teacher evaluation and much fear about how this data will be used. Typically both teachers and administrators oppose proposals to use student test scores or data about student achievement to evaluate a teacher's performance.[4] They cite a variety of reasons including the poor quality of some standardized tests, mismatches between the required curriculum and what is actually tested, and the impact on student achievement of variables that are beyond the school and teacher's control. They worry that poor performance on an individual measure in an individual year will be used against them in destructive ways. Parents and employers, however, do not agree. They argue that present evaluation practices give strong positive ratings to teacher whose students consistently produce low quality work or perform poorly on outside measure of achievement. Parents and employers wonder why evaluation of teaching proficiency seems wedded to examining the means that teachers use but not the ends they produce. Shouldn't teachers whose students do not make progress have to go, outsiders ask?

In the past, formal evaluation documents and performance criteria have contained few, if any, direct references to the link between teaching and results. Few even contained language indicating that teachers or administrators must hold themselves responsible for whether students learn. Teachers' unions could and did protect their members from discussions about whether practices were successful, meaning whether children learned, because such evidence was deemed inappropriate. Mediocre supervisors adopted the notion that it was somehow unfair to inject a discussion about student performance into the evaluation process because it was not the teacher's fault if children did not

---

[4]See "Public Agenda: Reality Check, Quality Counts," (*Education Week*, Vol. XVIII, Number 17, January 11, 1999), pp.102-105.

We do believe that mediocre instruction will persist unless supervisors and teachers jointly understand and pay attention to the connection between their efforts and student learning.

learn. These patterns are changing as more and more states attend to issues of accountability and as both national and local unions call for members to take responsibility for student learning.

We are not arguing that high stakes decisions about compensation, evaluation ratings and rankings, or future employment should be based solely on students' standardized test scores. Nor do we claim that resources should be invested in creating better systems and instruments to capture and track teachers' impact on student achievement. We do, however, believe that mediocre instruction will persist unless supervisors and teachers jointly understand and pay attention to the connection between their efforts and student learning. One of the ways to pay attention is to examine data from measures of student performance. These can range from the work in an assessment portfolio designed by a school district, to scores on state mandated or local testing, to performances undertaken to reach nationally set standards.

Results and how teachers achieve them need to play a key role in the evaluation process. That role can vary. Teachers and administrators, for example, can reasonably be expected to analyze a variety of available data about student performance and draw conclusions that will help them improve instruction. The conclusions and decisions based on that analysis should be reported in the evaluation process. The reporting may take the form of a memo jointly prepared by a group of grade level teachers that outlines a problem they have identified during their data analysis and the steps they plan to take to solve the problem. Perhaps it is a summary of notes from an interview conducted by the principal. Perhaps the administrator reports on a system that a teacher devised to track student progress on a standard and discussed at a staff meeting. In any of these examples, two practices are likely to differ from business as usual. The first is a direct discussion of student performance data as a source of evidence about teacher practice; the second is the use of alternate sources of evidence beyond simple classroom observation.

Asking for evidence that teachers are analyzing data and reflecting on their teaching in relation to that data is one way to put test scores and other assessment information into the evaluation process. Focusing on data-driven goal setting is another. Following the lead of the National Board of Professional Teaching Standards, for example, Montgomery County, Maryland's performance criteria ask teachers to select and set goals on systemwide accountability measures and produce "measurable growth in student achievement" towards the goals they have selected. The key here is that teachers and administrators are expected to have ongoing conversations about the way in which each is contributing to systemwide accountability at each stage of the multiyear cycle. Talking about whether your teaching works for students and how we know that is no longer taboo.

Defined as data and feedback, results not only help mediocre teachers see where their work falls short, they also validate and give courage to highly competent practitioners (Schmoker 1996). How do we build the kind of collective responsibility that schools seem to need in order to get results? Making performance data a legitimate focus of a collaborative or collegial conference between teachers and administrators helps. Having access to good quality longitudinal data helps. Having the conviction to name a pattern of poor performance, provide adequate credible evidence of that performance, and ask for improvement helps. Mediocre practitioners often unconsciously rather than intentionally deprive their students of opportunities to learn. Individuals who do not know enough about what kinds of student outcomes other teachers are getting or have not witnessed exemplary practice to be able to make a judgment about their own work are being deprived themselves. When they have adequate data and the requirement to make sense of it, those whose instruction is second-rate also have the chance to take charge of their own outcome and change.

Summary

The promise of these four reform movements does not come from their ability to sort, label, or select teachers. The promise comes from their potential for creating shared objectives, shared understandings about what works and does not work, and shared responsibility for student achievement. Each has the potential to help leaders achieve the goal of providing every student with an excellent teacher.

Epilogue
Voices of the Students

We shall not cease from exploration—and the end of all exploring will be to arrive where we started—and know the place for the first time. (T.S. Eliot *Four Quartets*)

We began this book by considering Becky's plea for "real teachers." We conclude by returning to students again in the hope of bringing stronger conviction and new urgency to our task of confronting mediocrity. Leaders may want to use these sample quotes to introduce the topic of mediocre teaching in their work with administrators and teachers.[1] Let's listen to students talking about their teachers.

Excellent teachers care about their students. They realize that their success depends on making personal connections.

Sherry, suburban high school, honors student

She cares about her students and is really interested in our learning. When I was sick for a few days last year, she called me up to see how I was doing. She told me not to worry about the term test—that she would work out a make-up schedule when I was feeling 100%.

Mediocre teachers often do not care about their students.

Diane, urban high school, honors student

I was so sick, almost fainting, she paid no attention. I was sitting in the front row. I didn't dare ask her for a pass to the nurse. She didn't care; she was going on and on, talking her lesson. She didn't care that I was really sick.

---

[1] All the quotes in this chapter come from videotape and audiotape footage from our interviews with students. Names have been changed.

Dot, suburban high school, general level student

I'd been absent for a couple days, so I asked her if I could get some one-on-one help during the class. We went over to a corner of the room, and I said that I really did not understand this. She yelled at me in front of the whole class "I can't believe you are a senior and you don't understand this!" I just got really upset and walked away. I was really hurt; it was totally inappropriate. I stopped asking questions.

Excellent teachers are passionate about their subjects. Whether it be learning how to teach reading or reading about how to teach learning strategies, excellent teachers are constant learners.

Brian, high school, college prep student

She loves her subject and is always talking about new bio theories. She brings in articles from the Science supplement section in the [Boston] Globe. She really loves biology. It's kinda contagious—you can't help but get a little interested.

Mediocre teachers seem to go through the motions and have lost their passion.

Bonnie, urban high school, honors student

He was a "burn-out teacher." He has been teaching too long, and he knew it, and he still taught in this style: "I'm here to teach, and don't ask questions, you're going to do it my way." He didn't listen to me. If I had a question he went right on. He had something in his ears, and he has been like that for years—just burned out.

Excellent teachers not only love their subjects but really care about whether their students are understanding the material.

Melissa, suburban high school student

Mrs. Smith is awesome. I think the difference between her and other teachers is that she cares about us not only as people but as students. She cares if we get it.

Mediocre teachers press on and don't care if students understand what they are teaching.

Connie, urban high school, college prep student

He went too fast. You couldn't understand—he wouldn't take questions from anyone. It was hard to learn when he didn't explain and just wrote things on the board—just notes that he was giving you. I transferred out.

Excellent teachers conceive of their work as being driven by student learning. They will persist with students willing to put in the effort until they are successful.

She is so patient. Last semester I was having real difficulty in understanding. . . . She sat with me three days after school. I kept saying it was impossible, but she stuck with me, and finally I got it. She was as happy as I was!

Mediocre teachers often give up on students.

Melinda, urban high school, college prep student
When you asked a question, she would not listen to you, and she would just keep on going. She would not spend the time to explain to you because she was too busy.

Excellent teachers find ways to connect material to students' personal experiences. They know this heightens motivation and helps students remember the material.

She is very demanding—nice but demanding. She makes the class relevant to our lives. When we were studying fermentation, she connected it to my running track and why I was so pooped out at the end of the 400 m race!

Mediocre teachers are more likely to center personal experiences on themselves.

Mary, suburban high school, honors student
My brother had him in '88 (my brother is much older than me), and he was fantastic. But every day now he talks about retirement even though it is 14 years away. He has gotten tired of doing the same thing. I know about his mortgage rate, his son, that he was in a graduating class of 234 students— we've heard it all. It's too bad because I know he used to be a good teacher.

Excellent teachers teach strategies. They teach students tools that can be applied in real circumstances independent of the teacher.

Bob, urban middle school student
He often takes time to talk about different learning preferences and gives us tips to help us not only in his class but in other subjects as well.

The mediocre teacher does not teach strategies or make relevant conections to students' lives.

Melanie, rural 8th grade student
Sometimes we read the chapter and do the questions, but she doesn't help and it doesn't seem to pertain to what she is trying to teach. I don't see what the point is.

Excellent teachers push kids to levels of high performance and spend time on significant learning.

Matthew, surburban 6th grade student
He made us work on sentence structure, paragraph development, and outlining skills for over a month to improve our expository writing for a major report. My writing improved after I learned about sentence types and paragraph organization rules. I have become confident about my writing.

Mediocre teachers occupy their students occupied with trivial work. These teachers' classrooms are characterized by the "sound and smoke of notetaking, answer giving, homework-checking, test taking and the forgetting that quickly follows... not much of high quality is being produced and not much intense engagement of the mind and spirit takes place" (Fried 1995, p. 2).

Mike, suburban high school, honors student

A lot of her quizzes were multiple choice, fill in the blanks: who said this quote on what page? What were they wearing? English should be more writing and interpreting and things like that. In literature there are more important things. How does it relate to what we do? What the author was thinking about when he wrote it?

Donna, suburban high school, college prep student

I had an English teacher [who said] "read 70 pages over the weekend." For the Monday quiz he picked up his book, thumbed through the 70 pages and found a question—he hadn't read it—he'd pick out insignificant things. For example, after reading 70 pages in Huckleberry Finn, he asked how fast the raft went down the river. I think that is insignificant. I complained. He said "If you had read it you would have known." It was as if he had not done the reading. If they (teachers) give up on learning how can they expect you to put in effort? It's harder to put forth effort if you see the teacher just sit there and not putting in effort. The teacher sets the mood.

A student from Ohio helps us to understand why we are committted to confronting mediocre teaching.

Bonnie, suburban 4th grade student

She was real mean. One time she asked me a question. I did not have a clue about decimals when we first started it. She called on me, "Just answer me." I said "I don't know it." "Just answer me, ANSWER it!" I do not do too well. If she asks you a question and you don't know, she will say what the answer is and won't explain how she got the answer, so when you take the test you don't have a clue. She will get really mad at you if you don't get it. When we start any subject, like decimals, she'll act like you should know it right away. Some kids get it right away, and they already know it because they have learned it from their older brothers and sisters. She goes right ahead with them and some people are like left behind. She does not answer questions that well. She uses words kids cannot understand so we cannot learn. My dad helps me, he makes it more easy. If I don't get something he'll go back with me. He says it in different words. She would go right on.

Leaders need to think about how to collect more sources of data from students. Deborah, a graduating senior, when asked by the interviewer "How could we help administrators do a better job in evaluating teachers?" said:

Go to the kids more for evaluation because we're the ones who sit there every day . . . we could give an honest opinion . . . ask the whole class and you could get a fair opinion. It is still important for administrators to observe, but ask the people who have been observing all year long!

A Final Thought

None of the mediocre teachers referred to by these students had received poor evaluations. Many of them were deemed excellent, and one of them was vigorously protected by a principal who viewed her responsibility as being a teacher advocate rather than a student advocate. If we as leaders ignore the problems, inflate performance ratings, and accept low standards, then what we expect is what we will get—mediocre performance. It is our competence, our conviction, and our control that will allow us to successfully confront mediocre teaching. The students quoted in this chapter and millions like them depend on us to provide excellent teaching for every classroom.

The 3 C's Supervisor's Survey on Competence, Conviction, and Control

In the blanks provided please rate yourself using the following scale:

```
4 = Expert
3 = Competent
2 = Basic
1 = Novice
```

1. Competence (knowledge and skills) in

A. _____ Capturing and documenting events during classroom observation, including literal note-taking

B. _____ Analyzing records of classroom observation to identify how events do or do not contribute to student learning

C. _____ Describing teaching using multiple sources of data

D. _____ Pinpointing problems and areas for improvement

E. _____ Designing improvement plans that are problem-based and include means of assessment

F _____ Avoiding rating bias, e.g., halo effect, leniency errors, severity error, etc.

G. _____ Writing evaluations that do not "sugar coat" issues of mediocre performance with tentative language, mixed messages, and vague generalizations

H. _____ Conducting difficult conferences and delivering negative information clearly and objectively

I. _____ Following contractual guidelines, timelines, and procedures

J. _____ Understanding and using appropriate local, state, and national standards as part of the evaluation process

K. _____ Defining and adhering to a clear vision of excellence when rating teaching performance

L. _____ Evaluating teacher's planning and thinking about objectives

TOTAL for Competence Score (48)
(Expert = 40+ Competent = 30+ Basic = 20+ Novice = 10+)

2. Conviction (belief) that . . .

1 = Lowest degree
2 = Moderate
3 = High
4 = Highest

A. _____   I have made a positive difference in improving mediocre teaching. (To rate a 4 you should be able to cite at least one instance of successful intervention in the last two years.)

B. _____   I am aware that while I may not be able to take on all cases of mediocrity I am committed to not looking the other way because the task is overwhelming. (To rate a 4 you should be able to cite at least one case in the last year where you took on a case of mediocre performance.)

C. _____   In my decision making I weigh the interests of students over teachers. (To rate a 4 you need be able to cite 2-3 examples when you made a decision unpopular with teachers but clearly beneficial to students.)

D. _____   Taking on substandard teaching is a high priority, and I am committed to building a track record of impacting mediocre or incompetent teaching.

E. _____   I have the endurance, fortitude, energy, and persistence to stick with a multiyear project involving confronting and following through on cases involving mediocre teaching.

F. _____   I believe that taking on mediocre teaching may be worth the long-term benefits in spite of the possible negative short-term impact in terms of school congeniality.

G. _____   I can balance treating the supervisee with regard and respect and dignity while questioning or not accepting his/her current level of performance.

H. _____   I have the committment, will, and stamina to lead throughout a process of confronting mediocrity and will seek out help when needed.

I. _____   My staff members would say that I am always pushing them to be better and that I have high standards.

TOTAL for Conviction (36 total)
(Highest = 30+ High = 25+ Moderate = 18+ Low = below 10)

3. Control

> 1 = Lowest degree
> 2 = Moderate
> 3 = High
> 4 = Highest

A. _____   The contract allows me to collect a wide range of data about a teacher's performance.

B. _____   I have control over the availability of human and financial resources needed to support an improvement effort.

C. _____   I believe I can allocate the time to address mediocre teaching if I need to.

D. _____   I have some control about my own goal setting for the year—and the number of major initiatives I undertake.

E. _____   I can have frequent access to and communication with key central office personnel.

F. _____   I have enough control over the implementation of teacher evaluation procedures.

G. _____   I can create or make use of an existing support network.

H. _____   I will have the full and continuing help of my central office and administrative colleagues if I take on mediocre teaching

I. _____   I am part of a culture that demands identification of and intervention with low performing personnel.

TOTAL for Control (36 total)
(Highest = 30+ High = 25+ Moderate = 18+ Low = below 10)

Reflections:

APPENDIX B

Unpromising Institutional Practices Survey

See Chapter 2 "Confronting Institutional Mediocrity" for more explanation of these practices.

Please rate yourself using the following scale. This practice is a pattern in my school/district:

> 1 = **Frequently**
> 2 = **Regularly**
> 3 = **Intermittently**
> 4 = **Rarely**

Transfer Practices

A. _____ **Transferring students whose parents complain** to a different class to smooth over a teacher problem.

B. _____ **Tailoring classes for low performing teachers** by giving low performing teachers smaller classes or higher or lower level classes.

C. _____ **Transferring teachers who are not performing at a high level to a different school** to alleviate one principal's problem (the dance of the lemons).
Note: *If teacher is transferred with a poor evaluation for a "second opinion," this might be appropriate. This "unpromising practice" is when there is a softening of the evaluation with the likelihood of transfer to another school.*

D. _____ **Transferring high maintenance children** out of a teacher's classroom to make the job easier for a low performing teacher.

Teacher Assignment Practices

E. _____ **Giving teachers with seniority the "best" classes and giving** novices the difficult classes. Assignments are based largely on seniority of teachers rather than needs of students or the needs of beginning teachers.

F. _____ **Assigning teachers into the same grade levels, course level, or courses** for five or more years. Fixed assignments for many years produce resistance to new assignments.

G. _____ **Changing teacher assignments every year or two.** This limits the time available to reach expertise at a subject or grade level or keeps a problem moving within the school.

H. _____ **Assigning teachers out of certification area.**

I. _____ **Using permanent substitutes in place of certified teachers.**

Evaluation Practices (For a more detailed analysis of evaluation procedures, see Appendix C "Grading Your Evaluation Procedures")

J. _____ **Making recommendations not connected to observation or data.** Example: "You must work to motivate your students" when no reference has been made to motivation in the report.

K. _____ **Inflating performance ratings:** Almost all teachers are excellent or rated above where they should be. Few if any are identified as unsatisfactory.

L. _____ **Overweighting nonteaching responsibilities in performance ratings.**

M. _____ **Writing observation and summary reports with mixed messages, "beat around the bush," and "glow and grow generalities."** Language is commonly characterized by "edubabble" such as "I enjoyed the lesson, but she must continue to work towards becoming more comfortable with her students."

N. _____ **Avoiding negative feedback even when warranted.**

O. _____ **Identifying only incompetent teachers for improvement.**

P. _____ **Identifying low performance only when there are parent complaints.**

Q. _____ **Failing to withhold salary step increase.** Most districts allow administrators to withhold salary increments for poor performance. (Frequently is a relative rating in this case. Frequently might mean one salary step increase withheld in a year.)

R. _____ **Basing evaluation on narrow sources of data** such as observation rather than, for example, teacher artifacts and student products.

S. _____ **Using daily lesson plans to suffice** for planning data when unit plans are a better source of planning data.

T. _____ **Awarding permanent contracts after three years for minimally competent performance.**

Cultural Practices

U. _____ **Practicing toxic blaming.** Teachers blame evaluators; evaluators blame unions; unions blame the school board when that group or individual is not present. (This creates a culture of blame and an anti-problem-solving ethos.)

V. _____ .**Failing to examine school and district patterns for evaluation ratings.** A low rating in this item means that there is rarely or never an examination of the patterns of evaluation ratings across a district.

W. _____ **Failing to provide formal induction support for new teaching staff.**

X. _____ .Expunging the record or writing a **glowing recommendation** for an individual who agrees to be counseled out.

TOTAL
Scoring: 85-96 Excellent 75-84 Good 60-74 Fair Below 60 Poor

Grading Your Evaluation Procedures

Assign appropriate number of points to each criterion.

Data Collection

A._____(5) **Evidence-based narrative** rather than checklist on observations. (If specifics in support of ratings are mandatory, give up to 2 points)

B._____(4) **Multiple means of collecting data** permitted (examples include: Professional Growth Questionnaire, Self-Evaluation, Peer Evaluation, Student Evaluation)

C._____(5) Systematic means for reviewing and analyzing **nonobservational data** (examples include: teacher's unit plan as well as lesson plan, student assignments, tests, samples of student work)

Standards and Criteria

D._____(5) **Clear criteria for performance standards** spelled out (examples include: effective teaching, collegiality and collaboration with peers, communication with parents and community, constant learning, performance of routine duties)

E._____(2) Includes **goal setting** as part of evaluation cycle

F._____(4) **Summary ratings limited to three** ("Pass, Fail, or Below standard." Give 3 points for two rating categories.)

G._____(5) **Reduction in force decision based on performance not seniority**

Cycles and Frequency

H._____(1) **Alternate years** or every third year cycle of evaluation for tenured teachers

I._____(1) Alternate year(s) has **alternative professional development choices** (e.g., something happens during the "off-year")

J._____(1) Formal evaluation every year for teachers in first 3 years

K._____(2) Requires at least **three full period observations for years 1-3**

Writing and Conferencing

L._____(1) Allows both **announced and unannounced** observations

M._____(2) Includes **pre-and post-conferencing** (1 point for post-conference only.)

N._____(3) **Postpones write-up** until after conferencing

O._____(3) Separates observation reports from final summary write-ups

Follow-up

P._____(4)   **Professional development** (examples include: common language framework, training on evaluation techniques)

Q._____(3)   Differentiated **"unsatisfactory"** **performance track with follow-up plan**

Support Structures and Accountability

R._____(5)   Evaluators are regularly **evaluated on their evaluations**

S._____(3)   Evaluator has **no more than 10-person caseload** in 1 year

T._____(3)   Provisions for **multiperspective evaluation**, e.g., principals and subject matter directors

U._____(3)   Principals are not on short-term contracts while teachers are protected by tenure. (Having principals on short-term contracts results in an unfair playing field and feeds into failure to confront teacher problems.)

Final Grade

A = 55+ B = 45-54 C = 35-44 Below 35 = Unsatisfactory

Grading Your Evaluation Procedures—Annotated Version

Assign appropriate number of points to each criteria.

Data Collection

_____(5)   **Evidence-based narrative** rather than checklist on observations. (If specifics in support of ratings are mandatory, give up to 2 points)
Checklists, unless they are anchored in behavioral specifics, are very unreliable. Many of the sources of error cited in Chapter 4 are likely to be present in checklist instruments. Narratives, however, are not inherently better than checklists. They must be substantiated by data and evidence rather than simply be a chronological narrative of the class proceedings.

_____(4)   **Multiple means of collecting data** permitted (examples include: Professional Growth Questionnaire, Self-Evaluation, Peer Evaluation, Student Evaluation)
It is recommended that all teachers be required to collect data from students and parents and carry out a self-evaluation as a piece of their evaluation.

_____(5)   Systematic means for reviewing and analyzing **nonobservational data** (examples include: teacher's unit plan as well as lesson plan, student assignments, tests, samples of student work)
It is important to include contract language that allows the evaluator to access teacher lesson and unit plans, student work, etc., as other sources of data are needed. It is best not to specify a definitive list but to have a clause that permits "observation and other documented source of data."

Standards and Criteria

_____(5)   **Clear criteria for performance standards** spelled out (examples include: effective teaching, collegiality and collaboration with peers, communication with parents and community, constant learning, performance of routine duties)
It is important to include nonteaching domains so that the summative evaluation can present a comprehensive picture.

_____(2)   Includes **goal setting** as part of evaluation cycle
Teachers need to take responsibility for their own learning and improvement. It makes sense to include a goal setting component. Note: Guard against limiting evaluation only to the goals set by the teacher. A New England district recently was limited to only evaluate and comment on the teacher's goals, They have since renegotiated their contract. Goal setting should be part of the evaluation but not the only focus of evaluation.

_____(4)   **Summary ratings limited to three** ("pass, fail, or below standard." Give 3 points for two rating categories.)
Instruments that ask evaluators to make four or five ratings are not valid. Fine discriminations are difficult to make. We recommend either "pass-fail" or perhaps the "pass, fail, excellent" system. The descriptions might be better as "satisfactory," "unsatisfactory," and "excellent." The most important thing is to be able to identify substandard performance. A three-rating sytem can work well if the default grade is satisfactory and not excellent. There is clear inflation of appraisal ratings. One midwestern district with 1400 teachers has only 2 unsatisfactory ratings and fewer than 25 satisfactory ratings. This is a good district, but all admit this is inaccurate. No wonder teachers get upset when their ratings are reduced!

_____(5)   **Reduction in force decision based on performance not seniority**
Almost all districts with or without collective bargaining agreements make RIF decisions based exclusively on seniority. We strongly recommend making performance the primary criterion and seniority a secondary factor. This allows districts to retain exceptional younger personnel. If performance is similar then, of course, seniority would be the determining criterion,

Cycles and Frequency

_____(1)   **Alternate years** or every third year cycle of evaluation for tenured teachers

_____(1)   Alternate year(s) has **alternative professional development choices** (e.g., something happens during the "off-year")
It makes sense for tenured teachers not to be formally evaluated every year. This frees time for administrators to do a more complete job with fewer staff members. Because of the influx of new teachers, we would recommend a three or four year cycle with structured choices for "off the summative years."

_____(1)   Formal evaluation every year for teachers in first 3 years
In many states tenure decisions occur after three years, so intensive evaluation is necessary during this period. Even where no tenure statutes exist, a skillful supervisor knows that getting rid of mediocre teachers early in their career is easier than later.

_____(2)   Requires at least **three full period observations for years 1-3**
Some contracts permit observation to be as short as 20 minutes, specify how many are announced or unannounced or forbid consecutive day visits. Since observations are still the major data base for most evaluation, a minimum of three seems fair and minimally reliable.

Writing and Conferencing

_____(1)   Allows both **announced and unannounced** observations

_____(2)   Includes **pre-and post-conferencing** (1 point for post-conference only)
While it is clear that the supervisor would not conduct a pre-observation conference for an unannounced visit, a post-observation conference is always recommended.

_____(3)   **Postpones write-up** until after conferencing

_____(3)   Separates observation reports from final summary write-ups

Follow-up

_____(4)   **Professional development** (examples include: common language framework, training on evaluation techniques)
It is helpful to have a common language and concept system upon which to base the district supervision and evaluation. This framework should support the criteria of good teaching spelled out in the evaluation document. Seminars and courses should be offered to teachers and administrators based on the same framework. Research for Better Teaching offers such a program.

_____(3)   Points awarded for a differentiated **"unsatisfactory" performance track with follow-up plan**
It is critical to be able to establish an improvement intervention plan.

Support Structures and Accountability

_____(5)   Evaluators are regularly **evaluated on their evaluations**
One of the major indicators of monitoring of mediocrity is the priority given to the evaluation of administrators on the quality of their observation and summative evaluation write-ups. The superintendent or his/her designee should draw samples of each evaluator's writing and make this a piece of his or her evaluation.

_____(3)   Evaluator has **no more than a 10-person caseload** in 1 year
A large caseload almost guarantees superficial and perfunctory evaluations. With the reduction in caseload comes an increase in the expectations for quality monitoring of teaching. The single best way to reduce caseload is to increase the number of trained evaluators and to use cycles that distribute the number of tenured evaluations over several years.

_____(3)   Provisions for **multiperspective evaluation**, e.g., principals and subject matter directors
Especially at the secondary level, it is recommended that each teacher gets a subject matter/curriculum observation as part of his or her evaluation as well as a more pedagogically based observation. This is especially important in light of the new standards-based testing that is growing in the country.

_____(3)   Principals are not on short-term contracts while teachers are protected by tenure. (Having principals on short-term contracts results in an unfair playing field and feeds into failure to confront teacher problems.)
Several states are eliminating tenure for principals, but few have done this for teachers. The unanticipated consequence is that some "unprotected" principals are less likely to confront the mediocrity of a "protected" teacher. The solution is to be found in granting high performing principals multiyear contracts.

Final Grade

A = 55+ B = 45-54 C = 35-44 Below 35 = Unsatisfactory

ASSISTANCE TEAM PLAN

Teacher   Teacher Representative   Supervising Principal   Curriculum Coordinator   Mentor Teacher   Nonsupervising Principal

Team Members

Signature:

Date:

Standard Area:

The Problem:

Performance Goals	Strategies Activities and Timetable	Support Structures	Data Collection Method and Sources	Evidence for Progress

Model Final Summary Evaluation Report Form[1]

Name:

Assignment: (school, grades, and or subjects)

Evaluator: (should be only one evaluator for each evaluatee; list name and position)

Supervisors: (list each by name and position)

This report covers from [insert month/day/year] to [insert month/day/year].

Cycle: check as many of the following as apply:

_____ nontenured	_____ tenured
_____ supervisory cycle	_____ evaluation cycle
_____ professional development plan	
_____ improvement plan	_____ remediation plan

Data Gathering Procedures: The evaluator should include a description of the data gathering procedures followed, including dates of observations and conferences, and a description of the sources of information other than that gathered on a firsthand basis, e.g., observation reports, memoranda letters, surveys, video or audio tapes, student artifacts, test results, etc.

List of Attachments: All attachments should be identified, e.g., "Letter from Mr. Doe to Principal Smith dated _____ ."" Memorandum dated _____ to Mr. Doe from Supervisor Jones Re: observation of _____ ."

Standards of Performance: Each performance standard should be identified, the evidence that substantiates the factual claims made by the evaluator should be reported along with an identification of the source and a judgment about whether the teacher satisfactorily demonstrates competence with regard to the performance standard. Common terminology such as "satisfactory or unsatisfactory;" "meets the standard or does not meet the district's standard" should be used with respect to every standard addressed in the evaluation report.

Overall Performance Rating:[2] _____ Satisfactory _____ Unsatisfactory

Recommendations: Evaluators should use this section to set forth expectations in any realm in which performance has been assessed as unsatisfactory or to include recommendations for growth and development for teachers whose performance has been rated as satisfactory.

---

[1]This sample evaluation report form includes all of the essential elements that should be included on a form of this type.
[2]The importance of including common language to be used for an overall performance rating cannot be overemphasized. Evaluatees often do not have a clear understanding that their supervisor considers that their performance is unacceptable. Similarly, evaluators sometimes use language that does not clearly and unequivocally express their assessment of the teacher's performance. Setting up a dichotomy such as "satisfactory" or "unsatisfactory" leaves no opportunity for misunderstanding insofar as the evaluator's overall assessment is concerned.

Date of Evaluation Conference: _____

Date Evaluation Report Was Given to the Teacher: _____

Evaluator's Signature: _____ Date: _____

Teacher's Signature:

My signature acknowledges receipt of this report on the date indicated and knowledge that it will be inserted into my personnel file. It does not indicate agreement or disagreement with its content. I understand that I have _____ days in which to submit a rebuttal statement, which will be attached to this report.

Teacher: _____ Date: _____

page ____of 2 pages

APPENDIX G

Performance Roles of Teacher and Related Competencies[1]

Source: California Teachers' Association, Six Areas of Teaching Competence *(Burlingame, Calif.: California Teachers' Association, 1964), pp. 18-26.*

ROLES OF THE TEACHER IN PROMOTING PUPIL GROWTH

Role 1: Director of Learning

1.1	Adapts principles of child growth and development to planning of learning activities.
1.11	Recognizes and deals with each pupil according to his needs.
1.12	Helps individuals acquire the skills of effective group membership.
1.13	Works closely with specialists, parents, and community agencies in the solution of physical and mental health problems.
1.14	Makes and uses pupil records in ascertaining needs, planning work, and guiding the learning process.
1.2	Plans teaching-learning situations in accord with acceptable principles of learning.
1.21	Provides effective and continuing motivation.
1.211	Develops cooperatively with pupils' objectives for large units of study, daily class work, and special activities.
1.212	Arranges for differentiated assignments to meet needs and abilities of individual pupils.
1.213	Uses a variety of instruments and techniques for keeping pupil informed of his progress.
1.22	Utilizes a variety of classroom activities.
1.23	Selects and uses a wide variety of instructional materials.
1.24	Provides abundant and varied opportunities for individual and group expression in appropriate creative fields.
1.25	Helps pupil make application of his experiences to many situations.
1.3	Demonstrates effective instructional procedures.
1.31	Provides a physical environment which facilitates learning.
1.32	Makes assignments skillfully.
1.33	Provides opportunities for wide participation.

[1]While there are numerous examples of performance standards for teachers that might have been chosen, this one is especially interesting both because of its source, i.e., the California Teachers' Association and the fact that it provides several examples of descriptors for each role and related competency identified. A key consideration in establishing competencies, criteria, or performance standards is to make certain that they are observable phenomena about which an evaluator can reasonably be expected to gather data either on a firsthand basis or through an examination of artifacts produced by the teacher or student.

1.4	Utilizes adequate evaluation procedures.
1.41	Carries on evaluation as an integral part of instruction.
1.42	Enlists cooperation of pupils and parents in developing programs of evaluation.
1.43	Uses a variety of devices and procedures.
1.44	Organizes and summarizes data for meaningful interpretation.
1.45	Reports to parents in terms of growth in knowledge, skills, attitudes, and social behavior.
1.46	Uses evaluative evidence to improve teaching-learning experiences.
1.47	Leads the learner to assume an important role in the evaluation of his own growth and development.
1.5	Maintains an effective balance of freedom and security in the classroom.
1.51	Shows an honest liking and sincere regard for boys and girls.
1.52	Emphasizes responsible group living with standards of conduct comparatively determined.
1.53	Develops relations among pupils that are cooperative and natural.
1.54	Provides opportunities for pupils to develop qualities of leadership and of self-direction.
1.55	Plans management of classroom routine as a worthwhile learning experience for pupils.

Role 2: Counselor and Guidance Worker

2.1	Utilizes effective procedures for collecting information about each pupil.
2.11	Makes effective use of informal procedures: anecdotal records, interviews, questionnaires, checklists.
2.12	Utilizes standard tests.
2.121	Is familiar with the more useful ones in his own field.
2.122	Selects those most appropriate for his purpose.
2.13	Is skillful in constructing and using informal tests and sociometric devices.
2.132	Appraises the characteristics of the test.
2.132	Interprets test results.
2.14	Provides pupils and parents with adequate reports.
2.141	Bases grades and reports on cumulative records.
2.2	Uses diagnostic and remedial procedures effectively.
2.21	Identifies learning difficulties.
2.22	Knows common diagnostic and achievement tests in own and related fields.

2.23	Administers and interprets diagnostic and achievement tests.
2.24	Selects appropriate remedial materials for instruction in relation to pupil's level of achievement.
2.25	Reveals ability to work correctively with the pupil at the level of his abilities, achievements, and interests at the given time.
2.26	Prepares and uses accurate and adequate records.
2.261	Makes case studies.
2.262	Keeps cumulative records.
2.3	Helps the pupil to understand himself.
2.31	Establishes effective relationships with individual pupils.
2.311	Utilizes suitable counseling techniques.
2.312	Maintains effective relationship with the home.
2.32	Assists the pupil in self-evaluation.
2.321	Helps him to understand his own abilities and limitations.
2.322	Guides him in the analysis of his personal problems.
2.323	Assists him in defining realistic goals.
2.324	Directs him to sources of information on vocational opportunities and careers.
2.4	Works effectively with the specialized counseling services.
2.41	Recognizes serious problem cases.
2.42	Refers serious cases to the specialist, with adequate background information.

LIAISON ROLES OF THE TEACHER

Role 3: Mediator of the Culture

3.1	Draws on a scholarly background to enrich cultural growth of pupils.
3.2	Directs individuals and groups to appropriate significant life application of classroom learning.
3.21	Utilizes his field of subject matter and/or general education in the solution of social, economic, scientific, and ethical problems.
3.22	Reveals the wide significance of his own subject matter field.
3.23	Develops an understanding of the interrelationships among the great disciplines.

3.3   Designs classroom activities to develop pupil ability and motivation for:

3.31   Finding democratic solutions to current social problems.

3.32   Recognizing and identifying key problems.

3.33   Understanding their interrelationships and defining the issues.

3.4   Directs pupils in learning to use those materials from which they will continue to learn after leaving school.

3.41   Teaches pupils to locate information on current problems.

3.42   Utilizes effective activities to develop pupil skill in using such materials in analyzing current problems.

3.5   Develops pupil attitudes and skills necessary for effective participation in a changing democratic society.

3.51   Uses democratic techniques and skills in teaching.

3.52   Provides for the use of democratic attitudes and skills by the pupils in the classrooms, through:

3.521   Teacher-pupil planning of problem units.

3.522   Development of effective discussion practices.

3.523   Guidance in effective committee and other group participation.

3.6   Helps his students acquire the values realized as ideals of democracy, such as:

3.61   Mutual respect.

3.62   Willingness and ability to cooperate in the solution of problems.

3.63   Willingness and ability to use intelligence in problem-solving.

3.64   Goals and standards for effective living in our culture.

Role 4: Link with the Community

4.1   Utilizes available education resources of community in classroom procedures.

4.11   Invites parents and other adults to share hobbies, talents, and experiences with students.

4.12   Utilizes field trips to draw on community resources.

4.13   Interprets community to pupils through his own field and incidental activities.

4.14   Reveals to the public the significance of the school program through pupil activities in classroom, school, and community projects.

4.15   Initiates students into community responsibilities appropriate to their age level.

4.2.	Secure cooperation of parents in school activities.
4.21	Knows when and how to obtain assistance for school or class affairs.
4.22	Conforms with policies of Parent-Teacher Associations and other cooperating groups relating cooperation with the school.
4.23	Encourages parents to visit regular classes and special school events.
4.24	Conducts individual and group parent conference with increasing skill.
4.3	Assists lay groups in understanding modern education.
4.31	Participates effectively with various socioeconomic groups.
4.32	Keeps parents and public informed of school activities through bulletins, class letters, and newspaper articles.
4.33	Initiates opportunities to discuss educational problems and accomplishments with friends, neighbors, and community acquaintances.
4.34	Accepts invitations to speak upon education subjects.
4.35	Communicates effectively with the public as well as with members of the profession.
4.4	Participates in definition and solution of community problems relating to education.
4.41	Contributes to service in the community.
4.42	Participates as a member of the profession in school betterment programs, bond issues, and legislative matters.
4.43	Draws upon reliable sources for information and assistance.

PROGRAM-BUILDING ROLES

Role 5: Member of the Staff

5.1	Contributes to the definition of the overall aims of the school.
5.11	Works effectively with the public to define school aims.
5.12	Interprets the relationship of school program and activities to the desired aims.
5.13	Articulates his classroom objectives to those of the school.
5.2	Contributes to the development of a school program to achieve its objectives.
5.21	Participates effectively in all-school curriculum developments.
5.211	Utilizes effective procedures in curriculum building.
5.212	Demonstrates familiarity with current curricular projects and patterns.
5.22	Articulates his classroom program to the school curriculum.

5.3	Contributes to the effectiveness of overall school activiites.
5.31	Participates in planning and guidance of student activities.
5.32	Assumes appropriate administrative responsibility for operation of the school as a whole.
5.4	Cooperates effectively in the evaluation of the school program.
5.41	Can define school aims in terms suitable for evaluation.
5.42	Participates in collection of relevant evidence.
5.43	Interprets the evidence to indicate needed revisions in program and aims.

Role 6: A Member of the Profession

6.1	Demonstrates an appreciation of the social importance of the profession.
6.11	Renders appropriate service to society beyond that for which he has contracted.
6.12	Contributes to the honor and prestige of the profession by his personal conduct.
6.13	Actively seeks to upgrade professional standards through selective recruitment and retention programs.
6.14	Interprets to others the goals and practices of the profession.
6.2	Contributes to the development of professional standards.
6.21	Takes part in the development of a functional code of ethics.
6.22	Adheres to the accepted code of ethics.
6.23	Helps to enforce the code of ethics in upgrading standards of professional behavior.
6.24	Supports an adequate system of certification and accreditation.
6.25	Helps improve preservice and in-service programs of preparation.
6.3	Contributes to the profession through its organizations.
6.31	Becomes a member of the organization.
6.32	Takes active part in the formulation of the organizational policies.
6.33	Supports the policy once formed until it is changed by the democratic process.
6.34	Seeks and supports legislative programs to improve the program of education as well as the economic and social status of the profession.
6.4	Takes a personal responsibility for his own professional growth.
6.41	Develops and tests more effective classroom procedures.

6.42   Keeps informed on current trends, tendencies, and practices in his field by use of professional literature.

6.43   Participates in conferences, workshops, etc., dealing with professional problems.

6.44   Enlarges his horizons through academic and nonacademic experiences.

6.5   Acts on a systematic philosophy, critically adopted and consistently applied.

6.51   Expresses a systematic philosophy of education held with deep personal conviction.

6.52   Identifies and clarifies the philosophical assumptions underlying various and conflicting policies for his work in the six roles of professional practice.

6.53   Explicitly utilizes his philosophical view in making consistent choices of educational policies and practices.

Bibliography

Andrews, Hans A. *Teachers Can Be Fired*. Chicago: Catfeet Press, 1995.

Airasian, Peter W., and Arlen R. Gullickson. *Teacher Self-Evaluation Tool Kit*. Thousand Oaks, Calif., Corwin Press, 1997.

Belton, Lorien. "What Our Teachers Should Know and Be Able to Do: A Student's View." *Educational Leadership* (September 1996): 66-68.

Berliner, David. "On the Expert Teacher: A Conversation with David Berliner." *Educational Leadership* (October 1986): 80–85.

Bridges, Edwin M. *Managing the Incompetent Teacher*. University of Oregon, Clearinghouse on Educational Management, College of Education, 1990.

Bridges, Edwin M. *The Incompetent Teacher*. Washington D.C.: Taylor and Francis, Falmer Press, 1992.

Bramson, Robert M. *Coping with Difficult People*. New York: Dell Publishing, 1981.

Brown, Genevieve, and Beverly J. Irby. *The Principal Portfolio*. Thousand Oaks, Calif.: Corwin Press, 1997.

Brooks, James Kimberly. *Termination of School Employees: Legal Issues and Techniques*. National School Boards Association, 1997.

Brinkman, Dr. Rick. *Dealing with People you Can't Stand, How to Bring Out the Best in People at Their Worst*. New York: McGraw-Hill, 1994.

Bruckerhoff, Charles E. *Between Classes, Faculty Life at Truman High*. New York: Teachers College Press, 1991.

Danielson, Charlotte. *Enhancing Professional Practice: A Framework for Teaching*. Alexandria, Va.: ASCD, 1996.

Darling-Hammond, L. "Educating Teachers: The Academy's Greatest Failure or Its Most Important Mission." Academe: *Bulletin of the American Association of University Professors* 85(l), 26–33.

DuCette, Joseph P., and M. Sue Whitlock. "Outstanding and Average Teachers of the Gifted: A Comparative Study." *Gifted Child Quarterly* (Winter 1989):15–20.

Elmore, Richard F., and Deanna Burney. "Staff Development and Instructional Improvement Community District 2, New York City." Paper prepared for the National Commission on Teaching and America's Future. Harvard University Graduate School of Education, March 1996.

English, F.W. Deciding *What to Teach and Test: Developing, Aligning and Auditing the Curriculum*. Newbury Park, Calif.: Corwin Press, 1992.

Fitzpatrick, K.A. *Indicators of School Quality Volume 1: Schoolwide Indicators of Quality*. Schaunburg, Ill. National Study of School Evaluation, 1997.

Fried, Robert L. *The Passionate Teacher.* Boston: Beacon Press, 1995.

Frase, Larry E. *Maximizing People Power in Schools: Motivating and Managing Teachers and Staff. Volume 5. Successful Schools.* Thousand Oaks, Calif.: Corwin Press, 1992.

Fuhr, Don. *No Margin for Error: Saving Our Schools from Borderline Teachers.* Dubuque, Ia.: Kendall/Hunt Publishing, 1996.

Fullan, Michael. *Change Forces.* Philadelphia: Taylor and Francis, Falmer Press, 1993.

Glafthorn, Allan A., and Linda E. Fox. *Quality Teaching Through Professional Development.* Thousands Oaks, Calif.: Corwin Press, 1996.

Grant, Gerald. *The World We Created at Hamilton High.* Cambridge, Mass., Harvard University Press, 1988.

Grove, Andrew S. *High Output Management.* New York: Vintage Books, 1983.

Hardy, Lawrence. "Why Teachers Leave." *National School Board Journal* (June 1999):13–17.

Howser, Michele A. "Reluctant Teachers: Why Some Middle Aged Teachers Fail to Learn and Grow." *Oregon School Study Council* (November 1989) 33(3).

Huberman, Michael. *The Lives of Teachers.* New York: Teachers College Press, 1993.

Jacobs, Heidi Hayes. *Mapping the Big Picture: Integrating Curriculum and Assessment K-12.* Association for Supervision and Curriculum Development, 1997.

Jones, Rebecca, "Showing Bad Teachers the Door." *American School Board Journal* (November 1997): 21–24.

Johnson, Jean, Steve Farkas, and Ali Bers. *Getting By: What Teenagers Really Think about Their Schools.* Report from Public Agenda, 1997.

Lawrence, C. Edward, et al. *The Marginal Teacher.* Newbury Park, Calif.: Corwin Press, 1993.

Manatt, Richard P. "Feedback from 360 Degrees: Client Driven Evaluation of School Personnel." *The School Administrator* (March 1997).

Manatt, Richard P., and Mari Kemis. "360 Degree Feedback: A New Approach to Evaluation." *Principal* (September 1997).

McLaughlin, Milbrey Wallin, and R. Scott Pfeifer. *Teacher Evaluation.* New York: Teachers College Press, 1988.

Millman, Jason. *Grading Teachers, Grading Schools.* Thousand Oaks, Calif.: Corwin Press, 1997.

Millman, Jason. *Handbook of Teacher Evaluation.* Beverly Hills, Calif.: Sage Publications, 1981.

Millman, Jason, and Linda Darling-Hammond. *The New Handbook of Teacher Evaluation.* Newbury Park, Calif.: Corwin Press, 1990.

Newmann, Fred M., and Gary G. Wehlage. *Successful School Restructuring*. Madison, Wisc.: Center on Organization and Restructuring of Schools, 1995.

Oakes, Jeannie. *Keeping Track: How Schools Structure Inequality*. New Haven, Conn.: Yale University, 1985.

Page, Reba Neukom. *Lower Track Classrooms*. New York: Teachers College Press, 1991.

Perkins, Peggy G., and Jeffrey L. Gelfer. "Portfolio Assessment of Teachers." *Clearing House* (March/April 1993).

Rogers, Dwight L., and Babinski, Leslie. "Breaking through Isolation with New Teacher Groups." *Educational Leadership* (May 1999).

Saphier, Jon, and Mary Ann Haley. *Activators*. Acton, Mass.: Research for Better Teaching, 1993.

Saphier, Jon, and Mary Ann Haley. *Summarizers*. Acton, Mass.: Research for Better Teaching, 1993.

Saphier, Jon, and Robert Gower. *The Skillful Teacher*. Acton, Mass.: Research for Better Teaching, 1997.

Schmoker, Mike. Results: *The Key to Continous School Improvement*. Alexandria, Va.: ASCD, 1996.

Shulman, L. S. "A Union of Insufficiencies: Strategies for Teacher Assessment in a Period of Educational Reform." *Educational Leadership* 46(3):8, 36–41.

Senge, Peter. *The Fifth Discipline: The Art and Practice of the Learning Organization*. Garden City, N. Y.: Doubleday, 1990.

Sizer, Theodore R. *Horace's Compromise: The Dilemma of the American High School*. Boston: Houghton Mifflin, 1984.

Stanley, Sarah J., and W. James Popham. *Teacher Evaluation: Six Prescriptions for Success*. Association for Supervision and Curriculum Development, 1988.

Steinberg, Laurence. *Beyond the Classroom*. New York: Simon and Schuster.

Stronge, James H. *Evaluating Teaching: A Guide to Current Thinking and Best Practice*. Thousand Oaks, Calif.: Corwin Press, 1997.

Stufflebeam, Daniel L., and The Joint Committee on Standards for Educational Evaluation. *The Personnel Evaluation Standards*. Newbury Park, Calif.: Corwin Press, 1988.

Sweeney, Jim, and Dick Manatt. "A Team Approach to Supervising the Marginal Teacher." *Educational Leadership* (April 1984).

Tucker, M.S., and J.B. Codding. *Standards for Our Schools: How to Set Them, Measure Them and Reach Them*. San Francisco: Jossey Bass, 1998.

Whitaker, Todd. *Dealing with Difficult Teachers*. Larchmont, N.Y.: Eye on Education, 1999.

Wiggins, Grant. *Educative Assessment: Designing Assessments to Inform and Improve Student Performance.* San Francisco: Jossey-Bass, 1998.

Wolf, Kenneth. "The Schoolteacher's Portfolio: Issues in Design, Implementation and Evaluation." *Phi Delta Kappan* (October 1991).

Wong, Harry K., and Rosemary Tripi Wong. *First Days of School.* Harry K. Wong Publications, 1991.

SKILLFUL TEACHING

Studying Skillful Teaching: Promoting Motivation, Learning, and Achievement (37.5 Hours)

For teachers, RBT's foundational program for building their capacity to improve their practices and students' achievement through lesson planning, high expectations, formative assessment, and cultural proficiency. Includes development of a common language related to the knowledge base on teaching and each state's professional standards.

SKILLFUL LEADERSHIP

Analyzing Teaching for Student Results (42 Hours, plus Site Visit)

For leaders to learn how to zero in on high-leverage teaching strategies that make a difference in student learning. Includes examination and use of a common language and concept system, the development of skills for classroom observation, and the capacity to identify and provide results-oriented reports and feedback that are credible and convincing.

Coaching for Sustainable School Improvement (CSSI) (24 Hours, plus Monthly Half-day Coaching Learning Community Sessions)

For instructional coaches to strengthen their coaching skills based on a partnership approach. Features the use of classroom video in the coaching relationship and incorporates the work of leading coaching expert Jim Knight.

Differentiated Conferencing (42 Hours)

For supervisors and coaches to develop the knowledge and skills to conduct meaningful and actionable conversations with teachers who are at different levels of professional maturity. From non-directive to directive and even to particularly difficult, this course develops a repertoire of skills that empower supervisors and coaches to grow their conferencing skills and match their clients with just-right approaches.

Evaluating Teaching for Student Impact (14-20 Hours, Tailored to Client Needs)

For school and district leaders to learn how to diagnose problems, communicate effectively, and draw on a repertoire of interventions to improve the quality of teaching. Samples strategies and approaches from the handbook by Platt and Tripp, *Strengthening Teacher Evaluation: Taking Action to Improve Ineffective Instruction,* aka *The Skillful Leader III* (2014).

Using Multiple Data Sources to Evaluate Teaching for Student Results (12 Hours)

For evaluators to learn how to use multiple data sources in their ratings of teacher performance to provide a comprehensive picture of a teacher and team practices and their connection to student learning.

SKILLFUL DATA USE

Data Coaching: Unleashing the Power of Collaborative Inquiry (37.5 Hours, plus Optional On-site Follow-up)

For Data Coaches and school/district leaders of Data Teams to learn how to lead a structured process of collaborative inquiry that increases professional community, effective uses of data, and student achievement. Based on *The Data Coach's Guide to Improving Learning for All Students: Unleashing the Power of Collaborative Inquiry* (Corwin Press, 2008) by Love, Stiles, Mundry, and DiRanna.

Formative Assessment for Results: A Team Approach (37.5 Hours)

For coaches, teacher leaders, teacher team facilitators, and administrators supervising coaches or teams to learn how to maximize the power of formative assessment by making its effective use the focus of teacher teamwork.

For further details on programs, including schedule, pricing, and registration, send email or call RBT.

Research for Better Teaching, Inc. • One Acton Place, Acton, MA 01720 • Phone +1 (978) 263-9449
Web: www.RBTeach.com • Email: info@RBTeach.com

SKILLFUL TEACHING

The Skillful Teacher: Building Your Teaching Skills (6th ed. 2008)
Designed for both the novice and the experienced educator, *The Skillful Teacher* is a unique synthesis of the Knowledge Base on Teaching, with powerful repertoires for matching teaching strategies to student needs. Designed as a practical guide for practitioners working to broaden their teaching skills, the book combines theory with practice and focuses on 18 critical areas of classroom performance. A must for instructional coaches and mentors.
by Jon Saphier, Mary Ann Haley-Speca, & Robert Gower

***The Skillful Teacher* Interactive Kindle eBook** (2008, Kindle 2012)
Available as complete *The Skillful Teacher* book or in 4 separately-orderable parts. Detailed search options or links to different chapters for instant answers to teaching dilemmas. Go to Amazon.com to purchase.
by Jon Saphier, Mary Ann Haley-Speca, & Robert Gower

Activators: Activity Structures to Engage Students' Thinking Before Instruction (1993)
This book is a collection of classroom-tested, practical activity structures for getting students' minds active and engaged prior to introducing new content or skills.
by Jon Saphier & Mary Ann Haley

Summarizers: Activity Structures to Support Integration and Retention of New Learning (1993)
This book is a collection of classroom-tested, practical activity structures for getting students cognitively active during and after periods of instruction.
by Jon Saphier & Mary Ann Haley

DVDs: *The Skillful Teacher Series* (2012)
Collections of videos that bring to life practical strategies for improving teaching, highlighting high leverage, 21st century skills from our "gold-standard" textbook, *The Skillful Teacher.* Volume 1A & 1B – Motivation skills from the Classroom Climate and Expectations chapters. Volume 2A & 2B – Planning and Error Analysis/ Reteaching skills from the Planning and Assessment chapters. Volume 3 – Instructional Strategies from the Clarity chapter. Included are introductory videos to the Map of Pedagogical Knowledge.
by Jon Saphier et al.

Poster: *Map of Pedagogical Knowledge Pyramid* (2009)
Full-color, 24" x 36" laminated poster. Support the professional development of your staff with this great visual of the foundation of good teaching. Display in teachers' room and training areas.

Mini-Posters: *Map of Pedagogical Knowledge Pyramid (pkg. of 25)* (2009)
Full-color, 8.5" x 11" laminated mini-posters, an instructional resource for every teacher.

SKILLFUL LEADERSHIP

The Skillful Leader: Confronting Mediocre Teaching (2000)
Based on ***The Skillful Teacher*** framework, this book is targeted to evaluators and supervisors who want a field-tested toolkit of strategies to improve, rather than remove, underperforming teachers. The text includes valuable legal notes and a model contract, case studies, assessment tools, and personal accounts of leaders in action.
by Alexander D. Platt, Caroline E. Tripp, Wayne R. Ogden, & Robert G. Fraser

The Skillful Leader II: Confronting Conditions That Undermine Learning (2008)
This important "Skillful Leader" book arms administrators and teacher leaders with step-by-step strategies to confront and raise the performance of teams and individuals who undermine student learning. The text includes methods of collecting data, strategies for intervention, and tips for hiring and training. Individual and community profiles, together with legal notes, provide practical tools for busy leaders.
by Alexander D. Platt, Caroline E. Tripp, Robert G. Fraser, James R. Warnock, & Rachel E. Curtis

Strengthening Teacher Evaluation: Taking Action to Improve Ineffective Teaching (The Skillful Leader III) (2014)
This work serves as a how-to handbook to accompany the best selling *The Skillful Leader: Confronting Mediocre Teaching.* Like its predecessor, the book offers dozens of illustrations, new cases, and sample documents plus legal advice to help evaluators confront ineffective instruction. It is a cover-to-cover guide for solving thorny teacher performance problems.
by Alexander D. Platt & Caroline E. Tripp

Research for Better Teaching, Inc. • One Acton Place, Acton, MA 01720 • Phone +1 (978) 263-9449
Web: www.RBTeach.com • Email: pubs@RBTeach.com

Beyond Mentoring: Putting Instructional Focus on Comprehensive Induction Programs (2011)
This book emphasizes the critical role of instructional practice in the induction support that is given to new and beginning teachers. Using RBT's model for the comprehensive induction of new teachers, educators are guided through the steps of developing an induction plan for new teachers and integrating the induction program with the district's professional learning community.
by Jon Saphier, Susan Freedman, & Barbara Aschheim

Talk Sense: Communicating to Lead and Learn (2007)
Barry Jentz shows how leaders can build the requisite trust and credibility for improving organizational performance. Typically, leaders "talk tough" to improve performance. When that doesn't work, they "talk nice" (or vice-versa). By learning to "talk sense", leaders can succeed in their efforts to improve performance.
by Barry Jentz

SKILLFUL DATA USE

The Data Coach's Guide to Improving Learning for All Students: Unleashing the Power of Collaborative Inquiry
(2008)
This resource helps Data-Team facilitators move schools away from unproductive data practices and toward examining data for systematic and continuous improvement in instruction and learning. The book includes a CD-ROM with slides and reproducibles.
by Nancy Love, Katherine E. Stiles, Susan Mundry, & Kathryn DiRanna

Using Data to Improve Learning for All: A Collaborative Inquiry Approach (2009)
This valuable handbook arms leaders with the tools for using data to improve student learning, with an emphasis on promoting equity within a culturally proficient school environment. The book contains detailed examples of schools that have demonstrated dramatic gains by building collaborative cultures, nurturing ongoing inquiry, and using data systematically.
by Nancy Love, Editor

Laminated Guide: *Data Literacy for Teachers* (2011)
For every teacher, Data Coach, and inquiry team. In a fold-out 8.5" x 11" laminated form, ready to be inserted in a notebook, the guide provides a simple framework to help teachers feel comfortable, knowledgeable, and skilled in effectively using a variety of data, including formative assessments.
by Nancy Love

Laminated Guide: *The Skillful Inquiry/Data Team* (2012)
For every grade level (elementary) or subject-area (middle and high school) team of teachers, plus school and district administrators. In a fold-out 8.5" x 11" laminated form, ready to be inserted in a notebook, this guide provides a proven-effective inquiry process and practical tools to maximize their impact on student achievement.
by Nancy Love

DVD: *The Skillful Data Use Series* (2012) Volume 1 Collaborative Inquiry: Connecting Data to Results. DVD collection of introductory instructional videos based on *The Data Coach's Guide* and *Using Data to Improve Learning for All* provides expert commentary, insights from successful implementations, and views of Data Teams in action.

Posters: *Unleashing the Power of Collaborative Inquiry* (2009)
Eight full-color, 24" x 36" laminated posters: (1) Using Data 19 Tasks, (2) Building the Bridge, (3) Using Data Diagram, (4) Data Driven Dialogue, (5) Data Triangle, (6) Logic Model, (7) Verify Causes Tree, (8) Drill Down Deep. Data is power!

OTHER RBT RESOURCES

John Adams' Promise: How to Have Good Schools for All Our Children, Not Just for Some (2005)
Curriculum reform, structural reform, funding reform, organizational reform—all these 20th-century efforts have failed to make a significant dent in the achievement gap and the performance of disadvantaged students, especially in cities and poor rural areas.
by Jon Saphier

How to Bring Vision to School Improvement Through Core Outcomes, Commitments and Beliefs (1993)
This practical guide provides a proven step-by-step sequence for generating consensus among parents and staff about a few valued core outcomes they want for all children. Then it shows how to achieve the concrete outcomes in the areas of school and family life.
by Jon Saphier & John D'Auria

Research for Better Teaching, Inc. • One Acton Place, Acton, MA 01720 • Phone +1 (978) 263-9449
Web: www.RBTeach.com • Email: pubs@RBTeach.com